FEDERALISM AND ETHNIC CONFLICT IN NIGERIA

FEDERALISM AND ETHNIC CONFLICT IN NIGERIA

Rotimi T. Suberu

UNITED STATES INSTITUTE OF PEACE PRESS
Washington, D.C.

Maps on pages xxii–xxiii are adapted with permission from *Wilberforce Conference on Nigerian Federalism,* ed. Peter P. Ekeh (Buffalo, N.Y.: Association of Nigerian Scholars for Dialogue, 1997), 68–69.

UNITED STATES INSTITUTE OF PEACE
1200 17th Street NW, Suite 200
Washington, DC 20036-3011

First published 2001

Printed in the United States of America

Library of Congress Cataloging-in-Publication Data
Suberu, Rotimi T.
    Federalism and ethnic conflict in Nigeria / by Rotimi T. Suberu.
        p. cm.
    Includes bibliographical references and index.
    ISBN 1-929223-28-5
        1. Federal government—Nigeria. 2. Nigeria—Politics and government—1960- 3. Ethnic conflict—Nigeria. I. Title.

JQ3086.S8 S82 2001
320.4669'049—dc21

                                                    2001039074

To my parents

Albert Oladimeji Suberu (1929–1991)
and
Mary Monilola Suberu

CONTENTS

AD: Alliance for Democracy

AFRC: Armed Forces Ruling Council

AG: Action Group

APP: All People's Party

CAN: Christian Association of Nigeria

CDC: Constitution Drafting Committee

COR: Calabar-Ogoja-Rivers state

FCC: Federal Character Commission

FCSC: Federal Civil Service Commission

FCT: Federal Capital Territory (Abuja)

FEDECO: Federal Electoral Commission

GNPP: Great Nigerian People's Party

LGA: Local Government Area

MNR: Movement for National Reformation

NCC: National Constitutional Conference

NCNC: National Council of Nigeria and the Cameroons

NDDC: Niger Delta Development Commission

NEC: National Electoral Commission

NPC: National Population Commission

NPN: National Party of Nigeria

NPP: Nigerian People's Party

NRC: National Republican Convention

NRMAFC: National Revenue Mobilization, Allocation, and Fiscal
Commission

OIC: Organization of the Islamic Conference

OMPADEC: Oil Mineral–Producing Areas Development
Commission

PDP: People's Democratic Party

PRP: People's Redemption Party

SDP: Social Democratic Party

SMC: Supreme Military Council

LIST OF TABLES

FOREWORD

MUCH OF THE FUTURE of the "third wave" of democratization—now a quarter-century old—will depend on the fate of a handful of large, pivotal states that are struggling with massive problems of governance and could swing either toward democracy or dictatorship in the coming years. Russia is struggling to resist the slide to authoritarianism under a young leader who suggests that only the return to tough, centralized power can fight economic and political decay. Mexico has just experienced a historic breakthrough to electoral democracy but now confronts huge challenges of economic and political reform. Brazil has made halting but significant progress toward more accountable government under the reform-minded leadership of President Fernando Henrique Cardoso. By contrast, however, democracy in Pakistan succumbed in the military coup of October 1999 to massive corruption, economic disarray, and mounting ethnic and sectarian tensions. The new democratic leadership in Indonesia is laboring with great difficulty to correct the abuses of authoritarian rule and hold the country together. In Africa, two countries dominate their subregions and generate powerful demonstration and diffusion effects across the continent. One is South Africa, which, in the face of enormous economic, racial, and public health problems, has nevertheless maintained a liberal democracy. The other is Nigeria.

Over the past four decades, no country in the world has had a more turbulent and tragic democratic experience than Nigeria. One of the most vibrant, pluralistic, and promising of the newly decolonized African states, Nigeria went from the jubilation of independence to the trauma of civil war in the space of less than seven years. When it became a major oil producer just after the civil war ended in 1970 and then saw its national income soar with the price of oil, the heavens seemed to be smiling on this complex land of three major nationality groups and hundreds of smaller ethnic and linguistic identities. During the 1970s, Nigeria was the rising power of Africa, headed for rapid development and international influence. As the oil income poured in, building sprouted everywhere, universities mushroomed, education surged, and nothing seemed impossible. It was a time of astonishingly rapid recovery from the physical and psychological devastation of the civil war. When corruption seemed to sour the whole project under the lax political leadership of General Yakubu Gowon, a military coup brought in a new set of leaders who seemed more purposeful and certainly more determined to return the country to civilian, democratic rule.

In retrospect, the 1975–79 political transition and the rebirth of democracy under the Second Republic can be seen as the high-water mark of political and economic promise in Nigeria's postindependence history. It was during those years of transition that the political energy, innovation, and flexibility of Nigerians produced a dramatically restructured federal system and a new democratic constitution with many creative and wise provisions to manage Nigeria's complex tensions. It was also during those years that oil income peaked at new, breathtaking levels. What political ingenuity and bargaining could not solve would be eased or washed away in the seemingly endless flood tide of oil revenue.

But the moment of hope and healing did not last long. Even as the oil revenue was pouring in, deep cracks were resurfacing in the edifice of Nigerian democracy. Despite imaginative constitutional engineering, ethnic cleavage and regional competition strained the country's party politics. The negative impacts of massive dependence on oil revenue became more glaring as the struggle for control of the country's oil wealth became the dominant theme of politics at every level. Massive corruption blighted politics and governance, distorting planning, depleting public accounts, and diverting funds from development projects into overseas bank accounts or shocking, vulgar displays of ill-gotten wealth. The public became cynical and disgusted. Politicians with too much at stake to risk defeat in an election resorted to brazen electoral fraud and violence. On December 31, 1983, not long after the first test of the Second Republic's ability to renew itself in a national election, the system came crashing down in a military coup to widespread popular celebration.

For the next fifteen long, brutalizing years, Nigeria struggled to return to democracy and to achieve the accountability and economic prudence that had eluded it during the Second Republic. For most of this time, the promise of economic and political reform was squandered under the duplicitous and murderous rule of two military dictators, Ibrahim Babangida and Sani Abacha. Now, early into what is hoped to be a long-lived Fourth Republic, Nigeria still confronts the basic questions of governance that have dogged it throughout its forty years of independence: How should federal institutions be designed to manage and contain the country's countless ethnic, subethnic, regional, and now increasingly religious cleavages? How should democratic institutions be reformed and bolstered to strengthen accountability and the rule of law? And how can the economy be restructured so as to unlock the country's immense developmental potential?

These are the same three broad challenges of governance with which the other pivotal "swing states" are struggling. As large and ethnically complex countries, they all must manage powerful cleavages based on territorial, ethnic, or, in some cases, religious identities. Some of them, like Nigeria and Indonesia, face the fundamental question of whether they can even hold together as one country. Related to this is the danger, faced especially by Pakistan and Nigeria, that prolonged failure to come to grips with the basic challenges of governance could so erode the moral and institutional fabric of public life that the state will essentially collapse. Increasingly, the three challenges of governance appear not as a coincidence of separate problems but as part of an organic whole. People do not trust the state and they do not trust one another. They have no confidence in the national project, in the institutions of economic and political life, and in the future generally. Consequently, every group, every faction and family, begs and bleeds the state for anything it can, as much as it can, as quickly as it can. When most of the country's wealth flows through the state because of a highly centralized and monolithic oil economy, the problem is intensified by several orders of magnitude.

This is the Nigeria that Rotimi Suberu grapples with in this landmark work of scholarship and political analysis. As the reader will discover from Suberu's comprehensive citations, federalism has long been a subject of intensive academic inquiry and political debate in Nigeria. In fact, no Nigerian problem has elicited more creative and heated discussion, and more searching scholarly attention, than the history, functioning, design, and restructuring of the country's federal system. Yet even against this rich backdrop of learned and at times distinguished contributions, *Federalism and Ethnic Conflict in Nigeria* stands out as the definitive treatment to date of an enormously complex and troubled history. Of course, Suberu's book has one advantage over previous works. As the most recent treatment, it offers the most up-to-date assessment of the evolution of Nigerian federalism and of the recent dangerous mutation of long-standing regional and ethnic cleavages into an increasingly polarized religious form: Muslim versus Christian. It is also the first work to take full stock of the enormous damage to the spirit and structure of Nigerian federalism done by the previous military dictatorships (1984–1999), with their relentless centralization of revenue and power and their repeated cynical ploys to generate some political legitimacy by creating more states and more local governments.

Suberu's work does much more than update previous analysis, however. In a balanced and dispassionate fashion, it weighs Nigeria's institutional experience in light of theories and the comparative experience of federalism. It also locates the travails of Nigerian federalism squarely within the broader context of Nigeria's distorted political economy. The fundamental obstacle to successful federalism in Nigeria is not the mere existence of multiple and deep sectional cleavages, but their incessant aggravation by an oil-based economy in which the central government controls and disperses (or fails to honor its legal obligations to disperse) most public revenue.

As Suberu shows throughout this splendid book, especially in chapter 3, the extreme centralization of control over revenue flows has fed the worst pathologies of Nigerian federalism. It has focused political attention excessively on control of the federal government. It has made the formulas for allocation of revenue vertically (between different levels of government) and horizontally (among the different states and the local government areas) an insoluble bone of contention. It has given the central government the ability to bring subordinate governments to their knees by withholding the revenue that is their lifeblood. In doing so, it has virtually erased a fundamental principle of federalism—that lower levels of government have some areas of autonomous authority that cannot be overridden by the center—and robbed subordinate units of any significant incentive to generate revenue of their own. It has also spawned profound grievances on the part of the oil-producing areas of the Niger Delta, from which much has been taken but little has been returned, except environmental disaster, economic destitution, and political repression.

As a result of all of this, Suberu maintains, Nigeria's "hyper-centralized" shell of federalism has gradually driven out any sense of civic or truly national commitment, leaving a shifting jumble of ethnic, regional, religious, and factional alignments to contend ceaselessly for power and resources. It is probably only the fact that the lines of cleavage do shift around, and up and down, that keeps the system from fracturing totally. But, Suberu carefully demonstrates, as more and more states have been created, politics has tended to become recentralized around the tripolar ethnic cleavage of Hausa versus Yoruba versus Igbo and, even more ominously, around the bipolar cleavages of North versus South and Muslim versus Christian. These developments have left the Fourth Republic besieged with the "clamor for radical political restructuring," including calls for confederation that would essentially dissolve the state of Nigeria.

Suberu points to many aspects of Nigerian federalism that are imaginative and hopeful. In principle, the multistate system disperses conflict and contains it within political subunits; fragments the solidarity of the three major ethnic groups; generates cross-cutting, state-based cleavages; and devolves resources down to lower levels of authority. Meanwhile, the "federal character" principle gives each group a role and a stake in the system. But these theoretical benefits of Nigeria's federal architecture have largely been vitiated by the intensely centralizing effects of federal government control and distribution of oil income. In such a system, every group must get access to federal power and resources in order to survive, and the major groups feel secure only when they control the national government and, hence, the presidency. In more truly federal systems, different regions and ethnic groups can afford to lose power at the center because they have resources of their own to work with and the structure of federalism shields them from excessive intervention and predation from the center. This fiscal autonomy and political insulation, Suberu demonstrates, is largely lacking in Nigeria.

What has emerged in Nigeria, Suberu convincingly tells us, is a highly superficial, vulnerable, and distorted federalism in which virtually all political imagination and mobilization is focused around the insatiable thirst for centrally controlled resources, for a piece of the "national cake." This frantic quest for resources—or what Babangida termed, in an ironically fitting allusion to his own governance, "the national cake psychosis"—has largely driven the proliferating movements for new states and local government areas, the conflicts over where to place new state capitals, the drive to "indigenize" public sector appointments at the state level, and the demands for pure proportionality (a "fair share") in the distribution of federal appointments, university admissions, and other opportunities and resources controlled by the center. As it has descended into an obsession with securing distributive shares, the "federal character" principle has proved divisive rather than integrative, undermining the integrity and capacity of every institution it has touched, including prominently the civil service and higher education. Sacrificing individual rights on the altar of group rights, it has nevertheless failed to benefit more than a narrow elite stratum of the disadvantaged groups. Moreover, as we see in chapter 6, when population is used as a major basis for allocating national revenue and legislative seats, distributing developmental projects, and creating new states and local government areas, the process of counting population inevitably becomes a political contest. The technical expertise necessary to execute a reliable, mutually accepted census is thus overwhelmed by the raw political muscle and deceit that gets mobilized in a zero-sum struggle for power and resources.

As this book emphasizes in its clarifying analysis and eloquent prose, there is no way out of this bedeviled and precarious situation except through democracy. The military has completely discredited itself as a political alternative, having abused federalism in practice and gravely distorted it in structure while systematically abusing human rights and plundering the country's wealth. A more viable Nigerian federalism can emerge only through constitutional reform and institutional innovation under civilian, democratic rule.

In his final chapter, Suberu reviews the ideas and proposals that have been offered for reforming Nigeria's federal system. Proposals to rotate or redesign federal executive offices miss the essential point, he argues. No constitutional revision can strengthen federalism and democracy in Nigeria unless it decentralizes power and resources. In short, several decades of "hypercentralization" must be reversed. An essential step, Suberu argues, would be to return to the states many of their original powers and functions, which must be entrenched through constitutional language giving the states exclusive jurisdiction in these matters. Control over local governments must be transferred from the center to the states, which should in turn devolve more power to the localities. Most of all, the system of revenue allocation must be reformed. Vertically, a greater share of national revenue must be assigned to state and local governments, and an independent, neutral administration must be given the authority to ensure that these lower levels of government receive the revenue due them. States and localities must also be given more authority to raise revenue of their own by shifting downward some taxes that are now exclusively federal. Horizontally, states and localities must be given incentives to generate internal revenue by having that criterion weigh more heavily in the allocation of national revenue. And more weight must be given to the "derivation" principle, so that the devastated oil-producing areas receive a greater proportion of the mineral wealth beneath them and offshore.

The logic of these reforms is strong and enjoys broad (although far from universal) support within Nigeria. However, no reform program can strengthen federalism and improve democratic governance in Nigeria unless it also addresses the related pathology of pervasive corruption and abuse of power. Unless transparency and the rule of law are strengthened so that political institutions work in practice at least somewhat as they are intended to in theory, no redesign of the federal system can achieve much good. That is why, Suberu emphasizes, transparency and bureaucratic professionalism and autonomy are so important in the administration of the country's system for raising and allocating revenue. In fact, procedures to ensure integrity and accountability and thereby to restrain power must extend to every major government institution if the enormous premium on controlling the state is to be reduced.

Yet corruption and abuse of power will be easier to control if power and resources are shifted downward, to levels of authority that are closer to the people and more visible. Then governance will begin to be redefined from an elite project to divide up "the national cake" to a public obligation to improve human welfare. Transparency and decentralization thus must proceed in tandem as the two fundamental pillars of political reform in Nigeria. Each goal requires powerful institutions of horizontal accountability that are insulated from the control of partisan politicians. An independent judiciary is particularly vital, Suberu notes. Not only must the judicial system enforce the laws against corruption, it must also defend the vertical distribution of power against encroachment from the center. What makes a system of government truly federal is that subnational units have some powers that are inviolable. Ultimately, only the courts can defend that boundary of authority against a self-aggrandizing center.

If the broad direction of reform is clear, the prospect is uncertain at best. No one should underestimate the gravity of the challenge confronting Nigeria during this Fourth Republic. Every previous attempt to make federalism and democracy work has failed. For the past two decades, each failure has sunk the country further into political, economic, and moral decay. As Suberu shows, the political and social glue that holds the Nigerian federation together is wearing thin. Yet there is no better alternative for Nigeria's future than true federalism. There is a tremendous amount at stake now—not only for Nigeria, but for Africa and the world—in making the institutions of Nigeria's federal democracy work this time and in redesigning them so they can work more effectively, with broader popular commitment. Those many Nigerians who appreciate the urgent need to establish a more viable federalism will find no better guide than this outstanding book.

LARRY DIAMOND
HOOVER INSTITUTION
STANFORD UNIVERSITY

PREFACE

THIS BOOK IS ABOUT THE DILEMMAS of the Nigerian system of federalism. It comes at a time of intensive agitation and extensive debate within Nigeria over the failure and future of the federation. At the heart of the Nigerian predicament, the book argues, is the development of an intensely dysfunctional system of centralized "ethno-distributive" federalism. The system is significantly rooted in the country's ethnic fragmentation and socioeconomic underdevelopment. But its unwholesomeness has been aggravated by the hypercentralization and broad institutional ruination arising from the overbearing influence of "soldiers and oil" on Nigeria's political economy.

To be sure, the contradictions of Nigeria's ethno-distributive federalism and political economy have been analyzed by several scholars, notably Daniel Bach and Richard Joseph. My modest contribution here involves the concerted dissection and discussion of the troubling conflicts that have plagued the Nigerian federal system in the four ethno-distributive arenas of revenue allocation, territorial reorganization, intergroup representation, and population enumeration. A further substantive concern of this study considers the challenges and possibilities of federal reconstruction and the mitigation of ethnic conflict in Nigeria.

This study has its roots in my doctoral research from 1986 to 1990 at the University of Ibadan into the instability of federalism in

Nigeria. The actual writing of the book began in 1993–94, when I was a fellow at the United States Institute of Peace in Washington, D.C. I am deeply grateful to the Institute for the fellowship, and for waiting so patiently and supportively for five years for the completion of the manuscript. For helping to make my one-year stay at the Institute such a rewarding and memorable experience, I am particularly thankful to Institute staff members Sally Blair, Barbara Cullicott, Joe Klaits, Timothy Sisk, David Smock, my "fellow fellow" Norma Krieger, and my superb research assistant, Curtis Noonan.

For nurturing and sustaining my interest in issues of federalism and political economy, I am indebted to four of my teachers at the Universities of Jos and Ibadan: Professors Busari Adebisi, John Ayoade, Isawa Elaigwu, and Aaron Gana. I am especially grateful to Professor Ayoade for the prodigious inspiration and meticulous guidance that he provided as my principal doctoral thesis supervisor. I hope the publication of this work will evoke some sense of tutelary pride and fulfillment in him.

My research into Nigerian federalism has also benefited, either directly or indirectly, from the facilitation, encouragement, example, advice, or comments of several friends, colleagues, collaborators, teachers, and students. Without the support or stimulation of such individuals, the burden of researching, reflecting, and writing in the often difficult Nigerian environment would have been much more unbearable. At the considerable risk of inadvertently leaving out the names of some important benefactors, I want to acknowledge the following persons: Ladipo Adamolekun, Wale Adebanwi, Bayo Adekanye, Adigun Agbaje, Rafiu Akindele, E. E. Alemika, Kunle Amuwo, A. S. Benjamin, Daniel Bach, Peter Ekeh, Jaye Gaskia, Alex Gboyega, Goran Hyden, Enemaku Idachaba, Jibrin Ibrahim, Chris Ikporukpo, Victor Isumonah, Arlene Jacquette, Darren Kew, Peter Lewis, Joshua Lincoln, Peter P. Melanchuk, Nereus Nwosu, Olatunde J. B. Ojo, Dele Olowu, Fred Onyeoziri, Eghosa Osaghae, Sarafa Ogundiya, Femi Omotoso, Marty Otanez, Femi Otubanjo, Oyeleye Oyediran, Tunde Oyekanmi, Alfred Stepan, Patrick Ukata, Ronald Watts, and, of course, Crawford Young.

I am grateful to my wife, Ibironke, and my children, Paul, Moyin, and Otito, for being ever so supportive and indulgent of my academic pursuits. I am also deeply indebted to my parents, to whom this book is dedicated, for their immeasurable contributions to my personal and professional development.

Special thanks are due to Dan Snodderly and my editor and friend, Peter Pavilionis, as well as their colleagues at the U.S. Institute of Peace Press, for their diligent management of this book project. For their useful and encouraging comments on the book's draft manuscript, I also wish to thank two anonymous and one not-so-anonymous reviewers commissioned by the Press.

In the course of the past ten years or thereabouts, Larry Diamond has been to me an indefatigable motivator, facilitator, mentor, and collaborator. He encouraged and supported my application for the Institute fellowship, and he has selflessly and generously promoted my work and research in numerous other ways. At the same time, Larry's own writings on Nigeria have been a tremendous source of inspiration to me and to a whole generation of students of the country's politics. The depth of his interest in Nigerian studies and in my own work is eloquently demonstrated in the fine foreword that he has crafted for this book. I owe him an irredeemable debt of gratitude.

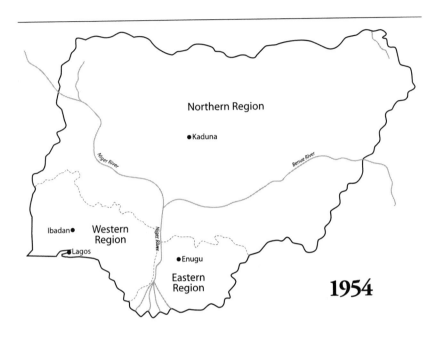

Northern Region

●Kaduna

Niger River

Benue River

Ibadan● Western Region

Lagos

●Enugu

Eastern Region

1954

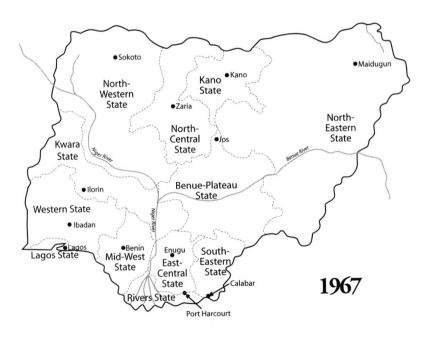

●Sokoto

●Maidugun

North-Western State

Kano State ●Kano

●Zaria

North-Eastern State

Kwara State

Niger River

North-Central State ●Jos

●Ilorin

Benue River

Western State

Benue-Plateau State

●Ibadan

Niger River

Lagos

●Benin

Mid-West State

Enugu

East-Central State

South-Eastern State

Calabar

Lagos State

Rivers State

Port Harcourt

1967

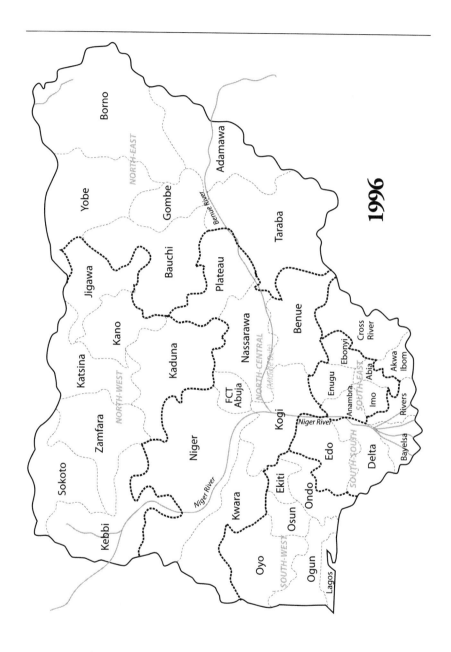

1996

A Political Chronology of Postindependence Nigeria

1960 Independence from Great Britain. Abubakar Tafawa Balewa serves as prime minister.

1963 Republic established. Nnamdi Azikiwe becomes president. Mid-West Region joins Northern, Western, and Eastern Regions.

1966 Military rule imposed after January coup. Establishment of Supreme Military Council (SMC), led by Major General Johnson T. U. Aguiyi-Ironsi from the southern Igbo ethnic group. Northern Muslim resentment leads to second coup in July. Colonel (later, Major General) Yakubu Gowon, heads the Federal Military Government.

1967 Gowon reorganizes Nigeria's four regions into twelve states.

May 1967 Eastern Region leader Lieutenant Colonel Odumegwu Ojukwu declares the region the Republic of Biafra; fighting ensues in July between rebels and Nigerian armed forces. State of emergency declared.

January 1970 Rebels surrender.

1975 Gowon overthrown in bloodless coup while attending Organization of African Unity conference. Brigadier Murtala Mohammed assumes the position of head of state and convenes Constitution Drafting Committee to develop a new constitution with the aim of establishing an "executive presidential system."

1976 Seven more states added to federation. Mohammed assassinated during an abortive coup attempt. Chief of General Staff Lieutenant General Olusegun Obasanjo takes over as SMC chairman and head of state.

1978 Constituent Assembly endorses draft constitution, which is promulgated by the Supreme Military Council after it makes a number of changes. Twelve-year state of emergency lifted, as is ban on political parties.

1979 Second Republic. Executive presidential system established under new constitution. National Party of Nigeria candidates Alhaji Shehu Shagari and Alex Ekwueme elected as president and vice president, respectively.

1983 Shagari re-elected, despite drop in oil income, excessive government spending, and widespread corruption. In December, senior military officers seize power.

January 1984 Major General Muhammadu Buhari sworn in as chairman of new Supreme Military Council, which launches "war against indiscipline."

1985 In the midst of severe political repression, the Buhari regime is deposed by senior SMC members. Major General Ibrahim Babangida installed as leader of Armed Forces Ruling Council (AFRC), which loosens press restrictions and encourages more open political system.

1986 Babangida announces five-year transition plan for return to civilian rule, including development of new constitution. Appoints "Political Bureau," made up of legal and political scholars, to recommend constitutional design and political reforms.

1987 Two new states—Akwa Ibom and Katsina—added to federation.

1989 Babangida lifts ban on party politics and announces new draft constitution recommended by Constituent Assembly. Citing "factionalism," he winnows thirteen parties seeking registration to two state-sponsored organizations, the Social Democratic Party and the National Republican Convention. New constitution for **Third Republic** is promulgated.

1991 Babangida announces decision to increase number of states in the federation to thirty.

1992 Following two rounds of invalidated presidential primary elections, Babangida announces replacement of AFRC with a National Defense and Security Council and the establishment of a Transition Council to prepare for presidential election and inauguration of civilian rule.

1993 In June presidential elections, Moshood Kashimawo Olawale ("M. K. O.") Abiola apparently wins, but a court injunction prevents announcement of results. Before stepping down as president in August, Babangida names Transition Council chairman Chief Ernest Shonekan as head of Interim National Government (ING). In November, Defense Minister General Sani Abacha takes over as head of new military administration after Nigeria's Federal High

Court declares ING unconstitutional. Abacha dissolves the country's bicameral legislature—the National Assembly—bans the two national political parties, and establishes a Provisional Ruling Council made up of senior military officers.

1994 Abacha convenes National Constitutional Conference (NCC), which gives preliminary endorsement to draft constitution and recommends return to civilian government no later than January 1, 1996.

1995 Final NCC report to the Abacha regime contains new draft of basic law but no timetable for its implementation. Abacha announces that his administration will cede authority to civilian government by October 1, 1998.

1996 Six more states—one in each geographic zone—added to federation, bringing total number of states to thirty-six.

1998 Abacha dies unexpectedly; General Abdulsalam Abubakar designated as his successor. Abubakar announces transition to civilian rule will be completed by May 1999. Government publishes NCC's draft constitution. Niger Delta region witnesses violent protests and occupations of oil production facilities.

1999 Abubakar declares **Fourth Republic** with adoption of new basic law based on the 1979 constitutional framework. Former army general Olusegun Obasanjo elected president in February. Return to civilian rule completed in May, with Obasanjo's inauguration as president for a four-year term and enactment of the new constitution. Mass violence erupts in northern region as Muslim-dominated states consider adopting Islamic legal codes; southern states experience anti-Muslim backlash.

1

INTRODUCTION

ANIEL ELAZAR HAS ARGUED that there are two kinds of federal systems—namely, "those in which the purpose of federalism is to share power broadly, pure and simple, and those in which the purpose of federalism is to give individual national communities a share in the power of the state."[1] Nigeria is perhaps the paradigmatic African case of the innovative use of federal principles and institutions to accommodate diverse communal constituencies within the power structure of the state. These communities are not primordial but have been shaped by the evolution and reconfiguration of the federal state itself, and it is the communal competition for access to state-controlled rewards and resources, rather than the simple fact of communal diversity, that provides the impetus to federalism in Nigeria.

The Nigerian federal system has always exhibited "peculiar" and "irregular" characteristics.[2] From the conventional perspectives of comparative federalism, the primary anomaly in Nigerian federalism is the domination of the country's politics by centralizing military elites who have ruled for more than two-thirds of the period since independence from Britain in 1960. Ivo Duchacek, for instance, argues that "the number of military coups d'état, followed by various tightly centralized controls, raises serious doubts about Nigeria's practice of federalism."[3]

The interventionist tendencies of what Donald Horowitz has

1

described as Nigeria's "bloated, greedy military" provide only a partial explanation for the peculiarities and pathologies of Nigerian federalism, however.[4] First, given the "irrepressible pluralism" of Nigerian society and the convulsive repercussions that attended the attempts to impose unitary rule in 1966, the country's military rulers have been constrained to "foster federalism, at least in some respectable way, rather than attempting to confront it at great political risk."[5] Thus, as Lawrence Rupley has observed, the country's military regimes have frequently been characterized "by a sensitivity to the diversity of opinions within Nigeria that is perhaps surprising to those who equate governance by soldiers with an intolerance for differences."[6]

Second, the centralizing tendencies that have reduced Nigeria into a "unitary state in federal disguise," to borrow a phrase from Gavin Williams and Terisa Turner, have not resulted from the military's tightly centralized controls alone.[7] The following must be numbered among other equally critical sources of overcentralization in Nigeria:

❖ The fact that the Nigerian federation "was not created by the coming together of separate states but was the subdivision of a country which had in theory been ruled [by the British colonial hegemon] as a single unit."[8]

❖ The unifying impact of the 1967–70 civil war, which, like the civil wars in the United States and elsewhere, produced a much stronger central authority with enhanced power and prestige.

❖ The ardent and generalized desire for rapid, state-led, and centrally coordinated development amidst pervasive economic scarcity.

❖ The overwhelming domination of the Nigerian economy by federally collected oil revenues, which account for some 80 percent of public finances at all levels of government and about 90 percent of the country's foreign exchange earnings.

❖ The continued intensity of distributive contention (as opposed to productive accumulation) in the Nigerian federation as the country's constituent governments and segments struggle relentlessly for the center's abundant financial resources and distributive largesse.

These distributive pressures are basic to an understanding of the four issues that constitute the focus of this study—namely, (1) the

intergovernmental sharing of revenues, (2) the reorganization of constituent state and local units, (3) the conduct and uses of population
censuses, and (4) the principle of "federal character," which prescribes
the equitable representation of the country's diverse segments in public
institutions. These four issues are in some way the pivots around which
have revolved the country's attempts to use the institutions and practices of federalism to mediate sectional political conflict and regulate
ethnic economic competition.

FEDERALISM AND CONFLICT MANAGEMENT IN NIGERIA

The essence of federalism is the constitutionalized or largely irrevocable
division of governmental powers and functions on a territorial basis
within a single country. More specifically, federalism entails the division
of power between central and constituent authorities, that the division
is entrenched in the constitution, that constituent governments
(regions, states, provinces, or cantons) have a share in central power,
and that the constituent units cannot be unilaterally abrogated by the
center.[9] In Nigeria, as in Switzerland, India, or Canada (especially in
relation to Quebec), federalism has developed in response to the need
for the accommodation of basic territorial ethnolinguistic or religious
diversity. Although Nigeria is recognized as one of the most ethnically
diverse countries in the world, however, the precise nature of the country's ethnolinguistic composition has remained a matter for conjecture.
Nevertheless, there is considerable consensus about the existence of
three major conglomerate nationalities that collectively account for
about two-thirds of the country's estimated population of 110 million:
the Muslim Hausa-Fulani in the North, the predominantly Christian
Igbo in the East, and the religiously bicommunal Yoruba in the West.
The rest of the population is variously believed to be made up of
between two hundred and four hundred "ethnic minorities," ranging
in size from several thousand to a few million and comprising adher-
ents of Christianity, Islam, and traditional indigenous religions.

The indeterminacy of Nigeria's ethnic configuration is really not
surprising. Like elsewhere in Africa, contemporary ethnicity in Nigeria
is hardly traditional or "rigid" in character. Rather, it is "an exceeding-
ly complex amalgam of multifaceted and interpenetrating identities"

that are still very much in the process of evolution and are ever "shift-ing up or down" in scale and intensity depending on the political or economic context.[10]

The key reason for the collapse of the asymmetric three region federal system bequeathed by the British at independence was precise-ly that it gave inadequate recognition to the multiplicity, complexity, and latent fluidity of ethnic territorial interests in the federation. Instead, this system reified the country's major tripartite ethnic cleav-age and transformed "a multiple ethnic balance of power," with no sin-gle ethnic group forming a majority, into a "federal imbalance" with the Northern Region alone comprising more than half the country's pop-ulation and three-quarters of its territory.[11] The consequences of this faulty structure included the ethnoregional polarization of party com-petition in the ill-fated First Republic (1960–66) and the eventual out-break of civil war.

Since the institution of a multistate federal system in 1967, how-ever, Nigerian federalism has arguably functioned to decentralize and defuse ethnic conflict in several ways.

First, by establishing the states (now thirty-six in number) as relatively autonomous arenas of political authority and resource compe-tition, federalism has served to devolve ethnic conflict away from the federal government or a few regional centers to the various state capitals. This devolution, in turn, has helped to localize ethnic conflicts in indi-vidual states and to lessen the possibility that such conflicts will engulf other constituent units or overwhelm the national political system. Thus pressures by Nigeria's Muslims for full official recognition of Islamic law have been largely contained by constitutional provisions that empower the states to establish Shari'a courts for their Muslim populations. Consequently, states in the Muslim-dominated North have been able to institute fairly elaborate systems of Islamic courts without provoking opposition from Christian or animist groups in other states or violating the basic secularity of the common federal arena.

This religious accommodation was endangered after the restora-tion of democratic rule in May 1999. Beginning with Zamfara state in October 1999, several northern states enacted or proposed legislation that would extend the scope of Shari'a law from personal and civil cases all the way to criminal matters. This implied drastic changes to the

North's pre-existing penal code, which was only partially based on elements of Shari'a. Despite the federal government's discouraging the push for strict religious law in the Muslim North, the judicial expansion of Shari'a eventually led to horrific sectarian and ethnoreligious bloodletting during early 2000, the exodus of several southern immigrants (mainly Christian Igbos) from the North, and even fresh talks about the confederalization or dissolution of the Nigerian entity. This explosive move to institute full Shari'a at the subfederal level notwithstanding, however, Nigeria's Christian and Muslim communities remained united in their commitment to preserving the religious neutrality or plurality of the federal center.

Second, multistate federalism in Nigeria has been used to fragment and crosscut the identities of each of the three major ethnic formations of Hausa-Fulani, Yoruba, and Igbo. Whereas the old regional system had institutionalized the demographic and political dominance of one of these ethnic groups in each region, the current thirty-six–state structure distributes the core population of each majority ethnicity among at least five states. This distribution has served to expose or activate important historical, territorial, or subethnic cleavages within the ethnic majority groups and to relegate them to smaller states that, unlike the old regions, are not large enough or economically strong enough to challenge the federal government. Although the major ethnic groups continue to demonstrate considerable internal cohesion as they compete with each other in bidding for supremacy in national politics, this ethnic solidarity is significantly less incendiary than the aggressive ethnic chauvinism that had expressed itself through the old regional system, fueled secessionist tendencies, and brought the country to the brink of disintegration.

Third, Nigeria's current federal institutional structure has operated to protect the numerous ethnic minorities from the direct hegemony of the bigger ethnic groups. Whereas the old regional system had denied the minorities the security of their own states or regions, the current thirty-six–state structure includes some fourteen states that are dominated by minority populations. Although it has not been possible to give each minority group a state of its own—and strident agitations for new states have persisted in many of the more ethnically heterogeneous minority-populated states—the multistate federal system has enabled "a variety of ethnic minority states to play an increasingly active role in a more fluid and decentralized polity."[12] This role of ethnic minorities has been particularly decisive in moderating and defusing the traditional rivalries and tensions between the country's three ethnic majority groups.

Fourth, as in many African countries that have sought to replace ethnic categories by administrative-territorial divisions as part of a state-building strategy, Nigeria's multistate federalism has promoted state-based identities as a cleavage that is independent of, and even competitive with, ethnic identities. This has been achieved by the distribution of homogeneous ethnic majority formations across many states and the incorporation of ethnic minority segments into heterogeneous units. This multistate structure does not eliminate ethnically homogeneous states; rather, it ensures that there is no state that contains all of the members of a major ethnolinguistic group to the exclusion of other states.[13]

The extent to which the ostensibly innocuous category of "statism" has been able to replace, rather than simply coexist with, the more explosive ethnoregional and religious identities is debatable, however. Much of the discussion on "statism" in Nigeria has focused almost exclusively on its negative role in generating discriminatory practices that exclude nonindigenous citizens (Nigerians residing in states other than their own) from state-controlled educational and bureaucratic opportunities available to indigenes. Nevertheless, Nigeria's use of constituent state units to dilute its combustible ethnic structure would appear to confirm the thesis that "successful multiethnic federal systems are those in which there is at least a certain level of divergence between the constituent units and the ethnic divisions."[14] This thesis, in turn, derives from the broader sociological theory that cleavages reinforcing, rather than crosscutting, one another tend to be additive and to result in the polarization and intensification of conflict. India is one country that has generally followed the principle of organizing its states on an ethnolinguistic basis. But the danger of sectional polarization in the Indian context is significantly diminished by the existence of crosscutting formations based on caste, sect, religion, and class.[15] The same sociological complexity exists in Switzerland, where linguistic and religious cleavages crosscut, rather than coincide with, one another.[16] In the absence of strong crosscutting cleavages in Nigeria, and given the country's relatively centralized ethnic structure (with three groups predominating), the decoupling of governmental from ethnic categories would appear to be an effective means of taming the "secession potential" that Charles Tarlton and Eric Nordlinger, among others, see as inherent in federalism's grant of autonomy to subnational constituencies.[17]

Fifth, and finally, federalism in Nigeria has functioned as a mechanism for devolving federally controlled resources and opportunities to diverse territorial constituencies and interests. Elazar, for instance, has called attention to the opportunities that the "politics of federalism offers . . . for extending economic benefits more widely than has otherwise been the case in the Third World."[18] Indeed, according to him,

> The Nigerian experience points to one of the real benefits of federalism in the developing world—the increased opportunity potentially provided by federal arrangements for the spread of development beyond the capital region, thus avoiding the common phenomenon of confining so-called national development to a single metropolis at the expense of the rest of the country.[19]

The dynamics of Nigeria's federalism have had less to do with the geographical dispersal of development from a central capital to regional jurisdictions than with plain, and increasingly fierce, interethnic struggles for centrally controlled resources and rewards. Moreover, the impact of this "ethno-distributive" approach to federalism has not been to spur local development efforts but to intensify the reliance of constituent segments and governments on central largesse in a way that has harmed rather than fostered the development of genuine federal relationships. Nevertheless, Elazar's remarks are useful in pointing attention to how federalism in Nigeria has been assimilated into a distributive strategy that is designed to channel central resources to ethno-territorial or sectional constituencies. His views echo the arguments of several close observers of Nigerian politics.

Nevertheless, such arguments say very little about the developmental, as opposed to the distributive, role of Nigerian federalism. Adele Jinadu, for instance, speaks of an "economic dimension" to Nigerian politics "whereby federalism is expected to equalize, as far as possible, the access of ethnic groups to public goods and to facilitate their active and meaningful involvement in and incorporation into the country's socioeconomic life."[20] According to Henry Bienen:

> The history of independent Nigeria had been one in which regions and ethnic groups struggled for shares of national revenue obtained first from the sale of commodity exports, especially groundnuts and cocoa, and then from small but growing oil sales. In so far as Nigeria has seen its politics governed by distributional issues, these have been communally defined for the most part and have centered on allocation from the center to the regions and states in the Nigerian federation.[21]

In his important study on *Politics and Economic Development in Nigeria,* Tom Forrest documents the primacy and pervasiveness of "distributive pressures, heightened by the existence of large centralized revenues, involving a struggle for shares in federal resources and representation at the center by individuals, communities and regions."[22] He explains that the "strength of distributive issues that have made up much of the substance of political debate and controversy and affected the allocation of resources is not explicable without reference to the evolution of the federal system and the structure of political competition."[23]

Of course, the emphasis on the ethno-distributive approach to federalism in Nigeria relates to broader structural features of African political economies. Here the forces of cultural segmentation, differential intersegmental modernization and mobilization under colonialism, resource scarcity, and state economic expansion have combined to make "politicized communal contention over economic distribution issues the prevalent form of politically relevant ethnicity."[24] Yet Goran Hyden suggests that experimentation with federalism has enabled Nigeria to avoid the closed and highly personalized forms of patrimonial ethnic politics that have become entrenched elsewhere on the continent. He contends that while patrimonialism encourages the practice of using the state primarily as a means to satisfy the patronage demands made by an elite cartel in the name of specific communities, Nigeria's federalism—in spite of its prebendal or ethnoclientelistic features—brings competitive community demands more effectively into the open and encourages the forging of impersonal rules and institutions designed to secure and broaden concepts of political justice, fairness, and reciprocity.[25]

Yet the primacy of distributive issues in Nigerian politics may reflect the federal system's role in taming or deflecting more incandesecent cultural-psychological or symbolic ethnic concerns. As Donald Rothchild explains, distributive struggles over fiscal allocations, the siting of infrastructure improvements, cabinet appointments, civil service recruitment, or appropriate allocative principles reflect negotiable conflicts among ethnic interests that share a common sense of destiny and a collective feeling of loyalty to the existing political order.[26] Subjective or symbolic conflicts over relative group status, cultural survival, identity, or territory, on the other hand, are nonnegotiable in character and often call into question the integrity, legitimacy, or normative authority of the political system. Nonnegotiable conflicts and the hegemonic or authoritarian state practices with which they are associated typically arise in hierarchically ranked, often racially polarized, plural societies devoid of any acceptance of the moral equivalence of the competing ethnic publics.

Such destructive conflicts can also develop in unranked ethnic systems, however, when ethnic representatives become intolerant and intransigent or when a regime becomes unresponsive or oppressive. Thus, "in some situations, ethnic groups begin with negotiable demands involving modest resource costs. If the state does not meet these claims, however, they can lead to extreme, nonnegotiable demands."[27] The Nigerian civil war is an apt illustration of the role that flawed institutional arrangements for managing state-ethnic relations may play in engendering otherwise avoidable catastrophic ethnic conflict. In brief, then, the salience of distributive issues in Nigeria today may argue for the success of the multistate federal system in channeling ethnic conflict along constructive, or negotiable, rather than destructive, or nonnegotiable, lines.

THE TRAVAILS OF NIGERIAN FEDERALISM

There is, however, growing recognition within Nigeria of what Daniel Bach has described as the "boomerang effects" of the country's federal practices.[28] The communiqué of a major national conference on Nigerian federalism, for instance, observed that the federal system was perched precariously on a "weak productive base."[29] This fragility was described as the logical outcome of diverse local or ethnoregional interests' preoccupation with distributing a shrinking "national cake" rather than producing a bigger one—that is to say, a preoccupation with distributive over developmental issues. In his 1992 federal budget speech, General Ibrahim Babangida referred to the country's structural enervation by a "cake-sharing psychosis" that has frustrated the autonomous and productive mobilization of grassroots resources.[30] But perhaps the most scathing critique of Nigeria's federal project is to be found in a December 1992 speech by Claude Ake, the country's foremost political scientist and political economist. His views, which reflect subtly on growing resentments by oil-rich minority groups at being the "milch cows" of the federation, deserve to be quoted at some length:

> [T]he habit of consuming . . . without producing . . . underlies our fanatical zeal for political power, and our political fragmentation. We seek political power avidly because it enables us to accumulate wealth without the bother of producing. We demand more and more states and local government areas because as each group divides itself, it appropriates more from the public coffers. We inflate population figures because the more we are the more we receive.
>
> Our predatory disposition has . . . ruined our state-building project. For us the state is not so much the incarnation of a corporate political identity as a battlefield. It is an arena where the different groups go, armed to the teeth, to battle for appropriation of what should be commonwealth. Every one takes from it, or tries to, and few ever give. Our predatory disposition constitutes the Nigerian state as a negative unity of takers in which collective enterprise is all but impossible. . . . Where does the wealth which we are for ever scheming to appropriate come from? We do not want to know. All we want to know is whether we can muster the power to appropriate it.[31]

A chief asset of federalism is that, in providing for the concurrent existence of multiple arenas of power, it disperses the stakes in political competition and reduces the intensity of the struggles for control of any one level or center of governmental authority. Thus in robust federal systems, the "game of politics is played vigorously and significantly in several places simultaneously" and "victories are seldom total or defeats irretrievable."[32] In Nigeria, however, economic resources and political power remain concentrated heavily at the central level. Although the current system of intergovernmental revenue sharing provides for the devolution of about half of federally collected revenues to the states and localities, the result of this distributive strategy has been to erode any sense of financial autonomy and responsibility at state and local levels without necessarily equipping these governments with adequate resources to discharge their socioeconomic responsibilities. Because of the absence of any truly autonomous niches of power and resources below the national plane, the competition for federal "political power in order to preside over the sharing out of the painlessly derived oil largesse becomes extremely vicious and destabilizing."[33]

In essence, Nigeria's deficient federalism cannot be absolved from the destructive "intensity of political conflict" most observers regard as the basic "threat to constitutional democracy" in the country.[34] Nigeria's recent turbulent political history has seen the collapse of two discredited civilian regimes, the military's eventual abortion of a protracted program of transition to a Third (democratic) Republic, and the swift crystallization of constitutional and communal challenges to the viability of the Fourth Republic. The same frenzied struggles for political power that have provided the pretext for the military's overthrow of civilian constitutions have led to several countercoups and convulsions within the military power structure itself. Concerned observers of these dismal political trajectories have long recognized that the inventive and extensive decentralization of powers and resources will be needed to secure democratic governance and political stability in Nigeria.[35] Yet other commentators appear to be daunted by what they see as the "structural intractability" and institutional imperviousness arising from the country's overwhelming dependence on centralized oil revenues.[36]

Given the dominant role that the distribution of central revenues plays in the operation of Nigeria's federal system, it is hardly surprising that the issue of revenue allocation has become a particularly explosive and contentious topic. The establishment of nine separate commissions on revenue allocation since 1946 has led to neither the development of an acceptable or stable sharing formula nor the elaboration of an appropriate framework of values and rules within which a formula can be devised and incrementally adjusted to cope with changing circumstances.

Interregional conflict over control of growing oil revenues was both an important source of friction in the final years of the First Republic and an underlying cause of the outbreak of civil war. The issue also engendered destructive interparty and intergovernmental conflicts during the Second Republic (1979–83). The latest twist to Nigeria's explosive revenue-sharing debates is the emergence of autonomist and separatist pressures among oil-rich communities in the southern ethnic minority states of Akwa Ibom, Bayelsa, Cross River, Delta, and Rivers. These communities, on which the country is dependent for about 80 percent of its oil production, are protesting both alleged neglect by the federal government and the use of their resources to subsidize other parts of the federation. Consequently, they have launched strident and sometimes violent movements for political self-determination and resource control in the oil-rich Delta region. These autonomist pressures were only partially moderated by recent revenue allocation policies that have sought to return higher proportions of oil revenues to the oil-rich areas through the partial restoration or recognition of "derivation" as a principle of economic entitlement.

Such autonomist stirrings would appear to provide strong support for Ronald May's thesis that federations incorporating small resource-rich units and large resource-poor units are especially likely to have their stability threatened by secessionist pressures from the wealthy segments.[37] Larry Diamond notes that "recurrent conflicts over the formula for distribution of federal revenue have been easier to settle than many other ethnic issues in Nigeria precisely because they have been quantifiable" or negotiable.[38] Richard Joseph, on the other hand, contends in his seminal work on *Democracy and Prebendal Politics in Nigeria* that "the presence of competitive regional and ethnic blocs of the population, a contest complicated by differences in language, religion and level of economic attainment, has rendered the issue of revenue allocation one of uncommon intensity."[39] Indeed, the issue's historic and ongoing involvement with separatist currents in the Nigerian federation is an apt illustration of the tendency for apparently negotiable distributive demands to assume a nonnegotiable, or disintegrative, character under the influence of inappropriate regimes or ill-motivated ethnic elites. One would like to agree with Philip Asiodu that the Nigerian federal system still has "a long way to go in meeting the claims of the oil producing areas, which see themselves as losing nonreplaceable resources while replaceable and permanent resources are being developed elsewhere largely with the oil revenues."[40]

The emphasis on the distributive aspects of federalism inevitably compels the concerted identification and elaboration of appropriate allocative criteria or principles. In Nigeria, as elsewhere in Africa, proportionality (that is, the allocation of central resources to constituent units or segments on the basis of relative population size) has been recognized as the best principle of allocation in terms of its universality and neutrality. Yet this distributive principle and the political struggles over the regional distribution of federal electoral constituencies have rendered the conduct and uses of population censuses the source of some of the most violently divisive conflicts in the Nigerian federation. Indeed, according to T. M. Yesufu, "the experience of Nigeria . . . suggests that in Federal states where regionalist feelings are strong, the political stakes of a census can be so high as to make the desirability of a statistically accurate count seem irrelevant."[41]

All of Nigeria's postindependence censuses (in 1962–63, 1973, and 1991) have provoked considerable ethnoregional suspicion and agitation. The lag of almost two decades between the conduct of the 1973 census, whose results were annulled amidst bitter interregional recriminations, and the organization of the 1991 census reflected some form of elite political consensus on the need to de-emphasize, if not completely avoid, what had become a major threat to the federation's stability. Although the 1991 census produced fewer polarizing outcomes than its predecessors, its results have nevertheless remained the object of considerable litigation and contention. It is open to question whether the Fourth Republic, already prematurely enfeebled by the regional and religious contention over Shari'a, can safely come through the conduct and outcome of a national census. Given the incendiary linkages between ethnoregional politics and census statistics in the country, the norm of decennial national population counts may be politically prohibitive in the Nigerian setting.

Partly in an attempt to sidestep the census quicksand, Nigeria's rulers have tried to impose an alternative distributive criterion—namely, the division of federal resources on an equal basis among the constituent governments of the federation. For most of the first phase of military rule from 1966 to 1979, for instance, half of the national revenues apportioned to the states was distributed on the basis of interunit equality and the other half shared on the basis of relative population. Quite predictably, the standard of interunit equality has been widely denounced for its inequitable impact on the economic fortunes of the country's more populous states. These strictures, in turn, have progressively nudged Nigeria's central authorities toward a policy of establishing states of approximately equivalent population, a strategy that has ironically merely accented the distributive importance of population statistics.

Indeed, as Martin Dent notes, "Nigeria is unique among federations in having deliberately sought to create regional units of roughly equal population."[42] While it has not been possible to establish states of exactly equal population, the degree of relative correspondence in the demographic size of Nigeria's constituent units is remarkable nevertheless. According to the provisional results of the 1991 census, the four most populous states in the federation at the time had a population of between four and five million each, while the four smallest states had a population of more than a million each. The remaining twenty-two states in the federation had a population of between two and three million each. This configuration was a far cry from the situation in the First Republic, when the Northern Region alone contained 53 percent of the federation's population. It is also a demographic distribution that is unusual for most contemporary federations, where the existence of dispersed demographic inequalities among constituent units, rather than the establishment of approximately equal units, is the characteristic norm.[43]

The official commitment to creating demographically equivalent constituent units and the practice of distributing central resources on an equal basis among states largely account for another exceptional feature of Nigerian federalism—namely, the persistent, pervasive, and politically irresistible pressures for the establishment of new states. As Elazar and Dean McHenry have shown, successful or mature federal systems are characterized by the relative stability or continuity in the boundaries of their constituent states. That does not mean that boundaries cannot be changed. It implies, rather, that such changes are normally implemented after a prohibitive or complicated constitutional process and are less frequent once the early cries for new states in the formative period of federation have abated. Even in India, where pressures for new states have not evaporated, politically important calls for fundamental changes in the number and shape of constituent units seem to have diminished significantly since the 1956 reorganization of states on a linguistic basis.[44]

Nigeria, unlike other federations, appears to be trapped in an endemic, unending, and seemingly intractable process of internal territorial agitations and reorganizations. There have been six state-creation exercises in the period since independence: In 1963, the three-region structure was changed to a four-region scheme via the excision of the Mid-West from the Western Region. In 1967, on the eve of civil war, the four regions were replaced with a twelve-state structure. In 1976, seven additional states were created to inaugurate a nineteen-state structure. In 1987, Katsina and Akwa Ibom were established as the twentieth and twenty-first states of the federation. In 1991, nine new states were created to establish a thirty-state structure. And in 1996, the number of Nigerian states increased to thirty-six with the creation of six new administrative units by the Abacha administration. Yet vigorous demands for more states, as well as new local government areas, are still being made by communities seeking easy access to central revenues. Of course, given the sheer multiplicity and fluidity of the territorial and cultural cleavages that can be used to justify the demands for new states and the federal resources they bring with them, there is no certainty that the state-creation process will ever be concluded in Nigeria.

It should be emphasized that, unlike in the classical federations of Canada, Switzerland, and the United States, the process of state creation in Nigeria has exclusively involved the fragmentation of existing units, including ethnically homogeneous states, rather than the incorporation of new units. Moreover, except for the 1963 reorganization, all state-creation exercises in Nigeria have been implemented by military fiat rather than by constitutional amendment and popular ratification. The arbitrariness that has invariably intruded into this method of implementing territorial reforms has fueled demands for more states by providing a moral weapon for communities contesting the legitimacy of the federation's internal boundaries.

It is widely conceded that the primary impact of the repeated proliferation and fragmentation of constituent units has been to reinforce centralizing tendencies in the federation. As Diamond rightly suggests, "the greater the number of states, the weaker and less viable individual states will become, with the direct consequence that the center would actually gather more powers and initiative."[45] However, one policy that has served to compensate for this overcentralization is the constitutional principle that prescribes the recognition of the country's "federal character," or plural nature, in the composition and conduct of key federal institutions and agencies. Although the federal character principle is sometimes interpreted to involve the equal devolution of federal developmental patronage to the states, its primary purpose is not to disperse resources away from the center but to establish an ethnically representative or inclusive center. Celebrated by some as a paradigm of creative ethnic-conflict management,[46] the practice of the federal character principle has also been denigrated by others as intellectually and morally crude, politically contentious, sectionally divisive, and institutionally destructive. According to Ladipo Adamolekun and John Kincaid:

> . . . the "federal character" concept has encouraged many Nigerians to view federalism not as a principle of noncentralized democratic government, but as simply a guarantee of ethnic and religious group representation in the institutions of government, no matter how centralized. Thinking federally and dispersing and sharing power accordingly among a multiplicity of governmental and nongovernmental institutions are thereby frustrated by a principle of power sharing that is simultaneously divisive and hierarchical. Thus, the military has been careful to maintain "federal character" practices even while centralizing power.[47]

The recurrent controversies over the appropriate modalities for implementing the federal character principle in Nigeria have come to epitomize all the tensions associated with the country's daunting national question. Thus, reflecting the recent surge of politicized interreligious agitations in the federation, current debates on the federal character principle have sometimes focused on the relative representation of Christian and Muslim segments in public institutions at both federal and, especially, state levels.

Until 1986, when the military administration of General Ibrahim Babangida arbitrarily enlisted Nigeria in the Organization of the Islamic Conference (OIC), Nigeria was noted for the remarkable amity between its large Muslim and Christian populations. This exemplary interreligious coexistence was sufficiently resilient to survive the political disagreements that developed during 1961–62 and 1977–78 over the institutionaliza-tion and constitutionalization of Shari'a. Since the OIC imbroglio, how-ever, Nigeria appears to have degenerated from a religiously peaceable to a religiously polarized federation. Aside from the bloody interreligious riots that have convulsed many northern cities since 1987, clashes which eventually provoked reprisal killings in the Igbo southeast during early 2000, a key manifestation of this polarized climate has been the increas-ing mobilization of religious identities behind the sectional struggles over the implementation of the federal character principle.

How This Work Is Organized

This introductory essay and the following chapter on the evolution of Nigerian federalism are designed to provide the analytical and histori-cal background to the study of conflict and federalism in Nigeria. The core chapters of the study—namely, chapters 3 through 6—are devot-ed to a discussion of Nigeria's continuing efforts to come to grips with the four contentious issues of revenue allocation; state (and local) reor-ganizations; intersegmental (including interreligious) representation, or the federal character principle; and population enumeration. To reiter-ate, all four issues are linked, in some way, to the attempts to mediate sectional political conflict and resource competition in the Nigerian federation. They have, however, also invariably served to underscore and intensify such conflict and competition. Much of the substance of the debate on Nigerian federalism revolves around the recurrent attempts to come to terms with these four sensitive subjects.

In discussing these issues, this study will, among other things, attempt to highlight the specific factors and forces contributing to their contentiousness, the perspectives and policies that have been developed to manage this divisiveness, the impact of the conflict-management strategies employed by various administrations, and the prospects for the continued mediation of the four contested issues under a political order that is stable, truly federal, and truly democratic.

The issue of federal institutional reform in Nigeria is a primary concern of this work. For all its flaws and failures, Nigerian federalism remains an "intensely living thing" and the "indispensable basis" for the country's continued survival as a single political entity.[48] Moreover, a key virtue of federalism as a political design that is based on "choice rather than accident" is the enormous possibilities that it offers for creative institutional renovation, experimentation, and adaptation on a continuing basis. Accordingly, the seventh and concluding chapter of this study is devoted to a discussion of the prospects and requisites for the creative elaboration and implementation of federalist reforms in the Nigerian experience.

2
THE EVOLUTION OF
THE NIGERIAN FEDERATION

FOUR DECADES AFTER its formal amalgamation into a single country under British colonial hegemony in 1914, Nigeria was finally established as a three-region federation under the 1954 Lyttelton Constitution. This constitution gave the country's three large but unequal regions substantial powers over internal policy and administration, while leaving external affairs and interregional issues largely to the center. In the interval between amalgamation and federation, Nigeria had been governed by the British as a unitary (albeit politically decentralized) state or, particularly after the Macpherson Constitution of 1951, as a quasi-federal entity. Underlying the decisive change in 1954 to a federal form of government were at least three closely interrelated but analytically distinct factors:

❖ The staggering diversity and sheer strength of ethnolinguistic forces in the federation.

❖ The differential regional impact of colonial administration, modernization, and mobilization.

❖ The enormous attraction that federalist guarantees of subnational autonomy had for the emergent, regionally based Nigerian "successor elites."[1]

The scale and intensity of Nigeria's ethnic diversity have become almost proverbial and will not be recounted here. Suffice it to say that British-created Nigeria was, and remains, "one of the most ethnically diverse countries in the world" and perhaps the most deeply divided of all the countries created in the course of the European occupation of Africa.[2] Although they had been interacting with one another in diverse ways since long before the colonial era, the several hundred Nigerian groups evinced sharp differences in geographical conditions, historical traditions, political institutions, and demographic configuration. Within Nigeria's borders were to be found, for instance, some 380 linguistic modes of communication, as many as twenty distinct geographical regions, and such divergent forms of political organization as clan communities, village republics, city-states, chiefdoms, kingdoms, and a caliphate.[3]

The most politically salient feature of Nigeria's ethnic diversity, however, was the distribution of ethnic groups into a relatively centralized ethnic structure, with the Hausa-Fulani, Yoruba, and Igbo formations predominating. As the rivalries among these three groups crystallized into bitter political struggles during the late colonial era (under the combined impact of economic competition and electoral mobilization), it became increasingly clear to all interested observers that only by some form of highly decentralized political arrangements could the major groups be accommodated within a single country. Nigeria's federalism, therefore, developed as an institutional response both to the federal character of the society (with its sharp territorial ethnolinguistic divisions) and to the explosive demographic configuration of the ethnic structure, which pitted three major nationalities in fierce competition with one another.

Yet Nigerian scholars have generally contested the view that the roots of Nigerian federalism lie in the primordial geography or cultural complexity of the country's society. Instead, they have placed greater emphasis on the legacy of British administrative regionalism or the colonial divide-and-rule syndrome. They argue, for instance, that the configuration of the three-region federation bequeathed by the British was rooted in the "pattern of colonial domination and the structures of colonial administration" rather than in the "natural" boundaries of Nigeria's constituent ethnic communities.[4]

This position deliberately underplays the fact that the three-region federation had been consciously designed to secure autonomy and hegemony for the country's three major nationalities. Although each region incorporated substantial numbers of ethnic minorities, each was dominated by a major ethnic group that constituted the political center of gravity of the regional government. Collectively, the three major ethnic groups were—and still remain—the main, but by no means the exclusive, competitors for power and privilege in the Nigerian federation.

In essence, the thesis that British administrative regionalism is the bedrock of Nigerian federalism often betrays an inadequate appreciation for federalism's deep roots in Nigeria's multinational, multireligious, multiregional, multicultural, and multilingual society. The thesis cannot satisfactorily account for the persistence of support for federalism in Nigeria after several years of independence from Britain and the dismantling of the colonially constructed tripartite regional system. What is more, this thesis oversimplifies the complex and ambivalent role of the British as a force for both integration and differentiation in Nigeria.

Far from being simply a divisive force, the initial historical role of the British was that of an agent of political integration and consolidation of the various Nigerian peoples. Through a protracted piecemeal and sometimes brutal process of colonial conquest and incorporation, the British brought the diverse Nigerian peoples together under the rubric of a modern economy and state. Moreover, despite the contradictory policies and pronouncements of many of its officers in northern Nigeria, it was obvious that the British government wanted to maintain Nigeria as a single political entity "and would have delayed independence if one or more regions had insisted on separation."[5] This "British intention for Nigerian unity,"[6] to borrow a phrase from Prime Minister Abubakar Tafawa Balewa, was motivated by diplomatic factors and, perhaps more important, by a desire to ensure the economic viability or financial profitability of the colonial project in Nigeria. Thus, the amalgamation of 1914 was motivated not only by the expectation that the South would benefit from the North's advanced system of native administration but also by a desire to combine the North's annual deficit with the South's financial surplus and put an end to the economically dysfunctional competition between the two regions.[7]

Having done so much to construct the Nigerian state, however, the British did relatively little to consolidate a Nigerian nation. Instead, British administrative policies intensified and reified the ethnic consciousness that the colonial regime's incorporation of divergent ethnic communities had been decisive in forging in the first place. Three aspects of British colonial policy were particularly decisive in unleashing centrifugal pressures for the disaggregation of the unitary colonial Nigerian state into a regional federation.

The first was the policy of indirect rule, which sought to administer the various Nigerian peoples through their traditional political institutions. This policy was elevated to the status of a dogma in the autocratic emirates of the North, where it was anchored in an elaborate and long-standing system of taxation and administration. In those parts of the country that lacked the hierarchical indigenous political forms of the emirate North, indirect rule often involved the invention or reification of strong tribal political institutions. The overall impact of this policy was "to reinforce the most conservative" features of local political institutions, perpetuate communal consciousness, and scuttle the forces that had been pushing toward interethnic integration or assimilation in the precolonial era.[8]

A second and related source of divisiveness in British colonial policy was the insulation and isolation of the emirate North from the forces of modernization producing transformative influences in the southern half of the country and, to a more limited extent, in the lower, "Middle Belt," sections of the North itself. A pact between the British and the Fulani emirs to sustain the system of indirect rule protected the theocratic authority of the latter from Christian missionary activity, modern electoral politics, and other forms of "corruptive" modern contacts with Europe or southern Nigeria. Thus, despite the amalgamation of 1914, direct official political intercourse between northerners and southerners did not take place until 1946, when the former were invited to participate for the first time in the advisory central legislative council in Lagos. This insularity ultimately engendered a combustible North-South duality. The most poignant expression of this dichotomy was the huge historical southern head start over the North in virtually every aspect of modernization, including education, per capita income, urbanization, wage employment, commerce, and industrialization. For instance, in 1951 "there was only one university graduate among Northerners, whereas there were hundreds of Yorubas, Igbos, and other Southerners with graduate and postgraduate degrees."[9] This uneven development, and the frenzied northern bid for political security that it entailed, was at the roots of much of the political turbulence in Nigeria during the fifties and sixties; it continues to haunt Nigerian politics even today.

The third and final source of centrifugal tendencies in British colonialism was the policy of administrative regionalism. The year 1939 saw the implementation of a long-agreed plan to divide Nigeria into the Northern, Eastern, and Western groups of provinces. The three provincial groups were subsequently transformed into administrative regions under the Richards Constitution of 1946 and progressively came to be regarded by the British as the "natural" regions or components of the incipient Nigerian federation. The "naturalness" of these regions derived from their rough demarcation by the lateral axis and southward confluence of the Benue and Niger Rivers, their broad coincidence with the three different routes by which the British penetrated and consolidated Nigeria after the cession of Lagos in 1856, and the demographic preponderance in each region of a major ethnic group.

Yet, as mentioned previously, each of the three regions also incorporated several ethnic minority groups, comprising roughly about a third of the regional population, who increasingly came to resent and protest the hegemony of the dominant ethnic nationality in their region. But despite pressures and proposals for territorial reforms by ethnic minority elites and a few concerned British officials, and despite southern apprehensions about the disproportionate size of the Northern Region, the conservative northern political establishment and the pro-northern British government remained inflexibly committed to the three-region structure.

Indeed, the 1958 British-appointed Willink Commission of Inquiry into the Fears of Minorities and the Means for Allaying Them was specifically instructed to make proposals for the creation of new regions "only as a last resort" and "if but only if no other solution seems to the Commission to meet the case."[10] Predictably, the commission reported in favor of retaining the three-region structure, arguing that new regions would produce new minorities, entail huge

financial costs in administrative overhead, and reify otherwise tran-
sient tribalist identities. It then expressed the pious optimism that a
constitutionally entrenched system of fundamental human rights and
the free play of political party rivalry would prevent blatant abuses of
ethnic minority rights or interests. Any hope for the satisfaction of
ethnic minority autonomist pressures was finally dashed at the 1958
London Constitutional Conference when the Colonial Office
explained that any proposals for immediate territorial reforms could
only mean the postponement of the agreed 1960 date for the granting of independence. Thus, although the conference agreed on constitutional provisions for creating new regions in the future, it
inevitably endorsed the tripartite regional structure that was to
become a source of great instability after independence.

British colonial policy essentially set the "regional mould" and
centrifugal basis for Nigerian federalism.[11] This conclusion is qualita-
tively different from the position that the British "governed Nigeria
into federalism" or the more grandiloquent formulation that "the
structures and ideological patterns of British colonialism carried within them a separatist orientation and a federalist fait accompli."[12] On
the contrary, forces other than British colonial policy were at play in
the instauration of federalism in Nigeria. The role of Nigeria's cultural complexity and centralized ethnic structure in generating pressures
for federalism has already been highlighted. The preferences and interests of Nigeria's nationalist leaders furnished another important
impulse for federalism.

As Ladipo Adamolekun and Bamidele Ayo have argued, Nigerian
federalism "resulted from a consensus decision reached between Nigeria's nationalist leaders and the British colonial authorities."[13] Beginning
with the landmark Ibadan General Constitutional Conference of 1950,
the Nigerian political class collaborated with the British to fashion the
basic outlines of a constitution for a self-governing Nigeria. At the conference, and in subsequent constitutional deliberations, the majority of
Nigeria's leaders increasingly and persistently emphasized the need to
grant the fullest autonomy to the country's component groups or
regions. Indeed, as Eme Awa has shown, these leaders behaved as if
"original sovereignty" lay with the regions, which could, therefore,
appropriately allocate functions to the center and reserve the residue to

themselves.[14] Billy Dudley's interpretation of this behavior is that "the Nigerian leaders were positively attracted by . . . the 'Wheare model'" of federalism and the experience of the United States on which it was ostensibly based. According to Dudley:

> The point . . . is not that they deliberately set out to adopt that model irrespective of sociological realities, but rather that they saw that formula as fitting in with those realities in a way in which Canadian, Australian, and Indian experience did not. . . . By accepting the "Wheare formula," Nigeria's leaders were then not merely copying an abstract model, but one which had been found to work successfully in the country which formed the basis for the model, a model which saw the essence of federalism in an institutional arrangement in which the component governmental units had equal and coordinate jural status.[15]

A basic impetus for this commitment to a system of strong constituent units was the sense of regional financial self-sufficiency engendered by the boom in international prices for regionally controlled agricultural commodities during the first half of the fifties. Indeed, the strongest supporters of the 1954 federal constitutional settlement were the political elites of the groundnut-producing North and the cocoa-rich West, the regions that benefited most from the commodity boom. The dominant Hausa-Fulani and Yoruba elements in these regions perceived federalism as a means of protecting regional power and resources from the poor but ambitious Igbo in the East. Indeed, until the 1950s, when openly regional parties developed in response to the inception of electoral competition and the progressive grant of internal autonomy to the regions, the Igbo had effectively dominated the nationalist movement through the enigmatic personality of Nnamdi Azikiwe—who would become the country's first president, albeit a ceremonial position—and his party, the National Council of Nigeria and the Cameroons (NCNC).

In essence, the Action Group (AG) assumed control of the Western Region government and the Northern People's Congress assumed control of the Northern Region government when these regions attained self-governing status in 1957 and 1959, respectively. The NCNC, on the other hand, progressively declined from being a nationwide movement with a formidable presence in the West to being a party of the Eastern Region, which had also attained full internal self-government in 1957.

Electoral competition in the immediate pre-independence peri-od, therefore, led to an unusual party system in which each region had its own party. From 1951 up to independence in 1960, government at the federal level was based on a coalition of two or more parties, an arrangement the Northern People's Congress dominated by virtue of the absolute population majority of its northern regional power base. Thus, when the office of prime minister was established in 1957, the leader of the Northern People's Congress in the central legislature, Abubakar Tafawa Balewa, became premier. After the 1959 federal elec-tions, the Congress-NCNC-AG grand coalition cabinet that he subse-quently established was replaced with a Congress-NCNC coalition government that ushered the country into independence on October 1, 1960.

FEDERALISM AND THE FIRST REPUBLIC, 1960–1966

The essential features of the 1954 Federal Constitution were retained under the 1960 Independence Constitution and the 1963 Republican Constitution. Although Nigeria did not formally become a republic until the introduction of the latter basic law (which substituted President Azikiwe for the British monarch as the country's head of state), the term "First Republic" is widely used by students of the coun-try's politics to designate the entire five-year, three-month duration (October 1960–January 1966) of the first postindependence civilian regime.

The Independence Constitution gave the federal government exclusive control of external affairs, defense, currency, mines and min-erals, and the major forms of communication and transportation. The constitution's list of concurrent central and regional powers included higher education, industrial and water-power development, the judici-ary, the police, and the regulation of labor, including the medical and legal professions. Unenumerated residual powers, including responsi-bility for a wide range of expensive socioeconomic programs in health, education, and agriculture, were left to the regions.[16]

Federalism in the First Republic was dominated by two contra-dictory trends: the growing economic and political ascendancy of the federal government and the vitiation of this centripetal current by the strengthening of the centrifugal pressures inherent in the federation's unwieldy structure and regionalized party system.

Developments in the pre-independence era, including the granting of self-governing status to the regions and the decision of the major party leaders to seek control of regional governments, had underscored the position of the constituent governments as the real locus of power in the Nigerian federation. With independence, however, a fully elected national government assumed responsibility for the federation's external defense and foreign policy and the coordination and supervision of national economic development. The coordinating role of the federal government in matters of economic development, in particular, invariably came to include the exercise of oversight functions that impinged on regional autonomy. Examples included the control of the surpluses of regional commodity marketing boards and the issuance of all external and internal public development loans. All this worked to increase the powers and enhance the prestige of the federation vis-à-vis the regional governments.

The growing subordination of the regions to the center in economic development matters was reinforced by the inelastic nature of regional tax revenues, especially personal income taxes, and the downturn in international prices for regionally controlled primary commodities after the late 1950s. Thus, except for the East (whose revenue position was enhanced by its share of royalties from the growing exploitation of oil located in its territory), all the regional governments experienced annual budgetary deficits for the greater part of the immediate pre-independence period through the First Republic. Indeed, external reserves for the regions fell from more than £120 million in 1954 to only £15.4 million in 1963.[17] Faced with declining revenues and expanding budgetary obligations, the regional governments increasingly turned to the center for financial aid and loans. The impact of these developments was "to make the regions conscious of a degree" of financial and economic "dependence" on the center.[18]

Political developments also underscored and reinforced the new power of the federal government. The Nigerian Constitution, like the Indian Constitution, contained emergency provisions that, if invoked, would enable the central authorities to assume extensive and intrusive unitary powers, including the appropriation of the executive and legislative functions of the regional governments. These powers were indeed activated in 1962, when the Congress-NCNC federal coalition government seized the opportunity of a split in the western-based AG to declare a state of emergency in the Western Region. This move was the "retribution for two and half years of the AG's opposition to the federal government and to the parties forming that government in their home regions."[19] The minority Mid-West area was subsequently excised from the Western Region and administered for six months by the federal government before local elections installed an NCNC government in the new region.

At the same time, the AG was systematically decimated and many of its leaders were humiliated and imprisoned for alleged treasonable offenses. The Congress-NCNC coalition then proceeded to restore to leadership positions of the Western Region government figures who, although enjoying little popular support, were willing to defer to the central government. These events were a "telling demonstration of what the federation can do to a region which is under the control of an opposition party."[20]

The growing fiscal and political supremacy of the center was, however, gravely distorted by the peculiar federal structure and party system. The large size and small number of constituent regional units made it "impossible in Nigeria for any real difference to exist between perceptions of regional power and calculations of national dominance."[21] In particular, the disproportionate size of the North enabled the party in control of that region, the Northern People's Congress, to project its regional dominance onto the federal arena. Thus, in the words of Billy Dudley, "with political power shifting to the centre, the real levers of power [were] actually to be found in the North. Federal superordination . . . in practice turned out to be Northern dominance."[22]

The First Republic is replete with examples of the manipulation of the inequitable federal structure by the northern political establishment to "consolidate its political control over the federation and its financial resources" and "to secure and enhance its class interests in competition against the political classes of the Eastern and Western Regions."[23] Thus, Dudley has shown that federal development spending during the First Republic was so heavily manipulated in favor of the Northern Region that the overall development prospects of the federation were invariably jeopardized.[24] The 1962–63 census crisis provided further evidence of the ability and determination of the North to go to any lengths to maintain its population majority and the political power that it conferred. The systematic obstruction of opposition campaigns in the North during the 1964 federal elections confirmed the futility of any electoral challenge to the political monopoly of the Northern People's Congress under the lopsided federal system. The frustrations and recriminations engendered by these elections culminated in a North-East (Congress-NCNC) polarization that foreshadowed the attempted secession of the Eastern Region barely three years later.

Apart from sowing conflicts among the regions and among the majority groups that dominated the regional governments, the federal structure also produced tensions between majority and minority groups within regions. The AG had sought to exploit these intra-regional ethnic tensions in a bid to mobilize support outside its Western Region base and win power at the center. The boomerang effects of this strategy were evident in the subsequent annihilation of the AG and fragmentation of the Western Region by the Congress-NCNC federal coalition. But besides fueling destructive interparty rivalries, the inequitable incorporation of ethnic minority segments into the federal structure also engendered violent ethnic minority protests within regions. The Western Region was generally believed to be at the threshold of an ethnic minority upheaval when the declaration of a state of emergency provided the opportunity for the excision of the Mid-West. In February and November 1964, riots by the minority Tiv in the Northern Region resulted in the death of an estimated 326 civilians and eleven policemen.[25]

The division of the country into three major regions, each dominated by one ethnic group and each controlled by a party based on that ethnic group, also produced a system of government and opposition that was destructively centrifugal. With each party using all the resources of the regional government to monopolize political participation and power in a region, "effective competition at the federal level means that at least one whole region or nationality group, and maybe more than one, will appear to be in opposition to the federal government."[26] Such a sense of ethnoregional isolation and alienation from the federal government was the predicament of the Yoruba for most of the First Republic, and it was the lot of the Igbo after the 1964 federal election crisis.

Finally, as Larry Diamond has argued, in a federal system with only a few regions "no serious political conflict could long remain contained within a single region."[27] The October 1965 Western Region elections that finally precipitated the collapse of the First Republic epitomized the failure of the federal structure to effectively diffuse and decentralize political conflict. Thus, the Western Region's slide into mass political rebellion and ungovernability, following the sordid rigging of the regional elections by an unpopular government, had a heavy impact on the entire federal system. Unwilling to humiliate the embattled pro–Northern People's Congress government in the West by reimposing emergency rule on the region, the federal government allegedly planned to invite the army to crush the opposition to the regional government.[28] On January 15, 1966, however, the First Republic was overturned in a bloody, but inconclusive, rebellion by a group of relatively junior, predominantly Igbo, military officers.

FEDERALISM UNDER THE FIRST PHASE OF MILITARY RULE, 1966–1979

The three military governments and four military heads of state that presided over this phase of Nigerian history can be demarcated roughly as follows:

- ❖ Major General J. T. U. Aguiyi-Ironsi, an Igbo, wrested power from the fumbling January 1966 putchists and ruled erratically for six months until he was assassinated in July following a bloody countercoup by officers from the North.

- ❖ Ironsi was replaced by Yakubu Gowon, an officer from an ethnic minority group in the Middle Belt (or Lower North), who presided over the federation through the civil war (1967–70) and post–civil war years until he was removed in a bloodless coup in July 1975.

- ❖ Gowon was succeeded by Murtala Mohammed, an officer from the Muslim Hausa-Fulani North, who was subsequently killed in the abortive coup of February 1976.

❖ Mohammed's deputy, General Olusegun Obasanjo, a Yoruba from Ogun state, presided over the final three years of military rule leading to the inauguration of the Second Republic in 1979.

The impact of these governments on the evolution of the Nigerian federation can be assessed in relation to three putative roles of the military in government as an instrument of centralization, a politically unencumbered initiator of basic structural and institutional reforms, and a purveyor and practitioner of national integration.

An underlying justification for military rule in Nigeria has involved the expectation that the centralized command structure of the military institution would function to counteract the centrifugal tendencies inherent in the country's complex ethnic composition. This expectation was carried to its logical conclusion by Ironsi's ill-fated Unification Decree of May 1966, which changed the formal designation of the military regime from "Federal Military Government" to "National Military Government," relegated the regions to groups of provinces, and unified the regional and federal public services. Ironsi's scheme incensed the North, which not only could not compete with the more educationally advanced South in a unified public service but was also still smarting from the loss of several of its prominent military and political leaders in the January 1966 coup. Anti-Igbo violence in the North in May was followed by Ironsi's murder two months later.

Although subsequent military governments were constrained to acknowledge the inviolability of Nigeria's federalism, this did not detract from the centralization inherent in military rule. Such centralization was evident in the legal basis of military rule as codified in the Constitution (Suspension and Modification) Decree No. 1 of 1966 and the Constitution (Basic Provisions) Decree No. 32 of 1975. Both acts empowered the ostensibly "federal" military regime to "make laws for the peace, order, and good government of Nigeria or any part thereof with respect to any matter whatsoever."[29] This clause suggests that the constitutional mandate of the central government is theoretically unlimited under the military. Thus even the most ardent proponents of the authenticity of Nigerian federalism under the military have been constrained to concede that "legally, Nigeria was and is unitary under military rule."[30]

Although they gave the center theoretically unlimited powers, however, the two acts also empowered the regional/state military governments to assume the constitutional responsibilities of their civilian predecessors in a modified form. Specifically, military governors were *delegated* the powers to make and implement laws with respect to residual and concurrent subjects under the old civilian constitution, with the proviso that state actions on concurrent matters should be preceded by consultations with the federal government. Because these decrees were nonjusticiable, however, even the modest autonomy envisioned for the states under the military remained insecure. In essence, the legal status of Nigerian federalism under military rule was profoundly ambivalent as the relevant enactments conferred seemingly absolute powers on the center, while simultaneously providing for the legal continuity and integrity of constituent governments, albeit in a radically modified form.

A consideration of the political, as distinct from legal, status of the states under the military underscores the ambiguous, even dubious, character of "military federalism" in Nigeria. Given the strictly hierarchical structure of the military establishment, the state military governments were invariably administered as part of a unified command structure. In particular, state governors were appointed and frequently redeployed by the head of the federal military government or the Supreme Military Council (SMC), a body that operated as the highest executive and legislative organ at the federal level.

Gowon's military governors did enjoy enormous powers and autonomy, however. This independence derived largely from the governors' membership in the SMC and the head of state's profoundly liberal and reconciliational leadership style. But all of this changed under the Mohammed-Obasanjo administration. The new government removed and humiliated Gowon's governors and banished their successors from the SMC. Henceforth, the state governors would be relegated to the National Council of States, a general intergovernmental body that was subordinate to the SMC, and placed under the supervision of the chief of General Staff or the deputy head of state.

These controls on the state governors were partially offset by certain features of "informal federalism" in the composition and operation of state military governments. For instance, the state governments were frequently, though not always, headed by military governors who shared significant geographical or cultural affinities with their respective states. Moreover, the co-optation of civilian commissioners and advisors into state military governments, and the pervasive elaboration of similar co-optation strategies at the federal level, helped to imbue these governments with a representative ethos that diluted military rule's inherent authoritarian and unitarian tendencies. Most important, the state governors usually enjoyed considerable freedom in the day-to-day running of the state's affairs. While this autonomy was especially visible under Gowon, the sheer difficulty of coordinating a country of Nigeria's size and complexity from a single center enabled all the military governors, once appointed, to acquire powers and privileges similar to those of regional princes in an essentially oligarchic federation.

While debate will persist about the real nature of Nigerian federalism under the military, there can be little doubt that legal and political organization of military government promoted an unprecedented process of centralization that radically modified the federal system but stopped short of formally or completely abrogating it. This centralization was accentuated by the military's distinctive capacity for swift and sweeping structural and institutional reforms. Unencumbered by the constitutional niceties and political haggling of a civilian democratic process, and prodded by its hierarchical command structure, the military introduced decisive changes in the internal territorial configuration of the federation, the system of revenue allocation, and the status of local governments.

Gowon's proclamation of a twelve-state structure (six each in the North and South) on May 27, 1967, was particularly historic. This decision at once extinguished the structural imbalance that had bedeviled the federation since 1954. The creation of seven additional states in February 1976 by the Mohammed-Obasanjo administration further accented the move toward a more horizontally balanced and vertically centralized federalism. The military's pursuit of centralized integration was also reflected in the administration's decision that same year to name Abuja—a centrally located and ostensibly ethnically neutral area in the former Northern Region—as the nation's new Federal Capital Territory (FCT), replacing the Yoruba-dominated southwestern city of Lagos as Nigeria's capital. It is widely conceded that these territorial changes would have been difficult to negotiate and consummate under civilian auspices.[31] Suffice it to add that the 1967 reorganizations, in particular, were greatly facilitated by the disproportionate representation and strategic location of ethnic minority elites within the power structures of the military-bureaucratic coalition that dominated national politics during Gowon's tenure as head of state.

As Lawrence Rupley has observed, "Changes in the nature of federal financial relations were among the most striking features of nearly fourteen years of military rule in Nigeria."[32] The major features of these centralizing financial reforms were (1) an augmentation of the financial resources and budgetary powers of the federal government as a result of the phenomenal expansion in federally retained petroleum profits tax; (2) the progressive replacement of the principle of regional derivation in the interstate allocation of federal revenues by such equity principles as population and interunit equality; (3) federal regulation or abolition, on grounds of macroeconomic planning, of such state revenue sources as produce sales tax, commodity export duties, cattle tax, and personal income tax; (4) the growing use of discretionary federal grants to offset the federation's erosion of the independent revenue-generating capacity of the states; (5) the direct or indirect funding by the federation of a variety of projects involving such residual or concurrent constitutional subjects as primary education, health, agriculture, industries, water supply, and housing; and (6) the consolidation of all important national revenues into a "Federation Account" to be shared on the basis of a 60:30:10 federal-state-local distribution formula.[33]

The provision for direct federal funding of the localities was partly designed to consolidate the important 1976 local government reforms in Nigeria. Apart from promoting the financial and functional empowerment of the localities, the reforms established a more uniform system of local government throughout the federation, circumscribed the formal political roles of traditional rulers and other unelected bodies in local government affairs, and generally sought to institutionalize the localities as the third axis of the federal administrative grid.[34]

These reforms of the local government system were presumably designed to lay the foundations for a stable system of participatory democracy, facilitate the achievement of broad-based grassroots development, ease the unrelenting pressures for the creation of new states, and provide some venue for popular participation under military rule pending the full restoration of civilian democracy. Yet, by providing for direct financial and institutional linkages between the center and the localities, and by ending the traditional powers of the states to determine the structure of local government, the reforms also served to augment the centralizing features of military rule.

However, the extent to which the military's policies of administrative centralization and political restructuring were accompanied by the development of a greater sense of national integration is debatable.[35] Although it presented itself, and was often portrayed by others, as an instrument of national integration, the initial impact of the military's intervention was to expose and exacerbate the organization's fatal fragmentation along ethnoregional lines and to accelerate the country's descent into a vicious civil war. Although the Igbo-led Eastern Region secessionist bid was successfully contained, the continued vulnerability of the military to sectional divisiveness was dramatized by the interregional imbroglio over the 1973 census and the volatile ethnoreligious undercurrents that infused the abortive coup of 1976 and the subsequent execution of the Middle Belt officers implicated in the putsch.

The military's image as an instrument of national integration was, therefore, gravely tarnished by its own internal sectional divisions and by its inability to contain the virulent ethnic theme in Nigeria's national politics. Yet there can be little doubt that, owing largely to the creation of states, the military bequeathed to the Second Republic a country that was more united than the unwieldy, regionally polarized entity it had inherited from the ashes of the First Republic.

FEDERALISM IN THE SECOND REPUBLIC, 1979–1983

Thanks to the innovative acts of constitutional planning that were undertaken during the final four years of military rule, Nigeria entered the Second Republic with federal institutions that diverged remarkably from those of the First Republic. The 1979 Constitution, which was fashioned by the military in collaboration with a Constitution Drafting Committee (CDC) and Constituent Assembly, included novel provisions that prescribed a substantial expansion in the legislative mandate of the federal government; the replacement of the First Republic's Westminster parliamentary system with an American-style presidential model; and the recognition of the country's federal character, or cultural diversity, in the procedures for electing the president, the formation of political parties, and the composition and conduct of public agencies.

In what C. S. Whitaker has characterized as a bold attempt "to nationalize control of the sources of Nigerian social power,"[36] the 1979 Constitution placed a total of sixty-five items within the exclusive legislative competence of central authorities. These items included twelve subjects that were on the concurrent list of the 1963 Constitution and thirteen other items that were appearing in the basic law for the first time. One of the new items empowered the federal government to establish and regulate authorities throughout the federation in order to promote the rather comprehensive objectives of public policy enumerated in chapter two of the constitution. Twelve substantive items were additionally brought within the purview of the central government by the constitution's list of federal and state concurrent legislative powers. In essence, these items allowed the federal government to legitimately intervene in virtually every matter of public importance, with the actual scope of the residual powers assigned to the states under the constitution becoming a function of "what the federal government voluntarily chooses to leave to the states."[37]

The desire to establish a more centralized and integrated polity was also an underlying motive for the change from parliamentary to presidential government in the 1979 Constitution. The drafters of the new constitution sought to replace the dual, divided, and weak executive of the First Republic with a single, effective symbol of federal executive authority and national unity. Moreover, a presidential system was regarded as more consistent with Nigeria's federalist traditions and democratic aspirations for at least three different reasons. First, the separation of powers between the executive and the legislature in presidential systems (unlike the Westminster practice of creating parliamentary executives) was considered to be more congruent with the federalist principle of constitutionally dispersed authority. Second, the coordinate status assigned to second legislative chambers in presidential federations (in contrast to the parliamentary tradition of establishing weak second chambers) was expected to give more effective protection to state and minority rights. Third, the presidential system's fixed electoral cycles (unlike the discretionary electoral cycles associated with parliamentary systems) would presumably be more effective in reducing the already enormous advantages of incumbency in the Nigerian setting.

At the Constituent Assembly, however, many members were more impressed by the familiar arguments against the value of presidentialism in deeply divided societies. In particular, these members echoed the view that the predominance of a single presidential figure would offer less scope for the accommodation of competing ethnic interests than was possible under the collegial cabinet of the parliamentary system.[38] To compensate for this limitation, however, Murtala Mohammed had advised the CDC to devise procedures to ensure "the president and vice-president are elected into office in such a manner as to reflect the federal character of the country."[39] The final constitutional document consequently required the president to win a quarter of the vote in each of at least two-thirds of the states in order to be elected directly. An elected president was also required to take cognizance of the federal character of the country in the composition and conduct of his government by appointing at least one person from each state into his cabinet. At state and local levels, the doctrine of federal character enjoined the relevant authorities to give adequate recognition to the "diversity of peoples" in their respective jurisdictions. Moreover, all registered political parties were not only prohibited from espousing or pursuing sectional agendas but were also required to establish offices in, and enlist officers from, at least two-thirds of the states.[40]

The innovations in the new constitution produced a mixed set of consequences. On the one hand, the multistate structure and the various federal character provisions in the constitution decisively reduced the structural inducement to ethnic and regional polarization in the Nigerian federation. According to Diamond:

> It is a matter of immense significance that the kind of ethnic and regional polarization that savaged the First Republic did not emerge in the Second Republic. . . . [E]thnicity remained the most salient political cleavage. But it was much more fluid and decentralized. National political conflict did not polarize around ethnic divisions. Rather, the experience of the Second Republic demonstrated that in a democracy, deep

cultural divisions, even a centralized ethnic structure, do not inevitably produce mass ethnic conflict. Cultural complexity can be managed and centrifugal forces contained by effective political structures.[41]

On the other hand, a wide range of conflicts during the Second Republic underscored the "boomerang effects" of some of the mechanisms that had been introduced to contain destructive divisiveness. The application of the federal character principle, for instance, came to be linked to such divisive conflicts or processes as (1) the legal dispute over the election of Alhaji Shehu Shagari as president in the 1979 election, (2) the controversy in the ruling National Party of Nigeria (NPN) over the rotation of the presidency among the country's geographic zones, (3) the pressures for the subordination of meritocratic standards to ethnopolitical criteria in admissions into educational institutions and recruitment into the bureaucracy, (4) the development of vigorous movements for the establishment of about fifty new states, and (5) the dramatic expansion in the number of local government areas from 301 to almost one thousand. To be sure, the crystallization of some of these pressures, at a time when the country was reeling from an unprecedented economic crisis caused by a precipitous fall in petroleum export revenues, functioned to undermine the quality of governance in the Second Republic.[42]

Moreover, the development of political opposition to the centralizing features of the 1979 Constitution and the bitter struggles between national and local elites for political advantage led to phenomenal conflicts between the NPN-controlled federal government and the states dominated by parties in opposition to the NPN. This intergovernmental row involved conflicts over the allocation and administration of federally collected revenues, the appointment of presidential liaison officers to the states, the involvement of the federation in such residual or concurrent issues as public housing and agricultural development programs, the control of the police and the maintenance of public order, the ownership and use of electronic media, and alleged federal political intervention in—or destabilization of—the "opposition" states' governments. Indeed, some of these governments were eventually uprooted in the rigged 1983 elections that established the hegemony of the NPN and precipitated a military coup at the end of that year.[43] Thus, as in the First Republic, the ruling elite at the center betrayed its weak commitment to federalism and toleration by crudely attempting to dislodge its opponents in the states.

FEDERALISM UNDER THE SECOND PHASE OF MILITARY RULE, 1984–1999

The coup of December 31, 1983 simply returned the country to the legal and political situation before the inception of the Second Republic on October 1, 1979. The period after 1983, like the 1966–79 era, was characterized by tendencies toward political and administrative overcentralization, the sometimes arbitrary imposition of sweeping structural and institutional changes, and the intermittent eruption of violent sectional tensions within the military establishment and the political system at large.

The return to an era of questionable and vulnerable federalism in Nigeria was epitomized by the administration of the states as part of the unified military command structure. According to one observer, the "federal structure of the country has been effectively dismantled by the appointment of governors as just another routine military assignment."[44] This subordination of the federal institutional structure to the military organizational superstructure was not significantly reversed by the introduction of the elaborate, but eventually aborted, program of transition to the Third Republic in January 1986 and the subsequent election of civilian state governors in December 1991. During most of the two-year period (December 1991–November 1993) of cohabitation of civilian governors and a military-dominated center, the latter effectively subordinated and constantly regulated the former. The political vulnerability of the democratically elected state governments was clearly dramatized in June 1993 when the federal government shut down several state-owned media organizations that had criticized the military's annulment of that month's elections to the Third Republic's inaugural presidency.

Equally symptomatic of the return to military federalism were the sweeping reforms and reorganizations of local and state administrations implemented after the collapse of the Second Republic. There were many key changes introduced to the local government system during this period:

❖ A doubling (from 10 percent in the Second Republic to 20 percent in 1992) in the proportion of the Federation Account allocated to the localities, an increase that was implemented primarily at the expense of the states whose allocations fell from 30 to 24 percent.

❖ The announcement of formal provisions for the direct, as distinct from indirect (that is, state-channeled), transfer of central statutory allocations to the localities.

❖ The abolition of state-controlled Local Government Ministries and Service Commissions as part of the move to eliminate or reduce intervention by the states in the local government system.

❖ The establishment of an approved national scheme of service for local government employees.

❖ The establishment of provisions and regulations in the federal constitution regarding the areas, structure, composition, jurisdictions, and election of local councils.

❖ The extension of the presidential system of government to the local government level.

❖ The realignment of local government boundaries with federal and state legislative boundaries.

❖ The devolution of increased responsibilities to the localities for primary education, health care, and local infrastructural improvements.[45]

While ostensibly promoting the cause of local decentralization, the primary impacts of these changes were to consolidate the move to a uniform national system of local government and to further constrain the scope for autonomous intervention by the states in the affairs of the localities. All this confirms the thesis that local government reforms in Nigeria have been consistent with the military's centralizing project and proclivities.

The autonomy of the states was eroded not only by reform of the local government system but also by the three rounds of state reorganization exercises (in 1987, 1991, and 1996) that increased the number of states in the federation from nineteen to thirty-six. The proliferation of constituent state units during a period of sharp statutory and extrastatutory cuts in their allocations from the Federation Account roused fears about the total collapse of Nigerian federalism. Significantly, the federal government used the occasion of the August 1991 reorganizations to impose a number of centralist directives that transferred key state-owned institutions to the federal government, dissolved major regional or interstate bodies, and placed a ceiling on the size of state cabinets. What is more, in announcing the 1996 reorganizations, the central authorities declared that, unlike in the past, no special "take-off" grants would be made available to the new units, which were consequently rendered financially despondent.

The implementation and crystallization of these centralizing measures and pressures coincided with a period of considerable governmental instability and sectional turbulence in the Nigerian federation. There were five different heads of state during the 1984–99 period: General Muhammadu Buhari (January 1984–August 1985), President Ibrahim Babangida (August 1985–August 1993), Chief Ernest Shonekan (August 1993–November 1993), General Sani Abacha (November 1993–June 1998), and General Abdulsalam Abubakar (June 1998–May 1999). All of them were beset by considerable ethnic, regional, or religious tensions.

The Buhari administration was removed in the wake of southern allegations of northern domination of the administration and of disturbing agitations for the recasting of the federation along confederal lines. The Babangida administration experienced and provoked the worst sectional, especially religious, tensions. In April 1990, for example, the nation was momentarily confronted with the specter of another civil war when disgruntled military officers sought unsuccessfully to remove Babangida from power and to expel the Muslim North from the federation. The military-backed interim civilian administration of Chief Shonekan was installed and displaced amidst sharp ethnoregional polarization over Babangida's annulment of the June 1993 presidential election, which was won by a southerner (the Yoruba Chief M. K. O. Abiola) for the first time in the nation's history. On succeeding the Shonekan government in November 1993, the Abacha administration was confronted with demands for convening a sovereign national conference that would re-examine the basis for Nigerian federalism and possibly undo the amalgamation of 1914!

In a bid to respond to this divisiveness, the Abacha administration convened a National Constitutional Conference (NCC) during 1994–95. The conference proposed the constitutionalization of the following accommodative solutions: the rotation of the presidency on a North-South basis; an expansion in the proportion of national oil revenues allocated on a "derivation" basis from less than 5 percent to at least 13 percent; the establishment of a Federal Character Commission to monitor and enforce equitable intersegmental representation in government; and the elaboration of a specific list of exclusive state legislative powers, as opposed to the previous constitutional practice of defining these powers as unenumerated or residual jurisdictions. These proposals, along with other changes, were codified in the 1995 draft constitution. Yet that constitution was really never enforced by the Abacha administration. Instead, assailed by the unrelenting clamor in the South for the revalidation of the 1993 presidential election results and for the radical restructuring of the federation, Abacha imposed an unprecedented regime of administrative centralization, ethnoregional domination, political repression, and arbitrary personal rule.

A reprieve from the tightening spiral of repression and strife came for Nigeria with Abacha's sudden death in June 1998. At the time of his demise, Abacha was scheming to civilianize his rule through a fraudulent democratization program. Yet his successor, General Abubakar, launched a revised program of transition that culminated in the inauguration of the Fourth Republic in May 1999. An important feature of this transition was the informal political compromise on a regional shift of power. Induced largely by the southern, especially Yoruba, angst over the annulment of Abiola's 1993 presidential election victory and the politician's subsequent death in detention in July 1998, this compromise effectively excluded persons from the politically dominant North from bidding for the Fourth Republic's inaugural presidency.

THE NIGERIAN FEDERATION SINCE 1999

The initial months of the Fourth Republic were dominated by renewed allegations of ethnoregional marginalization, a chain of bloody communal conflicts, and continued pressures for fundamental constitutional restructuring.

Far from heralding an era of interregional amity, the installation of the new civilian administration of Olusegun Obasanjo, Nigeria's former Yoruba military ruler, brought forth cries of marginalization from other sections of the country. Elements from the Muslim North, in particular, denounced the Obasanjo government for betraying the North's good faith in conceding political power to the South. This alleged betrayal involved the dismissal of several northerners from the military and the bureaucracy, the relocation of important federal institutions from the North to the South, and the disproportionate assignment of key ministerial appointments to figures from the president's Yoruba southwestern region (where, ironically, he had been overwhelmingly rejected for the rival Yoruba candidate, Olu Falae, in the 1999 presidential contest).

A more disturbing challenge to the stability of the new democratic dispensation involved the resurgence of interethnic, subethnic, state-ethnic, and ethnoreligious bloodletting, which claimed more than one thousand lives within the first year of the Fourth Republic. The deadliest and most publicized of these clashes included those involving the Ijaw, Itsekiri, and Urhobo communities in Delta state; Ijaws and Ilajes in Ondo state; the Jukun and Kuteb in Taraba state; Yorubas and Hausas in Oyo, Ogun, and Kano states; Muslim Hausas and non-Muslim minority or immigrant ethnic communities in Kaduna state; Christian Igbos and Muslim Hausas in Abia state; Aguleri and Umuleri Igbo communities in Anambra state; Ife and Modakeke Yoruba communities in Osun state; and the invasion and destruction by federal troops of the restive, oil-rich Odi community in Bayelsa state.

Mostly rooted in long-standing intercommunal competition for scarce resources and political control at the local level, these conflicts were often aggravated by the sectionally manipulative or provocative policies of political authorities in the period before and after the inauguration of the Fourth Republic. Several of these conflicts also involved the activities of new militant ethnic youth organizations. Among such "ethnic militias" were the Oodua People's Congress, the Arewa People's Congress, the Ijaw Youth Council, Egbesu Boys of Africa, Bakassi Boys, and the Movement for the Actualization of the Sovereign State of Biafra. This militarization and ethnicization of Nigerian youth culture was promoted significantly by the legacy of state repression and

impunity under military rule, by widespread socioeconomic immiseration and frustration, and by the sheer institutional disintegration or
failure of the national police and security agencies.

The Fourth Republic was also assailed by the unrelieved clamor
for radical political restructuring or fundamental constitutional change.
The 1999 Constitution for the new republic—essentially an updated
and amended version of the 1979 Constitution for the Second
Republic—was widely condemned as both illegitimate and inappropriate. Essentially, the 1999 Constitution was virtually imposed by the
Abubakar administration in defiance of public pressures for a truly
democratized constitution-making process. Moreover, the new constitution was regarded as too centralized to accommodate the country's
need for "true federalism," for effective economic and political decentralization.

The fragility of the new constitutional framework was both
underscored and aggravated by several political developments in the
first year of the new republic. These events included not only the introduction of strict Shari'a law in the Muslim North but also the virtual
disintegration of the new republic's three registered political parties—
the ruling People's Democratic Party (PDP), the All People's Party
(APP), and the Alliance for Democracy (AD); the development of par-
alyzing conflicts between the executive and the legislature, particularly
at the federal level; and the resurgence of intergovernmental conflicts
over the allocation of revenues, the control of the police, the use of central emergency powers, the status of local governments, the declaration
of public holidays, and the legislation of a national minimum wage.

In October 1999, President Obasanjo sought to respond to this
constitutional ferment by inaugurating an interparty "technical" committee on the review of the 1999 Constitution. The National Assembly
established its own rival committee on constitutional review in May
2000. Presumably, both bodies would propose specific amendments to
the 1999 Constitution. This parallel procedure, in turn, could damp-
en the clamor for the election of yet another constituent assembly to
write a new constitution or for the convening of a sovereign national
conference to restructure the Nigerian federation.

The case for incremental constitutional amendment, rather than
fundamental constitutional change or radical political restructuring,

would seem to be buttressed by some significant achievements of the new democratic dispensation. The induction of civilian rule significantly reduced the scope for the center's extraconstitutional erosion of the political authority and fiscal entitlements of the subfederal tiers. The oil-bearing states were conciliated by the partial implementation of the derivation principle and the establishment of a Niger Delta Development Commission (NDDC). The allegations of marginalization notwithstanding, the Obasanjo administration was far more ethnically inclusive and conciliatory than all the preceding military administrations since 1984. Above all, the inauguration of democracy tremendously expanded the space not only for the articulation but also potentially for the representation, accommodation, and moderation of competing ethnic claims.

If Nigeria's history is any guide, the greatest challenge for the Fourth Republic would involve its capacity for self-renewal through the electoral process. Unlike in the past, however, the costs of future electoral collapse and democratic breakdown could now include not only the tragedy of repressive military rule but also the danger of a potentially unmanageable escalation of current challenges to the very idea of a united Nigerian federation.

CONCLUSIONS

Three salient points should be highlighted in concluding this historical overview. First, a review of Nigeria's political history suggests that three basic factors shaped the instauration of federalism in 1954: the sheer diversity and complexity of the groups incorporated into Nigeria's British-drawn boundaries, the differential administration and modernization of the country under colonial rule, and the enormous attraction that federalist guarantees of subnational autonomy had for Nigeria's regionally based elite. While the character of British administrative policy provided the primary impulse for the regionalist federal arrangements instituted in 1954, the basic pluralism of Nigerian society and the preferences and interests of the Nigeria's political class largely account for the persistence of federalism since the country's independence.

Second, the outstanding achievement of the first phase of military rule in Nigeria was the transformation of the impossible and combustible regional federation of the First Republic into a more institutionally balanced multistate federal structure. Much of the appeal the concept of "military federalism" has enjoyed among students of Nigerian politics cannot be dissociated from this historic role of the military in repealing and replacing a "bizarre version of federalism," as Diamond describes it, that seems to have been "designed in such a way as to virtually guarantee its failure," as claimed by Arend Lijphart.[46]

Third, developments since the collapse of the Second Republic, in particular, would appear to provide strong support for the argument that the military may have outlived its usefulness for Nigerian federalism. Far from promoting national integration, the military's centralist reforms and reorganizations of the federal system severely eroded the viability and legitimacy of the Nigerian federation. In essence, the military's centripetal reconfiguration and manipulation of the federation produced a profound centrifugal backlash involving radical proposals for the restructuring, confederalization, or even dissolution of the Nigerian union. As the following chapters will attempt to show, however, an even more fundamental problem of federalism in Nigeria is the role of the federal system in institutionalizing, intensifying, and perpetuating the country's sectional struggles for distributive advantage.

3

THE POLITICS
OF REVENUE SHARING

L IKE SO MANY OTHER ASPECTS of its federal system, Nigeria's intergovernmental financial scheme exhibits a number of peculiar features. One important characteristic of this scheme is the relative
stability in the allocation of tax jurisdictions. Right from the inception of
intergovernmental revenue-sharing arrangements in 1946, Nigeria has
allocated the most important taxes to the federal government, with relatively less important taxing powers going to the subnational authorities.
This arrangement is based on the assumption that the subfederal units
are best left with those taxes that have a largely local impact, do not
endanger national macroeconomic policy, are relatively inexpensive to
administer, and have relatively stable yields.[1] Only sales tax, property tax,
and, more arguably, personal income tax readily satisfy these criteria in
the Nigerian context. Consequently, central authorities have been
responsible for the legal administration and collection of the most lucra-
tive revenue sources, including import, export, excise, business, and mining taxes.

A corollary of the allocation of the most important tax jurisdictions to the center is the heavy reliance on the redistribution of centrally
collected revenues (as distinct from the division of taxing powers) as the
predominant mode of intergovernmental financial relations in
Nigeria.[2] The need to redistribute central revenues to the states and

localities arises from the fact that, while the center controls the most important revenue sources, the subcentral governments bear the primary responsibility for such essential, expansive, and expensive social services as education, health, agriculture, and water. Consequently, Nigeria's states and localities have come to rely heavily on the statutory allocations from the center for their operational revenues. Indeed, with the exception of the relatively industrialized Lagos state, Nigeria's state and local governments depend on the center for an average 70 to 80 percent of their revenues. This extraordinary dependence is mediated only by the fact that central allocations to the states and localities take the form of unconditional, constitutionally guaranteed (that is, statutory) grants. It is, therefore, mandatory, rather than discretionary, for the center to share its revenues with the states and localities. Legally, the "federal government has no more right over the monies collected by it than the state and local governments."[3]

Nevertheless, a primary consequence of the dependence of all governments on centrally collected revenues has been to make the revenue-sharing system the source of deep political contention among all governments and segments of the country's populace. The primary purpose of revenue sharing in many other federations is to assist financially weaker states; it is a supplemental, rather than a primary, source of state financial resources. In Nigeria, however, "the revenue allocation issue is not a secondary matter, but a primary issue that is fundamental to the political stability of the country as a whole."[4] The exceptional political sensitivity of revenue sharing in Nigeria has been further compounded by the "lack of consensus on the criteria of distribution, the absence of reliable socioeconomic data, the rapid rate of constitutional and political change, and the extent to which revenue distribution is tied to perceptions of regional ethnic dominance."[5]

The balance of this chapter seeks to provide an analysis of Nigeria's contentious revenue-sharing politics and practices. The analysis focuses on three major dimensions of Nigeria's revenue-sharing system: the division of centrally collected revenues between the federal, regional, and local authorities (vertical revenue sharing); the distribution of central revenues among the states or their localities (horizontal revenue sharing); and key problems associated with the general administration of the revenue-sharing scheme.

VERTICAL REVENUE SHARING

In recent times, the issue of revenue sharing between the federal and subfederal governments has progressively emerged as the most contentious in Nigeria's fiscal federalism. The key issue in this debate has involved the problem of deciding how much of centrally collected revenues should be retained by the general government or devolved from the center to the states and their localities. The attempt to resolve this issue has pitted the forces of federal financial hegemony against those of regional economic autonomy.

The issue of federal-regional fiscal relations received its first formal attention in the Richards Constitution of 1946, which sought to give the nation's three administrative regions "a large measure of financial responsibility."[6] Consequently, under an arrangement devised by the financial secretary to the Nigerian government, Sir Sidney Phillipson, certain locally collected and region-specific revenues (mainly direct taxes, government fees, and rents) were declared as regional revenues, while the nondeclared revenues (export, import, excise, and business taxes) were assigned to the center. The arrangement also provided that "each region would receive, in addition to the full amount of its share of declared regional revenues, a block grant from the nondeclared revenue" in rough proportion to its relative contribution to such central revenues.[7]

Although the Phillipson scheme made relatively large revenues available to the three regions, the subfederal governments remained in a weak financial position vis-à-vis the central government because the latter had an overriding claim to nondeclared revenue that accounted for more than two-thirds of total Nigerian revenues in 1948–49. Indeed, for the greater part of the 1946–51 period, the proportion of centrally collected revenue transferred to the regions was less than 20 percent.[8] This highly centralized financial arrangement reflected the essentially unitarist (albeit decentralized) character of the Nigerian state under the Richards Constitution, and the subordinate (rather than coordinate) status of the regions vis-à-vis the center.

A move toward more decentralist financial arrangements was made following the report of the 1951 Hicks-Phillipson Commission. But the new arrangements brought only marginal improvements in the fiscal fortunes of the regions vis-à-vis the center. In 1952–53, the regions received only 25.8 percent of total central revenues, up from 17.2 percent in 1951–52.[9] In essence, the central government still retained a disproportionate share of central revenues for its own use, and it continued to exercise financial hegemony over the regions.

It was only in 1954, with the introduction of a federal system, that a genuinely decentralized system of revenue sharing emerged. The primary difference between the new revenue-sharing regime and its predecessors did not lie in any fundamental changes in the division of tax jurisdictions between the center and the regions, however; the power to tax and to vary the rates of taxes on the most important revenue sources remained firmly with the federal government. The financial status of the regions was bolstered via the statutory reallocation of centrally collected taxes to the regions on the basis of the contribution of each region to revenues from such taxes. Thus, one-half of general import, excise, and export duties and all revenue receipts from import duties on motor fuel and mining rents and royalties went to the region of origin. The financial strength of the regions was further augmented by the regionalization of the commodity marketing boards and the division of the accumulated reserves of these agencies (about £75 million) between the regions. Moreover, regional control of the boards gave the regions virtually unimpeded powers to fix producer prices and impose sales taxes, thereby inhibiting the traditional jurisdiction of the center on export taxes.[10]

With these changes in the revenue allocation system, it was not surprising that the regions came to assume a position of financial parity, if not predominance, vis-à-vis the central government. Thus, "whereas in 1951–52 . . . regional revenue was only 24 percent of central government revenue, under the 1954 fiscal system the federal and regional governments shared the total current revenue sources of Nigeria on about a fifty-fifty basis."[11] Although the Raisman Commission of 1958 endorsed the continued allocation of a substantial proportion of central revenues to the regions of derivation, however, the era of regional financial power did not last for long. Instead, the collapse of international commodity prices, the increasing budgetary burden imposed by state-funded social services, and the general expansion in federally retained revenue receipts led to a reassertion of the center's financial hegemony by the late 1950s. Thus, although there was a general expansion in public finances during this period, the expansion was more pronounced at the federal level than in the regions. Between 1959 and 1960 and 1961 and 1962, for instance, the revenues of the federal government increased by 31 percent, while those of the Northern, Western, and Eastern Regions' governments increased by 26, 21, and 29 percent, respectively.[12] Furthermore, during the 1963–66 period, the federal government consistently generated budgetary surpluses, while the Northern and Western Regions had difficulty in balancing their budgets.

The increasing fiscal vulnerability of the regions led the 1964 Binns Fiscal Commission to recommend an increase in federal allocations to the regional governments. The commission proposed two options for resolving the financial problems of the regions: (1) an annual grant of £3.75 million to the regions for the four-year period from 1965 to 1969, or (2) an increase by five percentage points (from 30 to 35 percent) of the proportion of general import duties and mining rents and royalties paid into the interregional Distributable Pool Account. The latter recommendation was adopted, going into effect from April 1966.[13] But this concession to the regions was largely superficial. In the words of Adebayo Adedeji, "Having regard to the increased financial need of the regional governments due to increased responsibilities—a fact which the commission admitted—the additional payments recommended by the commission were obviously minimal."[14]

The growing financial dilemma of the regions was exacerbated by the developments that followed the intervention of the military in January 1966. The centralizing imperatives of military rule, the fragmentation of the regions into smaller states in 1967, the emergency created by the 1967–70 civil war, and the growing importance of the oil industry all combined to promote the forces of fiscal centralization.

Under Decree 13 of 1970, excise duties on tobacco and petroleum products and import duties on motor fuel, which were previously returned to the states of origin, were now shared equally between the federal government and all the states. And in 1971, the federal government assigned to itself all rents and royalties from offshore oil operations, thereby depriving the oil-rich littoral states of their entitlement to 45 percent of these revenues.

Apart from encroaching on the states' share of central revenues, the military also instituted measures that drastically limited the capacity of the states to maintain or mobilize independent revenues of their own. In the course of the first phase of military rule from 1966 to 1979, the military took over the entire marketing board system, "abolished export duties and sales taxes on agricultural produce, reduced poll taxes to a uniform level throughout the country, standardized personal income tax rates throughout the country (removing from state governments the power to vary rates), introduced a uniform fuel price (reducing the power of state governments to impose petroleum sales taxes) and abolished pools, betting, casino and gaming taxes."[15] Although the federal government sought to compensate for these confiscatory policies through an expansion in discretionary financial devolutions to the states, such awards could hardly salvage their financial integrity. "Justified on the grounds of achieving national macroeconomic control," concluded Pauline Baker, "these measures had an enormous impact on the federal structure, leaving a legacy of unprecedented dependence from which the states have not yet recovered."[16]

A poignant indication of the unrelenting centralization of the financial system during the 1970s was the fact that the federal share of total public (federal and state) revenues increased from 48 percent in 1954–55 to 63 percent in 1974–75. Similarly, regional dependence on central revenues increased dramatically from about 56 percent during the 1953–65 period, to about 80 percent during the 1970–79 period.[17]

In the closing years of the first phase of military rule, the federal government instituted a basic change in the revenue-sharing scheme. In line with the recommendation of the Aboyade Committee on Revenue Allocation, all federally collected revenues were consolidated into a newly created Federation Account, mentioned previously. The account was to be shared among the center, the states, and (for the first time in the nation's revenue-sharing history) the localities according to formulas to be determined by the National Assembly or other appropriate federal agencies. While allowing the states and the localities to partake in such previously federally retained revenues as petroleum and business profits taxes, the new arrangement created a more tightly integrated national revenue-sharing scheme by making all the governments collectively dependent on the Federation Account. Moreover, the federal government continued to retain a disproportionate share of revenues in the Federation Account under the 60:30:10 revenue-sharing formula adopted during the last six months of the first era of military rule.

With the transition from military to civilian rule in October 1979, the state governments predictably sought to regain some measure of constitutional autonomy and fiscal capacity. Seeking to reassert their rights to generate independent revenues, several state governments revived such previously abolished independent revenue sources as poll, community, and casino taxes. But more important, all the state governments vociferously argued for a drastic reduction in the center's share of federally collected revenues in the Federation Account. As the Okigbo Commission on Revenue Allocation noted in 1980:

> All the memoranda as well as oral evidence received from the states pointed to the same direction, namely, that under the revenue allocation scheme in force during the period 1970–80 too much money was . . . concentrated in the hands of the Federal Military Government. This . . . put the states in financial difficulties from which they now seek an escape. . . . Of the nineteen states with which we held discussions, only three conceded up to 50 percent of the Federation Account to the Federation; a few of the other sixteen put the share of the Federation as low as 28 percent but most of them recommended a proportion of between 40 and 45 percent.[18]

Yet the states were only marginally successful in their quest for more equitable revenue-sharing arrangements (see table 1). The initial revenue allocation act that was ratified by President Shehu Shagari on February 2, 1981 assigned 58.5, 31.5, and 10 percent of the Federation Account to the center, the states, and the localities, respectively, after the special funds were divided among the center (3.5 percent) and the states (5 percent). Following spirited legal challenges by the Bendel state government and other opposition-controlled states, the revised revenue law adopted in January 1982 increased the allocation to the states by only 3.5 percentage points. In essence, the states were assigned only 35 percent of the Federation Account (including all special funds), while the center continued to retain more than one-half (precisely, 55 percent) of the account for its own use.[19]

But even the modest financial gains made by the states during the Second Republic were reversed after the reimposition of military rule at the end of 1983. In particular, the Babangida administration pursued a

Table 1. Vertical Allocation of the Federation Account

Items	Initial 1981 Act (Nullified by Supreme Court in October 1981)	Revised 1981 Act	1990	January 1992	June 1992 to date	NRMAFC* Proposals	Proposals of the NCC Committee on Revenue Allocation
Federal Government	55	55	50	50	48.5	47	33
State Government	26.5	30.5	30	25	24	30	32.5
Local Government	10	10	15	20	20	15	20
Special Funds†							
A. Derivation‡ (Mineral-producing states)	2	2	1	1	1	2	–
B. Dev. of Mineral-Producing Areas	3	1.5	1.5	1.5	3	2	6.5
C. Initial Dev. of FCT Abuja§	2.5	–	1	1	1	1	2
D. Gen. Ecological Problems	1	1	1	1	2	0.5	2.5
E. Stabilization	–	–	0.5	0.5	0.5	0.5	0.5
F. Savings	–	–	–	–	–	2	–
G. Other Special Projects	–	–	–	–	–	–	3.0
Subtotal of Special Funds	8.5	4.5	5	5	7.5	8	14.5
TOTAL	100	100	100	100	100	100	100

Sources: Adapted from *New Nigerian,* February 26, 1981; T .Y. Danjuma, "Revenue Sharing and the Political Economy of Nigerian Federalism," *Nigerian Journal of Federalism* 1, no. 1 (1994): 57; and National Constitutional Conference, *Report of the Committee on Revenue Allocation* (Abuja, September 1994), 13 and 30.

*The National Revenue Mobilization Allocation and Fiscal Commission, inaugurated by General Babangida in September 1988 under the chairmanship of retired Lieutenant General T. Y. Danjuma.

†Since 1984, the specified percentages of special funds for derivation and mineral-producing areas have been applied only to mineral revenues in the Federation Account and not to the totality of the account.

‡In 2000, in deference to the provisions of the 1999 Constitution, 13 percent of onshore mineral revenues in the Federation Account was paid to the mineral-producing states in lieu of the specified statutory allocations for derivation and the development of mineral-producing areas.

§Abuja enjoys the statutory status of a state for revenue-sharing purposes and, therefore, partakes in the states' share of the Federation Account.

policy of expanded financial devolution to the localities at the expense of the states. Thus, while the local governments' statutory share of the Federation Account increased from 10 percent in 1983 to 15 percent in 1990 and 20 percent in 1992, the states' share declined from 35 percent to 24 percent during the same period. Meanwhile, the federal government retained 48.5 percent of the Federation Account for its own use, while assuming direct or indirect responsibility for the administration of another 7.5 percent of the Federation Account designated as special funds.[20]

The declining financial position of the states after the reimposition of military rule was further aggravated by the center's egregious violation of revenue allocation laws. Under the Babangida and Abacha administrations, in particular, the central military government simply ignored constitutional provisions that required it to pay all federally collected revenues (with the minor exception of the income taxes of military, police, and diplomatic personnel and residents of Abuja, the Federal Capital Territory) into the Federation Account for redistribution among the three tiers of government. In 1997, for instance, federally collected revenues amounted to 452 billion naira (which replaced the pound as Nigeria's unit of currency in 1973), out of which only 208 billion naira was paid into the Federation Account. Similarly, out of an estimated total federal revenue of 424 billion naira in 1998, only 189 billion was earmarked for intergovernmental sharing.[21] Because of the center's extraconstitutional diversion of huge amounts of federally collected revenues into so-called "dedication" or "reserve" accounts, federal external debt service obligations, and other "priority projects," the subfederal governments received "only about half of what they ought to receive from the Federation Account."[22]

Further contributing to the fiscal recentralization of the 1984–99 period of military rule were such developments as the replacement of the state-administered sales tax with a federally administered value added tax in 1994, the unilateral revisions or reduction of personal income tax rates by the center, and the regulation of the residual taxing powers of the states through the promulgation of the Taxes and Levies Decree of 1998.

Because of these centrist regulations and manipulations, especially the underpayment of federal revenues into the Federation Account, the federal government's share of public expenditures expanded

dramatically from 52 percent in 1983 to 74 percent in 1995, while the
state governments' share declined from more than 40 percent to less
than 20 percent during the same period.[23] A major consequence of the
military's disengagement from the administration of the economy in
1999 was to put an end to the more egregious abuses of revenue allocation that had existed since 1984. Some administrative manipulations
still persist, however. What is more, pressures for the alteration of the
entire vertical revenue-sharing formula in favor of the subfederal tiers
have continued and even intensified.

Indeed, the continued appropriation of a disproportionate share
of the Federation Account by the federal government at a time of
expanding administrative costs and increasingly unsustainable spending obligations at state and local levels has galvanized fervent nationwide opposition to the revenue-sharing system. The Political Bureau—
a presidential panel made up mostly of political scientists that coordinated the debate on Nigeria's political future during 1986 and 1987—
reported general public support for a revenue-sharing scheme that
would put the federal and states' share of the Federation Account at 40
percent apiece, with the localities receiving the remaining 20 percent.

The bureau also referred to "a considerable body of opinion advo-
cating the reallocation of fiscal powers among the three tiers of government to give more powers to the local government and states in the collection of revenue from their areas of jurisdiction."[24] The Revenue
Allocation Committee of the 1994–95 National Constitutional
Conference proposed the allocation of only 33 percent of the Federation
Account to the federal government, with 32.5, 20, and 14.5 percent for
the states, localities, and special funds, respectively. In December 1999,
some members of the Senate Committee on States, Local, and Boundary
Affairs proposed an allocation formula that would give the states and the
localities each 35 percent of revenues in the Federation Account, leaving
the federal government with only 30 percent.[25] In a June 2000 statement,
the "thirty-six state governors of the federation . . . condemned the current revenue allocation formula as being unduly favorable to the Federal
Government and called for a reduction of the Federal Government's
share from 48.5 percent to 30 percent."[26]

In short, the present centralized arrangement for revenue sharing
is largely lacking in political legitimacy and is unlikely to survive any

future independent technical review or popular constitutional conference. Meanwhile, the formula for horizontal revenue sharing has also
produced considerable contention and opposition.

HORIZONTAL REVENUE SHARING

Until the hardening of state-based opposition to the financial hegemony of the central government in the 1970s, the most sectionally
explosive issue in Nigeria's fiscal federalism involved the conflict over
the appropriate formulas for the interstate sharing of centrally collected revenues. Although now partly eclipsed by vertical revenue
sharing conflicts, the debate over horizontal revenue sharing has
never been far from the epicenter of Nigeria's federalism. Indeed,
according to Adedotun Phillips, "The major problem of intergovernmental revenue sharing in Nigeria has always been the formula for
sharing revenue among regions and states, that is, the horizontal revenue sharing scheme."[27]

While vertical revenue sharing debates have revolved around the
determination of the relative proportions of centrally collected revenues
to be allocated to the center and the subnational governments, horizontal revenue-sharing conflicts have involved the issue of the appropriate principles to be used in sharing central revenues standing to the
credit of the states or their localities.

Since 1946, probably close to twenty principles of horizontal revenue sharing have been developed, none of which has enjoyed complete acceptance. These principles can be divided into two broad categories: *efficiency principles*, designed to allocate resources rationally to
the most economically efficient units, and *equity principles*, designed to
equalize the fiscal capacities of constituent units by redistributing
resources on explicitly political grounds. Among the efficiency principles of horizontal allocation are derivation, independent revenues,
absorptive capacity, tax effort, and fiscal efficiency. Equity principles
include even development, national interest, continuity in government
services, minimum responsibility of government, financial comparability (among governments), primary school enrollment or the social
development factor, national minimum standards, equality of access to
development opportunities, and land mass/terrain.

As in many other developing countries, Nigeria's revenue-sharing practices have emphasized equity over efficiency principles. This bias reflects a widely shared official commitment in Nigeria, and elsewhere, to the use of equalizing fiscal transfers and other redistributive strategies to maintain national unity and reduce interregional economic disparities. Yet there has been a lack of consensus in Nigeria over the appropriate choice or mix of equity principles and over the degree of recognition that should be given to efficiency principles in the overall revenue-sharing scheme. In this debate, the subnational governments have predictably sought to canvass those revenue-sharing principles most supportive of their particular interests. As the Okigbo Commission put it in 1980:

> In the memoranda presented to us by the states, each state made its case for allocation mostly in terms of those factors that suit its particular characteristics: population in states like Oyo, Borno, Kano, Sokoto; geographic area in states like Gongola, Kwara; population density in states like Lagos; derivation in states like Bendel, Cross River, Imo, Ondo and Rivers. . . . If we can call all of this a pattern, it is that each state is looking at its own interest singularly by proposing to the Commission as the dominant principles of allocation those which give it the most advantage over other states.[28]

Since the reconstitution of the regions into states in 1967, however, Nigeria's horizontal revenue-sharing practices have been dominated largely by six principles of entitlement—namely, equality of states, population, social development factor, land mass and terrain, derivation, and internal revenue generation effort (see table 2).

Equality of states

This principle effectively entered into Nigeria's revenue-sharing practices after the creation of twelve states in 1967. Faced with the problem of sharing revenues among the newly created states, the federal government simply divided the share of the old North equally among the six successor states to the region. But, for some reason, this principle was not explicitly invoked in sharing revenues among the six new states in the South. Following the end of the civil war, however, the norm of interstate equality in revenue sharing was elevated to a general principle of allocation throughout the federation.

Table 2. Horizontal Revenue Allocation Formulas

Principles	Percentage Weight Assigned					
	1970 to 1980	Initial 1981 Act	Revised 1981 Act	1990 to date	Proposals of NRMAFC	Proposals of NCC Revenue Allocation Committee
Equality of States (Minimum Responsibility of Government)	50	50	40	40	40	30
Population	50	40	40	30	30	40
Social Development Factor	–	–	15	10	10	–
Internal Revenue Generation Effort	–	–	5	10	20	10
Land Mass and Terrain	–	10	–	10	–	10
Population Density	–	–	–	–	–	10
TOTAL	100	100	100	100	100	100

Source: New Nigerian, February 26, 1981; and National Constitutional Conference, *Report of the Committee on Revenue Allocation* (Abuja, September 1994), 14 and 30.

As previously noted, throughout the 1970s, one-half of federal revenues assigned to the states was shared equally among them, while the other half was distributed on the basis of population. Although the weight assigned to the equality principle was reduced to 40 percent in 1981, the principle remains the single most important factor in the horizontal revenue allocation formula.

The norm of interunit equality has been defended on various grounds.[29] First, the principle gives recognition to the reality that each of the states has to sustain a basic, minimum set of public functions and institutions, irrespective of its size or population. It is in this regard that the norm of state equality is often referred to as the principle of minimum responsibility of government. Second, the standard of state equality upholds a fundamental axiom of symmetrical federalism, according to which each unit in the federation is constitutionally and legally equal to any other unit. Third, compared to other principles of entitlement, the equality principle is virtually unmatched in its simplicity, verifiability, certainty, ease of applicability, and nonreliance on the use of technical and often unavailable socioeconomic data.

Fourth, given the commitment of successive federal administrations to establishing states of relatively equivalent populations, the principle of interunit equality does not necessarily produce per capita imbalances in revenues available to the states. Fifth, the equal distribution of revenues among states of relatively equal populations could promote the basic goals of equity, even national development, and national integration. Sixth, and finally, the application of the equality principle helps to reassure or compensate states that are not populous, large, or rich enough to benefit from other principles of fiscal allocation.

In spite of its seemingly obvious advantages, however, the principle of equality has provoked profound criticisms. According to the noted economist and member of the Okigbo Commission on Revenue Allocation, Adedotun Phillips, while the equality principle "is the easiest to use," it is also "the most difficult to defend."[30] One major drawback of the equality principle is its spurious assumption of comparability or equivalence in the conditions of the states. On the contrary, no two states are exactly equal in economic circumstances, geographical conditions, or population. Thus, despite the long-standing official commitment to the creation of states of approximately equal populations, it has not been possible to make all the states exactly or nearly identical in such a fashion. Under current revenue-sharing arrangements, Lagos (with a 1991 population of 5.6 million) gets an equal share of 40 percent of the states' portion of statutory grants in the Federation Account along with Yobe (with only 1.4 million people). Under the impact of the equality principle, high-population states essentially have remained relatively underfunded on a per capita basis in relation to the low-population states. Predictably, the more populous states have been the most persistent and strident opponents of the equality principle.

A second major limitation of the equality principle is the strong, unremitting pressures it generates for the creation of new states. The application of the equality principle means, in effect, that a greater share of federal revenues can be obtained by the fragmentation of an existing state into two or more units, each of which can then claim its equal share of the portion of the Federation Account that is distributed on the basis of interunit equality. Quite obviously, the perennial pressures for the establishment of new states are unlikely to cease until the equality principle is either abrogated or drastically de-emphasized.

A final weakness of the equality principle is that it provides no incentive for the states to mobilize independent revenues of their own and thus encourages the tendency toward fiscal lethargy at the subnational level. A principle that guarantees each state substantial revenues by virtue of the simple fact that it constitutes a governmental unit in the federation can only induce a sense of complacency among the states.

Population and the social development factor

Population has been a long-standing—and contentious—principle of revenue allocation in Nigeria. As far back as 1946, for example, the Phillipson Commission recommended the use of the population principle, along with derivation and need, in sharing central revenues among the regions. Subsequent commissions also emphasized the importance of the population factor, if not explicitly then implicitly through the recommendation of such surrogate measures as need, primary school enrollment, number of adult male tax payers, or the social development factor.

From 1970 to 1980, half of federal statutory grants to the states were distributed on a population basis. In 1981, however, the weight attached to the population factor was reduced to 40 percent. In 1990, the principle was further relegated to a weight of 30 percent. Notwithstanding this decline, aggregate population remains the second most important factor of allocation (after interunit equality) in Nigeria's horizontal fiscal federalism, and population-related factors (primary school enrollment, ratio of hospital beds to population, and so forth) remain the single most important set of factors shaping the country's revenue-sharing practices.

The justification for the relatively strong emphasis on population is not far-fetched. To virtually all of Nigeria's officials, population is the veritable indication of expenditure obligation and "all things being equal, the more people there are in a state, the greater would be the need for the provision of services and amenities."[31] Moreover, the use of population statistics, which are potentially relatively easy to assemble and verify, helps to obviate the need for more technical and often inaccessible socioeconomic data.

But the population principle has been extensively and severely criticized. First, the use of the population principle in revenue allocation has been an important source of the political sensitivity and contentiousness surrounding population statistics in Nigeria. Consequently, the country's census exercises have often degenerated into fierce ethnic and regional contests, and the resulting population figures have usually been severely tarnished by actual or alleged acts of falsification or inflation.

Second, the use of unreliable, controversial, or outdated population data tends to distort the revenue-sharing system. For the almost three decades between 1964 and 1991, for example, the Nigerian federal government relied on projections from the 1963 census figures in making population-based grants to the states. Yet it was widely known that the figures were cynically and extensively inflated and may have been rendered even more dubious by probable changes in the composition and distribution of the nation's population since the organization of the 1963 census.

Third, several critics have argued that raw aggregate population data may say little about the economic circumstances or need of a state. To be meaningful and useful, it is argued, the population principle must incorporate such characteristics of the population as sparsity, density, age composition, rural-urban distribution, and so on. Until the introduction of the social development factor, however, these characteristics were largely neglected in the implementation of population-based allocations in Nigeria.

Fourth, many of the smaller Nigerian states complain that they have been unfairly shortchanged by the use of the population factor. They contend that while a large population may mean a heavy expenditure obligation, such a population may also imply a higher taxable base. So far, however, the use of the demographic factor in resource allocation in Nigeria has focused exclusively on the expenditure-inducing aspect of the population equation, ignoring its possible revenue-generating dimension.

Finally, contrary to the expectations of those who advocate population as the ultimate principle of equitable distribution, allocation on a population basis is only "moderately equalizing" because it provides no positive assistance in reducing the disparity between wealthy and poor regions but, rather, merely prevents it from increasing.[32] Alternative principles of allocation must, therefore, be implemented if effective equalization is to be achieved.

Since it was introduced under the revenue-sharing scheme of the Second Republic, the social development factor has mitigated some of the weaknesses associated with the use of raw population data. Under the 1981 Revenue Allocation Scheme, the social development factor was defined to comprise direct and "inverse" primary school enrollment and was assigned a weight of 15 percent. To assist the states in maintaining those of their population already in school, direct primary school enrollment was assigned a weight of 11.25 percent. And to compensate or encourage those states that have lower primary school enrollment relative to population, inverse enrollment (or the proportion of children of primary school age not yet in school) was assigned a weight of 3.75 percent.

In 1989, however, the Revenue Mobilization Commission reduced the weight attached to the social development factor by five percentage points and introduced fundamental changes in the factor's composition and computation. Simply put, the 10 percent weight now allocated to the social development factor is divided among education, health, and water in the ratio of 4:3:3, respectively. The education component of the social development factor was defined to include direct primary school enrollment and direct and inverse secondary school enrollment. The health component gave equal recognition to the direct and inverse proportion of hospital beds per state, while the allocation for water supply was divided equally between the "average annual rainfall (for state's headquarters for the five most current years) and the territorial spread of water supply in the state."[33]

Derivation and the compensation
or protection of mineral-producing areas

The derivation principle has aroused perhaps the most heated arguments in Nigeria's revenue-sharing debates. The derivation, or origin, principle of distribution stipulates that a significant proportion of the revenues collected in the jurisdiction of a subnational government should be returned to that government.

The derivation principle dominated revenue-sharing practices and politics during the early stages of federation in Nigeria. In the late 1950s and early 1960s, for instance, all export duties on agricultural commodities and import and excise duties on tobacco and motor fuel were simply returned to the region of production or consumption. But the derivation principle soon came under severe criticism for very obvious reasons.

Basically, the principle had a detrimental impact on interregional equity and national unity. It tended to make the rich regions richer and to arouse invidious opposition and resentment from the relatively less endowed regions. The application of the derivation principle to the allocation of growing oil revenues during the 1970s accented the economically inequitable and politically contentious nature of the principle. The approved estimates of statutory grants for the 1974–75 fiscal year, for instance, allocated 241 million naira to the oil-producing states of Rivers and Mid-West, which had a combined population of 4.1 million, whereas the Western, East-Central, North-Western, and North-Eastern states, with a total population of 30.2 million, received only 102.3 million naira under the same scheme.[34] This imbalance was the result of a policy that returned 45 percent of onshore oil rents and royalties to the states of derivation or production. But such egregious asymmetry in the financial fortunes of the states only served to galvanize opposition to the derivation principle and nudge the central government into downgrading the principle in favor of a revenue-sharing strategy that increased the amount of resources available for distribution among all the states.

Apart from its economically inequitable impact and politically contentious nature, the derivation principle has also been criticized for restricting the capacity of national authorities to initiate and implement redistributive or macroeconomic reforms, requiring the use of often unavailable economic data regarding the interregional consumption and production of goods, often rewarding units not on the basis of any superior productive effort but by dint of geography, and unleashing political counterpressures against the free mobility of goods and services in the federation.[35]

Given these limitations, it is not surprising that the derivation principle has sometimes been condemned as the "devil" of Nigeria's fiscal federalism. Even before the growth of oil revenues made the application of derivation more contentious and invidious, Adebayo Adedeji had denounced the principle in the following frequently quoted words:

> The derivation principle bedeviled the development of a rational and equitable system of revenue allocation in Nigeria. It . . . poisoned intergovernmental relationships and . . . exacerbated interregional rivalry and

conflict. Perhaps more than any other single factor it . . . hampered the development of a sense of national unity and common citizenship in Nigeria.[36]

Both the Aboyade Committee and the Okigbo Commission recommended the elimination of the principle from Nigeria's revenue-sharing practices. Only the intervention of the NPN federal government, which enjoyed considerable electoral support among the southern ethnic minority oil-producing states, ensured the survival of the derivation principle during the Second Republic, when 2 percent of funds in the Federation Account was assigned to the mineral-producing states on the basis of derivation. Quite obviously, the principle has suffered a systematic decline. Whereas in the late 1960s, excise and import duties on tobacco and petroleum products were transferred wholly to the state of derivation, today these revenue receipts are paid into the Federation Account, which is shared on the basis of principles that give only relatively marginal recognition to the derivation criterion.

Similarly, the proportion of oil revenues allocated on a derivation basis declined from 50 percent of mining rents and royalties in 1969, through 2 percent of the Federation Account in 1981, to only 1 percent of mineral revenues in the account during the period from 1989 to 1999. Moreover, as far back as 1971, all offshore mineral revenues were vested in the federation, thereby depriving the littoral oil-producing states of their previous claim to about half of the rents and royalties from these revenues.

The systematic downgrading of the derivation principle has fueled criticisms from ethnic minority elites in the oil-producing states who see the decline of derivation as just another expression of oppression and domination of minorities in the Nigerian federation. In the words of the Second Republic governor of Rivers state, Melford Okilo:

> Derivation as a revenue allocation criterion is not new to this country. It featured prominently when cocoa, groundnut, etc., were the main sources of revenue for Nigeria. But derivation as a principle of revenue allocation has continued to be deliberately suppressed since crude oil became the mainstay of the country's wealth . . . simply because the main contributors of the oil wealth are the minorities.[37]

This ethnopolitical interpretation is echoed by at least two noted students of Nigeria's revenue-sharing policies, who argue as follows:

"'Derivation' was defeated because the oil wells were located in a few southern states with little political clout."[38] "The speed with which the derivation principle paled into insignificance with changes in both the source of revenue and its location left no one in doubt that revenue allocation is a political power game."[39]

Nevertheless, the decline or delegitimation of the derivation principle has occurred in tandem with a growing recognition of the need to devise a system of special grants (as opposed to shared revenues) to compensate the mineral-producing areas for the ecological and social costs of oil extraction. As extensively documented by the elites of the mineral-producing states and areas, these costs include the loss of agricultural land, the destruction of aquatic life, and the pollution of the general environment, all of which have resulted from oil spillage, gas flares, the construction of oil pipelines, and related oil-producing activities.

In 1977, the Aboyade Committee recommended that 3 percent of the Federation Account be allocated to the mineral-producing areas and to other communities beset by ecological or related problems. Some three years later, the Okigbo Commission proposed devoting 2 percent of the Federation Account to the amelioration of the mineral-producing areas' special problems. Although this amount was increased to 3 percent of the Federation Account in the initial (and eventually nullified) 1981 Revenue Allocation Law, it was eventually reduced to 1.5 percent in the revised 1981 Revenue Allocation Act endorsed by President Shagari in January 1982. Following persistent and increasingly strident demands by the oil-producing communities, however, the Babangida administration, in June 1992, increased the special fund for mineral-producing areas to 3 percent of mineral revenues in the Federation Account.[40]

Under the revenue-sharing arrangements in effect in 1999, only 4 percent of mineral revenues in the Federation Account was exclusively allocated to the mineral-producing areas and states (that is, the 3 percent special fund for the rehabilitation of mineral-producing areas plus the 1 percent of mineral revenues paid to the oil-producing states on the basis of derivation). Disenchanted with this negligible allocation, spokespersons for the oil-producing states and areas demanded the following:

❖ The return to the affected oil-producing areas of all oil rents and royalties (that is, all federally collected oil revenues except the petroleum profits tax).

❖ The payment by the federal government and the oil companies of reparations to the oil-producing communities for past and ongoing expropriation, despoilment, or neglect of these communities.

❖ The abrogation of all legal instruments, including constitutional provisions, that vest in the federal government ownership and control of all the country's onshore and offshore minerals, oil, and natural gas.

❖ The discontinuation of the distinction between onshore and offshore oil revenues in the application of the derivation principle.

❖ The enactment of appropriate legislation that would require the state-backed multinational oil companies to protect the environmental rights and identify with the developmental aspirations of their host communities.

❖ The establishment of new states, localities, and other appropriate developmental entities in the oil-producing areas as a means of improving the capacity of government to respond adequately and promptly to the special problems and needs of these areas.

❖ As an ultimate solution to the problems of the oil producing communities, the recasting of the federal structure along more genuinely federal or confederal lines to give the oil-producing communities greater political and economic autonomy.[41]

The campaign for the rights of Nigeria's oil-producing communities was most effectively prosecuted and popularized (both nationally and internationally) by Ken Saro-Wiwa, a noted writer and leader of the Movement for the Survival of the Ogoni People, which published a trenchant "Ogoni Bill of Rights" in 1990. In November 1995, the Nigerian military government provoked severe international strictures and sanctions when it executed Saro-Wiwa and eight other Ogoni activists following their questionable convictions for the May 1994 mob murders of four progovernment Ogoni leaders.

By the time of Saro-Wiwa's execution, however, the oil-producing areas' demands for economic rights had yielded an important concession: In October 1995, General Abacha formally approved, but did not

implement, a "consensus resolution" of the 1994–95 National Constitutional Conference that "the principle of derivation shall be constantly reflected in any approved formula as being not less than 13 percent
of the revenue accruing to the Federation Account . . ." directly from
any natural resources.[42] This resolution was eventually codified as section 162(2) of the 1999 Constitution for the Fourth Republic. In April
2000, the federal government began implementing the provision,
retroactive to the beginning of the year.

The payment of the 13 percent derivation revenues to the oil-
producing states marked perhaps the first major achievement of the
Fourth Republic in the federalist management of regional conflict. Yet
misgivings persisted in the oil-producing areas over many aspects of the
derivation revenues: the choice of January 2000 (rather than May
1999, when constitutional rule was restored) as the effective date for
the commencement of the new derivation rule, the continuing exclusion of offshore oil revenues (estimated at about 40 percent of total oil
revenues in 2000) from the derivation rule, the failure to directly
involve the oil-producing localities and communities (as distinct from
the states) in the devolution of the derivation-based revenues, and the
alleged attempts by the Obasanjo government to frustrate the effective
funding of the NDDC as a centrally coordinated agency for respond-
ing directly and specifically to the ecological and developmental problems of the oil-producing communities.

Land mass and terrain

Land mass and terrain have usually been advocated as legitimate principles of revenue sharing by two groups of geopolitical interests in the
federation—namely, the large and relatively sparsely populated states of
Nigeria's North (which account for some 70 percent of the country's
territory) and the states of the swampy, oil-rich Delta region of the
country's South. These interests contend that their extensive or difficult
geographical terrain imposes additional budgetary obligations, which
should be partly offset by the revenue-sharing scheme. Except for a
short-lived appearance in the nullified 1981 Revenue Allocation Law,
however, the principle of land mass/terrain did not figure in Nigeria's
revenue-sharing scheme until 1990, when it was virtually unilaterally
imposed by the Babangida administration.

Since 1990, land mass and terrain (three main terrain types are recognized: wetlands, plains, and highlands) have been assigned a combined weight of 10 percent (5 percent each for land mass and terrain) in the interstate allocation formula. Two major problems beset the utilization of land mass as a factor in horizontal revenue allocation. The first relates to the predictable southern opposition to the very obvious advantage that the factor of land mass confers on the North. As a counterpoise to this northern advantage, and given the reality that the South is far more densely populated than the North, southern delegates at the 1994–95 National Constitutional Conference pushed for the introduction into the horizontal sharing formula of the countervailing factor of population density—a variable that can only further complicate the politicization of population data in Nigeria. The second major problem with the principle of land mass and terrain pertains to the surreptitious manner in which it was introduced. Thus Gini Mbanefoh has suggested the need to provide more legitimacy for the principle, perhaps through a more open public discussion and endorsement of its merits. "In the meantime," Mbanefoh has concluded, "either the use of the principle should be suspended or the weight assigned to it generally reduced."[43]

Internal revenue-generation effort or independent revenues

There is a growing realization in Nigeria of the need to induce or encourage the states to generate or mobilize independent revenues of their own so they will come to regard federal allocations as supplemental to, rather than as the major source of, their revenues. Such an outcome would have the distinct advantage of reducing the intensity and destructiveness of current intergovernmental and intersegmental competition for centrally controlled resources.

The importance of autonomous revenue generation by the regions and states was emphasized in the reports and recommendations of most of the revenue allocation commissions since the 1950s, especially the 1953 Chick Commission; the 1977 Aboyade Committee; the 1980 Okigbo Commission; and the 1989 National Revenue Mobilization, Allocation, and Fiscal Commission (NRMAFC). But it was not until the Second Republic that the principle of independent state revenues was explicitly and formally incorporated into Nigeria's revenue-sharing scheme.

Under the interstate sharing formula of the revised 1981 Revenue Allocation Act, the principle of internal revenue generation effort was assigned a weight of 5 percent, in line with the recommendation of the Okigbo Commission. The 1989 NRMAFC report, however, recommended that the weight be increased to 20 percent. The Babangida administration reduced NRMAFC's proposed new weight by half and shifted the remaining weight of 10 percent to the new principle of land mass and terrain.[44]

Two main problems have plagued the application of the principle of internal revenue generation effort. First, given the absence of reliable data on the budgets and economies of the states, there has been a great deal of confusion regarding the proper measure for ascertaining the internal revenue generation effort of the states. After a protracted search for an adequate measurement of independent revenues, NRMAFC eventually settled for what it described as a practical, incremental indicator of internal revenue effort: the percentage increase in internal revenues generated by a state in a specified period over the preceding period.[45] This measure of independent revenue effort differs significantly from the measure recommended by the Okigbo Commission (the ratio of total internal revenues to total expenditures) or the measure approved by the Shagari administration (the ratio of internal revenue to recurrent expenditures).[46] NRMAFC did recognize the inconclusiveness of the search, and it proclaimed its receptiveness to any novel ideas for measuring and enhancing the autonomous fiscal capacity of the states.[47]

The second fundamental problem involves the intensive opposition to the principle of internal revenue generation by several states, particularly in the relatively economically backward North, that "feel they have little room for increasing their internally generated revenue either because they are poor or because they have fully exhausted their revenue sources."[48] This is probably the key reason that the Babangida administration opted to fix the weight for internal revenue generation effort at 10 percent, instead of the 20 percent recommended by NRMAFC.

ADMINISTRATIVE PROBLEMS OF FISCAL FEDERALISM

An abiding problem of revenue sharing in Nigeria is the absence of an appropriate and acceptable framework of administrative institutions for managing, reviewing, and adjusting the system of intergovernmental financial relations in general, and disbursing designated special funds or grants in the Federation Account in particular.

Virtually all of the ad hoc panels on revenue allocation since the Phillipson Commission of 1946 have emphasized the need to establish a permanent technical fiscal commission in Nigeria. Such a commission is expected to perform a number of important functions, some of which were delineated by the Okigbo Commission as follows:

> (i) To maintain and administer the Federation Account.
> (ii) Keep under continuous study and review the federal fiscal system and the financial relations between the Federation and the states, and between the states and local government councils.
> (iii) Constantly review the bases of revenue sharing among the three levels of government, among the states in their own behalf, and among the states for the benefit of their local government councils.
> (iv) Propose changes in the scheme for revenue sharing.
> (v) Ensure compliance with the revenue sharing scheme and report thereon to the National Assembly.
> (vi) Supervise the administration of loans to the states.
> (vii) Undertake any studies or duties that may be supplementary to, or necessary for, the proper discharge of the duties enumerated in i-vi above.[49]

In its White Paper on the Okigbo Commission Report, the Shagari administration showed very little enthusiasm for the idea of a Permanent Fiscal Commission, which would have put an end to the federal government's direct administration of the Federation Account.[50] Meanwhile, the government's management of the Federation Account became the source of bitter disputes during the Second Republic, as several opposition-controlled states complained of irregularities and abuses in payments into the account.

Intergovernmental financial relations in the Second Republic were beset by several other administrative problems. In particular, bitter and protracted intergovernmental disagreements developed over the administration and management of the special funds in the Federation Account for the development of mineral-producing areas and the amelioration of environmental problems throughout the federation. Because both funds had been legally designated under the Revenue Allocation Law as monies allocated to the states, some of the state governments sought a direct and overriding say in the administration of these funds. The federal government, on the other hand, tried to establish special federal agencies to administer the funds, in line with the recommendation of the Okigbo Commission. Legal challenges by the Bendel state government stymied the federal government's move, and in October 1982 the Supreme Court prohibited the central administration from managing the two funds. Thus political and legal conflicts in the Second Republic prevented the administration and disbursement of the funds for improving mineral-producing areas and tackling related environmental problems.[51]

After the collapse of the Second Republic at the end of 1983, the military administration of General Buhari simply established special ad hoc federal committees to administer the controversial funds. Following the inception of the Babangida administration in August 1985, however, three far-reaching measures were taken to resolve some of the key administrative problems of fiscal federalism in Nigeria.

First, NRMAFC was established in 1989 as a permanent body to develop, monitor, and review an appropriate system of revenue collection and distribution.

Second, a permanent statutory agency, the Oil Mineral–Producing Areas Development Commission (OMPADEC), was established in June 1992 to administer the 3 percent of mineral revenues in the Federation Account approved by the Babangida administration for the rehabilitation and development of mineral-producing areas. The commission had its headquarters in Port Harcourt and state offices in Abia, Akwa Ibom, Cross River, Delta, Edo, Imo, Ondo, and Rivers states. The commission's board consisted of twelve members, all but two of whom were indigenes of the mineral-producing areas.

Third, the government unveiled plans and proposals to establish a new national body to replace the National Emergency Relief Agency and administer the 2 percent of the Federation Account set aside for environmental problems or disasters throughout the federation.[52]

In spite of these measures, major problems still bedevil the administration of federal finance in Nigeria. The composition of NRMAFC, for example, has remained deeply problematic. Originally designed to operate as a purely technical agency, NRMAFC is now in danger of degenerating into an unwieldy, overpoliticized body. When the commission was first inaugurated, it had eight members and a secretary. The initial structure was consonant with the recommendation of the Okigbo Commission, which had envisaged a fiscal commission comprising "not less than four but not more than eight members selected so as to reflect federal character of the country."[53] Unfortunately, the desire to reflect Nigeria's federal character has led to the distortion of NRMAFC's composition. Thus, in line with the general tendency to interpret the federal character clause as requiring the representation of every state, NRMAFC now consists of a chairman and one member from each of the country's thirty-six states. As T. Y. Danjuma, the commission's chairman, noted in December 1992, the introduction of the principle of equal state representation into the composition of NRMAFC means that "if . . . new states were to be created in the future, the size of the commission will further increase," thereby making the body even more unwieldy and its decision-making process more cumbersome and time consuming.[54]

Moreover, NRMAFC has not curtailed irregularities in the center's administration of the Federation Account. For example, the commission could not stop the egregious underpayment of federally collected revenues into the Federation Account under the Babangida and Abacha administrations, in particular. While such manipulation was directly related to the extraconstitutional nature of military rule, irregularities in the management of fiscal federalism have not been uncommon under civilian governments. In May 2000, for example, the Delta state government decried the continuation under the new democracy of the practice by which past military governments deducted Nigeria's external debt service obligations from federally collected revenues *before* these revenues were shared vertically among the country's three governmental tiers. This practice shortchanges the subfederal authorities because they collectively account for less than 30 percent of Nigeria's external debt stock of about $33 billion.[55]

Part of the explanation for the inability of NRMAFC to restrain the center's manipulation of revenue-sharing administration lies in the commission's charter as a federally appointed (or presidential) rather than truly intergovernmental body. Moreover, there is a contradiction between the constitutional responsibility of NRMAFC to oversee the administration of the Federation Account and the practical centralization of this responsibility in the federal Ministry of Finance, which coordinates the activities of the intergovernmental Federation Account Allocation Committee.

Another unresolved administrative problem of Nigeria's fiscal federalism involves the development of an appropriate and acceptable mechanism for the management of special funds generally and the special allocations to the oil-producing communities in particular. For example, Saro-Wiwa and other spokespeople for ethnic minorities in oil-producing areas assailed OMPADEC for not giving adequate representation to the recognized leaders of the oil-rich areas. More fundamentally, these ethnic minority activists denounced OMPADEC as an insignificant concession to the resource-endowed communities and as a ploy by the federal government to pre-empt the legitimate claims of these communities to a substantial share of the wealth extracted from beneath their soil. Here is how Saro-Wiwa summed up the commission's purpose:

> OMPADEC is illogical, an insult, and an injury. If you have your own money, why should government set up a commission to run your money? . . . They are treating us like babies here. . . . OMPADEC is [designed] to bait us and destroy our will to resist injustice.[56]

Indeed, OMPADEC came to acquire considerable notoriety for its mismanagement of developmental projects in the Niger Delta. It was replaced with the NDDC following the inauguration of civilian rule in 1999. Yet the final ratification of the NDDC bill by the National Assembly in June 2000 was preceded by several portentous conflicts: between the federal executive and the legislature over the funding arrangements for the NDDC and the modalities for appointing members to it, and among the oil-producing areas over the location of the commission's headquarters and whether the commission should cater to only the core Niger Delta states (Akwa Ibom, Bayelsa, Delta, Cross River, and Rivers) or to all oil-producing states (the aforementioned Niger Delta states plus Abia, Edo, Imo, and Ondo). These conflicts, coupled with the earlier failure of OMPADEC, reinforced cynicism about the appropriateness of a centrally coordinated, as opposed to state-based, response to the problems and demands of the oil-producing areas.

The state-based option was largely upheld by the important decision of the Obasanjo government to pay the 13 percent derivation revenues to the oil-rich states, instead of paying all or a substantial part of the revenues into the NDDC, as initially proposed by the government. Yet, again, that decision instantly raised fears about the possible short-changing of the immediate oil-bearing communities, some of which constitute ethnic or ethnoterritorial minorities in their respective states. Nonetheless, transferring the revenues directly to the oil-bearing localities would involve enormous administrative or logistical complications and could exacerbate intercommunal conflicts. All this would seem to support the need for an agency like the NDDC *and* for innovative measures to transform the commission into a truly inclusive, intergovernmental, decentralized, and democratized instrument for addressing the developmental and environmental problems of the oil-producing communities.

An entirely different general problem of revenue allocation administration in Nigeria involves the fiscal arrangements for local governments. Since the inclusion of the localities in the national revenue-sharing scheme in the late 1970s, the accepted arrangement for disbursing their share of central revenues has been to divide the allocation among the states on the basis of the interstate revenue-sharing formula. The state governments would then transfer the allocation, along with 10 percent of their internal revenues, to their respective localities on the basis of a formula devised by individual state assemblies or any other appropriate state-level agencies. Growing evidence that the state governments were diverting central revenues meant for their localities, however, led the Babangida administration to decide on the direct transfer of central revenues to the local governments. Yet all evidence suggests that the direct funding of the localities has been difficult to implement in practice. Thus state governments continue to serve as the "clearinghouse" for the local governments' share of central revenues, which is still disbursed on the basis of the same formula as the interstate sharing formula.[57] Not surprisingly, the continuing mediation of federal-local financial relations by the states is denounced by many localities as a negation of their constitutional and financial autonomy.

A final administrative and political problem of revenue allocation in Nigeria involves the anomalous and potentially contentious place of the Federal Capital Territory of Abuja in the revenue-sharing scheme. Apart from partaking in federal statutory devolutions as if it were "one of the states of the federation," Abuja is entitled to regular subventions from the federal government's budget through the Ministry of the Federal Capital Territory. The territory is also assigned 1 percent of the Federation Account through a special fund for its initial development. In addition, Abuja's local government council areas are entitled to federal statutory allocations to the nation's localities. Apart from complicating the unresolved question about the proper administrative status of Abuja, the federal territory's multiple access to the Federation Account, in a context of continuing financial insecurity and vulnerability at the subfederal level, has become truly invidious.

CONCLUSIONS

Basically, three major problems beset Nigeria's revenue-sharing politics and practices. The first relates to the persistence of imbalances in the vertical sharing of revenues: The federal government controls a disproportionate share of federally collected revenues to the chagrin of the states and localities whose independent revenue sources have remained grossly inadequate. This vertical imbalance not only engenders intense opposition from the states and localities, it also unleashes strong pressures at all levels of Nigerian society to win political control of the center and its disproportionate financial largesse.

The second problem of revenue allocation in Nigeria revolves around the unfulfilled quest for acceptable, equitable, and rational principles of horizontal allocation. Despite the concerted and protracted efforts to devise an adequate scheme, Nigeria's horizontal revenue-sharing formulas still suffer from several flaws: the continuing heavy reliance on the two simplistic and politically counterproductive principles of population and interunit equality, the dearth of reliable socioeconomic data to sustain the application of more rational principles of allocation, the absence of adequate inducements for the states and localities to mobilize independent internal revenues, and the very limited compensation of the mineral-producing areas for the ecological risks and social costs of oil production.

The third fundamental problem is that Nigeria's revenue-sharing practices are beset by a weak institutional or administrative framework. In other words, Nigeria lacks appropriate institutions for the rational management of the revenue-sharing system, for the disbursement of special funds or grants in the Federation Account, and for securing the financial integrity and autonomy of the localities. All things considered, Nigeria still has a long road to travel in its search for a politically acceptable, socioeconomically equitable, and technically reasonable system of revenue allocation.

4

THE STRUGGLE
FOR NEW STATES
AND LOCALITIES

I<small>N UNDERTAKING A DISCUSSION</small> of the dramatic struggles for new states and localities in Nigeria, it is useful to begin by delineating the key features of this phenomenon.

First, the creation of constituent units in Nigeria has assumed a cyclical or self-perpetuating character, with each reorganization operating largely to provoke pressures for further reform. This perennial character of territorial reforms is unusual in most other major federations, where initial periods of internal territorial changes have usually been followed by the achievement of relative stability and an elite political consensus regarding the shape and number of constituent units.

Second, while changes in the territorial configuration of the classical federations often entailed the "incorporation of external units to an initial core," federal territorial reforms in Nigeria have exclusively involved the fragmentation of pre-existing regions or states into two or more constituent units.[1] Thus each exercise in the reorganization of state boundaries in Nigeria has led to the pullulation of smaller and weaker units of constituent governments, the proliferation of narrower administrative-territorial identities, and the consolidation of centralized federal power.

Third, far from being the outcome of an elaborate process of public debate, popular ratification, or constitutional amendment, new states in Nigeria have been established mainly by military fiat. To be sure, the military's decisions on the shape and number of constituent units have been guided by a number of officially enunciated principles, such as the need to ensure some equivalence in the population of the states and the desirability of creating geographically compact constituent units. Moreover, the implementation of territorial reforms via the executive action of national military authorities has enabled the country to avoid the intractable constitutional difficulties and protracted political controversies often associated with the implementation of territorial reforms under civilian auspices. Nevertheless, this "executive" method of territorial reorganizations has also led to considerable arbitrariness in the choice of new states and localities, their areas or composition, and their seats of government. The result of this arbitrariness has been to undermine the legitimacy of state and local boundaries and to fuel pressures for further territorial reforms by aggrieved or disadvantaged segments of the population.

Fourth, whereas state boundaries in many multiethnic federations often reflect the territorial distribution of ethnic communities, the boundaries of the Nigerian states have hardly coincided with ethnolinguistic territorial cleavages. The incongruence between ethnic and state boundaries in Nigeria is not the result of a natural divergence between ethnic and territorial identities. Despite the country's long history of interethnic migration and even assimilation, Nigeria's ethnolinguistic groups remain predominantly territorially concentrated, not territorially intermixed or dispersed. Rather, the divergence of ethnic and state boundaries in Nigeria has resulted from a federalist state-building strategy that has sought to break up the country's three major ethnic groups into several states and to substitute ostensibly innocuous administrative divisions for presumably more fraught ethnic identities.

Finally, it is the generalized struggle by diverse sectional constituencies for an ostensibly more equitable distribution of national developmental patronage, rather than the quest by distinct cultural communities per se for political autonomy, that has become the overriding rationale for the reorganization of state and local boundaries in Nigeria. Thus some of the major reasons that often inform demands for new constituent units in Nigeria are that such units would "promote development" and ensure "a more equitable distribution of development undertakings."[2] But while giving satisfaction to the clamour of communities for federal financial allocations, amenities, and opportunities, the creation of new states and localities also speaks to the class interests of sectional elites. Quite obviously, it is these elites who benefit most from the proliferation of political posts and the multiplication of bureaucratic opportunities ensuing from the creation of new constituent units. Indeed, according to Daniel Bach,

> Accumulation and enrichment have become the key words and the ultimate justification in the process of establishing new territorial entities—whether they be states or local governments. Creating a new state means the establishment of a civil service, the distribution of contracts for the construction of a new secretariat with its roads and infrastructures, a new hospital, staff schools and houses, possibly a university, not to mention the establishment of parastatals, of a television station and a newspaper.[3]

The distributive imperatives that now overwhelmingly dominate the generalized pressures for new states in Nigeria were largely dormant during the early years of the state creation movement in Nigeria in the 1950s and 1960s. During this period, the demands for new states came predominantly, though not exclusively, from the nation's ethnic minorities, who sought political autonomy from the regionally hegemonic ethnic majority groups. Undoubtedly, such ethnic minority agitations reflected the quest by minority group politicians for "power and its material gains" and a concern by ethnic minority communities for protection against alleged discrimination in the distribution "of the rewards and resources of an expanding economy and state: contracts, loans, scholarships, processing plants, water supplies, street lights, schools, hydroelectric projects."[4]

Yet, while most of the contemporary demands for new states and localities come from ethnic majority groups seeking greater access to central resources and positions, the early cries for states were not only made by ethnic minority elites in the name of political autonomy from majority groups but were also actively resisted by the majority groups. To better understand the processes by which the movement for territorial reforms in Nigeria was transformed from an ethnic minority political project into a generalized strategy of distributive sectional struggles, let us examine the major territorial reforms in Nigeria since the creation of the Mid-West in 1963.

THE STRUGGLE FOR ETHNIC MINORITY STATES
AND THE CREATION OF THE MID-WEST REGION

To reiterate, the initial pressures for new states in Nigeria arose from the opposition of the nation's ethnic minorities to the British-constructed tripartite regional structure, which entrenched the hegemony of the Hausa-Fulani, Yoruba, and Igbo nationalities in the Northern, Western, and Eastern Regions, respectively. The more prominent of these minorities included the Kanuri, Nupe, Tiv, Igala, Jukun, and the Ilorin-Kabba Yoruba in the North; the Edo, Urhobo, Ijaw, Itsekiri, and the Western Igbos in the Western Region; and the Ibibio-Annang, Efik, and Ijaw in the East.

Fearing or alleging "political repression, socioeconomic discrimination, and even cultural extinction by the majority groups," the minority groups sought independent regions or states of their own in which their minority status would be mitigated, if not completely eliminated.[5] In the Northern Region, for instance, the Tiv and other peoples of the lower North called for the creation of the Middle Belt state, the Kanuri agitated for a Bornu state, while the Ilorin-Kabba Yoruba sought a merger with their kith and kin in the West. In the Western Region, the Urhobo and other non-Yoruba groups demanded a Mid-West state. And in the East, the Ibibio-Annang, Efik, and Ijaw spearheaded the movement for the Calabar-Ogoja-Rivers (COR) state.

Although the 1958 Willink Commission of Inquiry into the Fears of Minorities and the Means of Allaying Them recommended against the creation of new regions, the issue of ethnic minority states remained a dominant theme of federal politics into the immediate postindependence era. For one, Nigeria's Independence Constitution included provisions for the creation of new states. The constitution in effect provided that an act to create a new state must be passed by two-thirds of the members of each house of the bicameral federal legislature and accepted either by each house of a majority of the regions or by each house in two regions, including any region that would lose territory to the new state.[6] However, the act can take effect only if 60 percent of voters in the proposed new region give their approval in a plebiscite and if the proposal is again ratified by each house of at least two regions. Although these provisions appeared to be cumbersome, they were not impossible to meet as long as the support of the dominant political parties could be enlisted behind the movement for new states.

If the constitutional provisions kept the possibility for new states open, the interparty competition for electoral advantage helped to sustain and invigorate the movement for these states. For the two major southern parties in particular, the declaration of support for new regions was indispensable in their efforts to win electoral support outside their narrow ethnoregional bases, as well as to end the North's hegemonic position in the federation. Consequently, the Yoruba-led Action Group aligned at various times with such ethnic minority movements as the United Middle Belt Congress, the Borno Youth Movement, and Ilorin-Talaka Parapo in the North, and the Efik-led United National Independence Party in the East. A desire to win and retain the support of these allies transformed the AG from an exclusively Yoruba-oriented party into the most consistent and vociferous supporter of new ethnic minority states in the federation. Similarly, the National Council of Nigerian Citizens' main allies outside its Igbo-dominated Eastern Region base were the various parties committed to the separation of the Mid-West from the Western Region, including the Benin-Delta People's Party, the Mid-West State Movement, and the Otu-Edo.

Given its vested interests in the continuance of regional federalism in general and the disproportionate size of the North within this system in particular, the Northern People's Congress consistently opposed not only the creation of new regions in the North but also the inclusion of any provisions for new states in Nigeria's constitution. Nevertheless, for purely strategic reasons, the Congress came to be closely associated with movements that supported the creation of new states in the southern regions. Indeed, as will be shown, the support of the Congress was ultimately decisive in the creation of the Mid-West from the Western Region in July–August 1963.

It is widely acknowledged that the Mid-West Region was created for reasons that had more to do with interparty rivalries than with any genuine desire to ameliorate the problem of minorities in the old West.[7] Specifically, the establishment of the new region was the result of a joint move by the Congress-NCNC federal coalition government to annihilate the AG and decimate its base in the Western Region.

The processes leading to the establishment of the Mid-West were initiated in April 1961 when the NCNC made a motion in the House of Representatives calling for the establishment of the region. Unwilling to tarnish its own image as a supporter of ethnic minorities, yet conscious of the political motives behind the NCNC's bill, the AG tried unsuccessfully to amend the motion to call for the simultaneous creation of the COR and Middle Belt states, thereby shoring up its political base by diluting the Congress-NCNC bases of support.

By early 1962, the NCNC's Mid-West motion had been endorsed by the federal parliament and the parliaments of the Northern and Eastern Regions. The AG-controlled Western Region, however, withheld its consent. When it became apparent that the Mid-West would be created without its approval, the Western Region challenged the legality of the proposed legislation on the Mid-West state. It argued in the Supreme Court that the constitution had intended a majority of the regions to mean three out of four (and not two out of three) and that the Eastern Region legislature had been improperly constituted and, therefore, was incompetent to endorse the Mid-West motion.[8] Many AG leaders also argued that the hasty and politically motivated manner in which the creation of the Mid-West was being pushed by the Congress-NCNC coalition would lead to administrative and financial chaos in the new state, the political victimization of AG supporters in the area, and the development of new minority problems.[9]

With the breakup of the AG and the declaration of a state of emergency in the West in May 1962, however, the federally appointed administrator of the region withdrew the West's legal opposition to the creation of the Mid-West. Thereafter, the remaining procedures for establishing the Mid-West were implemented. An interim federal administration in the area of the proposed new region was established with the mandate to conduct a referendum on the proposal; in July 1963, 89 percent of the registered electorate in the Mid-West voted for the creation of the new region. Inaugural elections to the Mid-West parliament were conducted in February 1964, and the NCNC predictably assumed control of the new legislature. It proceeded to form the Mid-West's first cabinet under the leadership of Chief Dennis Osadebay, who had headed the region's interim administration since the 1963 plebiscite.[10]

It was clear to all interested observers that the creation of the Mid-West out of the West, which was the smallest of the three regions, was a partial and brazenly partisan response to the ethnic minority movement for new states. The minorities in the East and North were not granted their statehood demands and continued to chafe under the oppressive hegemony of Igbo and Hausa-Fulani respectively. Indeed, the 1963 Independence Constitution made the creation of new regions virtually impossible by requiring the approval of any future territorial changes by three of the four regional legislatures, including the legislature of the region losing territory.[11] In essence, it was not until the collapse of the First Republic and the imminent disintegration of the federation in 1966–67 that an opportunity was, once again, provided for a reorganization of the federal system.

GOWON'S CONSTITUTIONAL COUP AND THE ESTABLISHMENT OF NIGERIA'S TWELVE-STATE STRUCTURE

A major theme of official discourse in the wake of the First Republic's collapse was the reorganization of the federal structure to provide a more viable basis for any future attempts at civilian rule. In February 1966, for instance, General Aguiyi-Ironsi established a Study Group on Constitutional Review under the renowned constitutional lawyer Chief Rotimi Williams. Among other tasks, the study group was asked to investigate and make recommendations regarding the sources of divisive regionalism in the First Republic, the relative merits and demerits of unitarism vis-à-vis federalism in the Nigerian context, and the possible future territorial divisions of the country.[12]

However, the work of the Williams Study Group was pre-empted by Ironsi's subsequent abrogation of the federal system and reconstitution of the country into groups of regional provincial administrations. The head of state's unitarist policies were widely perceived to be part of a scheme to replace northern Hausa-Fulani domination under the lopsided federal system of the First Republic with Igbo hegemony under an even more obnoxious unitary system.

The July 1966 countercoup, however, not only put an end to Ironsi's unitarist scheme but also put in power at the national level ethnic minority elements with a vested interest in the creation of a multistate federal system. Indeed, in a statement in November 1966 elaborating his political agenda for the country, Nigeria's new head of state, Lieutenant-Colonel Gowon (an Angas from the minority-populated Middle Belt in the North) made this contention:

> It is quite clear that our common need in Nigeria is that no one Region or tribal group should be in a position to dominate the others . . . [and] no Region should be large enough to be able to threaten secession or hold the rest of the Federation to ransom in times of national crisis. . . . [T]here is no doubt that without a definite commitment on the states' question, normalcy and freedom from fear of domination by one Region or the other cannot be achieved.[13]

Gowon went on to enunciate five principles for the creation of new states:

❖ No one state should be in a position to dominate or control the central government.

❖ Each state should form one compact geographical area.

❖ Administrative convenience, the facts of history, and the wishes of the people concerned must be taken into account.

❖ Each state should be in a position to discharge effectively the functions of the existing regional governments.

❖ It is essential that new states be created simultaneously.[14]

Gowon then concluded that "given the present size and distribution of the Nigerian population and resources," the application of the aforementioned five principles would lead to a division of the country "into not less than eight and not more than fourteen states."[15]

Gowon's speech was made in the wake of increasingly autonomist and secessionist pressures by the Odumegwu-Ojukwu–led military government in the Eastern Region. The region was embittered by the killing of Ironsi and other Igbo military officers and of thousands of Igbo and other easterners living in the North during and after the July 1966 countercoup that installed Gowon in power. Thus, while Gowon was able to persuade conservative Hausa-Fulani elements in the North to accept his scheme for a multistate federal system, the proposal was denounced by the Eastern government as an attempt to balkanize the region and undermine its opposition to what it saw as a Northern-dominated and anti-Igbo federal military government. This Eastern opposition to state creation was given partial satisfaction by Decree No. 8 of March 1967, which made it unlawful for the central authorities to legislate on the "territorial integrity" of a region without the express consent of the head of the federal military government and all of the four regional military governors.[16]

Yet, as it became increasingly obvious that the Eastern Region was determined to secede from the country, Gowon made this proclamation on April 24:

> I want to make it abundantly clear that in the event of Lt. Colonel Ojukwu carrying out his threat to secede, this will be a clear signal in the first place to create a COR state for the protection of the minorities in Eastern Nigeria whom we know do not want to part from the rest of the country. This action of creating the COR state will be backed by the use of force if necessary.[17]

Thus on May 27, 1967, the very day the Eastern Region's Consultative Assembly gave Ojukwu the mandate to declare the region the Independent Republic of Biafra, Gowon proclaimed a state of emergency in the federation and announced the division of the country into twelve states. In his words:

> I am promulgating a decree which will divide the Federal Republic into twelve states. The . . . states will be six in the present Northern Region, three in the present Eastern Region, the Mid-West will remain as it is, the Colony Province of the Western Region and Lagos will form a new Lagos state, and the Western Region will otherwise remain as it is.[18]

Because the States Creation Decree of 1967 (Decree No. 14) was clearly a violation of Decree No. 8 of the same year, Gowon's action in reconstituting the federation has often been characterized as a constitutional or legal coup. Yet this singular action marked a decisive turning point in the history of the Nigerian federation for a number of fairly obvious reasons.

Most of all, Gowon's reorganization gave considerable satisfaction to the long-standing demands by minority communities in the Northern and Eastern Regions for new states. The twelve-state structure included the Benue-Plateau, Kwara, and North-Eastern states, which accommodated the interests of the Middle Belt, Ilorin-Kabba, and Kanuri northern minorities, respectively. The creation of the Rivers and South-Eastern states similarly responded to the demands of agitators for the COR state in the old Eastern Region. In essence, of the twelve states Gowon established, at least six were dominated by former regional ethnic minority groups.

The new state structure also undermined the secessionist bid of the Eastern Region by gaining the support of non-Igbo minorities in the region for the new Rivers and South-Eastern states. Moreover, with the fragmentation of the East into three states, the Igbo heartland of the secessionist movement now consisted of only the East-Central state, which was cut off from the immense oil wealth and strategic seaport of the new Rivers state. Thus to many observers, Gowon's decision to establish a multistate federal system was less a comprehensive attempt to solve the nation's minority problems and more an emergency, last-minute measure to scuttle the Eastern Region's secession. Although Gowon's move failed to prevent the declaration of secession and the outbreak of the Biafran war, it did contribute decisively to the federal government's ultimate success in preserving Nigeria as a single entity.

Additionally, by constituting Lagos and its colony province into a new state independent of the old Western Region, Gowon's twelve-state formula essentially cut off the region from the sea and dampened the autonomist sentiments of those Yoruba leaders who had threatened to stay out of the Nigerian federation in the event of the East's secession. Moreover, the creation of Lagos state gave satisfaction to those in the new state who never really regarded the area as a part of the West and were not enamoured of the centrifugal tendencies in the old region.

The abrogation of the regions also ended the structural imbalance in the composition of the federation and reduced southern fears of northern domination of the country. Furthermore, the subdivision of the North and South into six states each helped to convey a sense of North-South parity and to pre-empt any feelings of domination or discrimination that may have resulted from the disproportionate concentration of new states in one half of the country.

Finally, the inauguration of the twelve-state system effectively marked the beginning of Nigeria's transformation from a peripheralized federal system into a centralized federation, or even what some have characterized as a highly decentralized unitary state. Having been virtually unilaterally established by the center, and lacking the size and resources of the old regions, Nigeria's new constituent state units became increasingly dependent on the center for financial sustenance and political direction. In short, the 1967 reorganizations left a legacy of political centralization and federal superordination that was difficult to reverse in subsequent years.

Yet the twelve-state structure was bound to be controversial and inconclusive. The reorganizations had relied heavily on old colonial-era provincial boundaries, were hastily implemented, involved many compromises and uncertainties, and were widely thought to be provisional. Gowon himself confessed that the circumstances in May 1967 "did not allow for consultations through plebiscites."[19] Instead, he committed his administration to the establishment of a States Delimitation Commission "which will ensure that any divisions or towns not satisfied with the states in which they are initially grouped will obtain redress."[20]

Indeed, many imbalances and contradictions still existed in the demographic configuration and cultural composition of the new states. The North-Eastern state, for example, was larger in area than all the six southern states put together, and it contained 18 percent of the country's population.[21] Culturally, some of the states contained populations that considered themselves ethnically incompatible with the dominant groups in their respective states: "Igalas sought separation from Kwara state, the Lere from North-Eastern, the people of southern Zaria from North-Central, the Urhobo, Isoko and Itsekiri peoples from the Mid-West, the Ijebu from the West, and so on."[22] These separatist pressures were greatly strengthened by the Gowon formula for financial devolutions to the states (one-half on an equal basis among the states and one-half on the basis of population), which held out the prospect of expanded federal revenue allocations to successful candidates for statehood. By 1973, "agitation for the creation of states had reached . . . a feverish point" throughout the Nigerian federation.[23]

Given these rising pressures, the Gowon administration was conflicted, reflecting the increasing torpidity and indecisiveness that beset the regime. It committed itself to the resolution of the states issue as part of a proposed (but eventually rescinded) plan of recivilianization and as a means of ensuring even development and bringing government closer to the people, but it could not take a definitive decision on further reorganizations. Indeed, the Boundary Delimitation Commission promised by the head of state in May 1967 was never appointed. The simmering demands for the reform of the twelve-state system were never decisively addressed until the removal of Gowon and the inception of the Murtala Mohammed administration in July 1975.

THE ESTABLISHMENT OF THE NINETEEN-STATE STRUCTURE

Barely a week after coming to power on July 29, 1975, Brigadier Murtala Mohammed appointed a six-person panel, under the chairmanship of Supreme Court Justice Ayo Irikefe, to inquire into the necessity or desirability of creating additional states and to advise on the delimitation, viability, and administrative capitals of any proposed new constituent units.

In its report, published early in 1976, the Irikefe Panel acknowledged the intensity of "ethnic loyalty, mutual suspicion and even hatred among the diverse peoples which make up Nigeria."[24] However, the panel advised against creating states on the basis of ethnic divisions or suspicion. Indeed, the panel "treated ethnicity as the least important of the criteria" that should form the basis for the state-creation exercise.[25]

While acknowledging the weak financial base of virtually all the Nigerian states, the panel opted to assess the viability of any proposed new states in demographic and spatial, rather than economic, terms. Indeed, according to the panel, "each state was not, and should not, be required to function as a self-contained or self-sufficient unit. . . . [T]he country as a whole constitutes a single economic system and so long as this system is viable, the viability of the component units can be assured through the redistributive actions of the Federal Government."[26]

In one of its most frequently quoted statements, the panel argued that the "basic motivation in the demand for more states is the desire for rapid economic development" and that "all other reasons adduced by state agitators are . . . mere rationalization to achieve the basic purpose of development."[27] Yet the panel noted that economic development may not necessarily be enhanced by the creation of states. Many groups simply saw the creation of states as a "booty-sharing exercise" that would diffuse or distribute public positions, perquisites, facilities, and related preferment among sectional elites and their constituents.[28] In essence, part of the solution to the repeated agitation for more states and the desire for basic development, according to the panel and the government, lay in the existence of good state governments committed to the equitable distribution of development undertakings and related opportunities among their populations.

Yet the panel recommended the creation of more states "because there was a very strong movement for it and the political stability of Nigeria cannot be guaranteed if new states are not created."[29] But states were to be created only "where the demand has been long, strong, and widely articulated and where the population and the area justify such an action and where administrative convenience and security are assured."[30]

In the final analysis, the Irikefe Panel recommended the establishment of a nineteen-state structure to be constituted as follows:

❖ The North-Eastern and Western states fragmented into three states each.
❖ The Benue-Plateau, East-Central, North-Western, and South-Eastern states split into two states each.
❖ Lagos merged with Ogun, one of the three proposed successor states to the Western state.

The recommendations of the panel were largely, but not fully, accepted and implemented by the government, which indeed announced a nineteen-state structure in February 1976 and inaugurated it the following April. But the government did not approve or implement the panel's recommendations that the South-Eastern state be split into two (Cross River and Akwa Ibom) and that Lagos should be merged with the new Ogun state. The government argued that the fragmentation of the South-Eastern state "would not be in the best interest of all concerned in the long run" and that the size and population of the proposed new Cross River state did not justify such a split.[31] However, in line with its policy of renaming the states to help de-emphasize old geopolitical symbols and sentiments, the South-Eastern state was redesignated Cross River state.

In the case of the proposed merger of Lagos with Ogun, the government rejected the proposal on the grounds that the "people of Lagos would be going into the state as a minority after enjoying statehood for a period of nine years."[32]

The government's decisions diverged from the Irikefe Panel's rec-ommendations in a number of other respects. For instance, while the panel had recommended the inclusion of Ijesha and Ife in Ondo state to prevent possible domination of the new state by the Ekiti, the gov-ernment resolved to put these two groups in the already unwieldy Oyo state.[33] Similarly, the Nasarawa and Lafia divisions in the North were made a part of Plateau state, rather than being included in Benue as recommended by the Irikefe Panel.[34] In addition, although the panel had recommended that the area of the old Onitsha province be divid-ed between Anambra and Imo states, the government opted to put the province completely in Anambra.[35] Indeed, only half of the twelve major interstate boundary adjustments recommended by the panel were eventually implemented by the government.[36]

In essence, while the government had intended the nineteen-state structure to be a fairly permanent arrangement, there was deep oppo-sition to the structure among communities that felt inadequately accommodated within it. Opposition to the nineteen-state system was particularly strong among the following groups:

❖ The indigenes of the proposed new Cross River state, whose state-hood aspirations had been endorsed by the Irikefe Panel, only to be rejected by the government.

❖ The peoples of the North-Central state (now renamed Kaduna), where the state bureaucracy had become polarized along the old provincial divisions between Katsina and Kaduna.

❖ The Igbo political class, which condemned a situation in which the Igbo dominated only two states (Anambra and Imo) against approximately five states each in the areas populated by the two other majority ethnicities of Hausa-Fulani and Yoruba.

❖ The peoples of the Mid-West state (now renamed Bendel), who complained that the state had not been subdivided since it was carved out of the Western Region in 1963.

❖ The peoples of some of the more populous or sectionally frag-mented states like Kano, Kwara, and Rivers, who sought new states on the grounds of balanced access to developmental proj-ects and interethnic equity.

Any suggestion for the reform of the nineteen-state structure was, however, unacceptable to the Mohammed administration, as it was to the government of General Olusegun Obasanjo, the chief of the General Staff who filled out Mohammed's term of office following the latter's assassination in February 1976. While admitting that "its decisions cannot please all those affected," the administration argued that a further "proliferation of states will make nonsense of the whole exercise" and warned that it would not condone "any future agitation, emotional outburst or provocative demonstrations on the matter."[37]

Thus, following the demonstrations for new states that took place during the visit of General Obasanjo to Kaduna in July 1977, Alhaji Nuhu Bamali and Alhaji Isa Kaita, noted lobbyists for the New Kaduna and Katsina states, respectively, were relieved of their positions in the Kaduna state government.[38] This was followed in June 1978 by the abrupt termination, with the tacit approval of the federal military government, of the proceedings of the Constituent Assembly following attempts by some of its members to insert provisions for the creation of four new states (Akwa Ibom, Wawa or Enugu, Katsina, and Kogi) into the 1979 Constitution.[39]

The popular pressures for new states could not be ignored by the democratically elected civilian government that succeeded the military administration in October 1979. Far from easing with the inception of civilian rule and the lifting of the ban on political parties, these pressures surged under the impact of partisan electoral mobilization and the new constitutional principle of federal character, which opened up new opportunities in federal representation and resource allocation to successful aspirants for new states.

For the parties of the Second Republic, therefore, the creation of new states was an issue they could either pragmatically exploit or perilously ignore in the struggle for electoral advantage. Indeed, the National Movement, the precursor to the National Party of Nigeria, had specifically exploited the issue to mobilize diverse sectional elites behind the party's bid for power in the 1979 elections. On assuming control of the federal government, the party predictably transformed the issue of new states into a national political project. To be sure, the states issue became "the most prominent and volatile issue in the 1979–83 legislative period and into the 1983 electoral campaign."[40]

Yet, for reasons that shall be discussed, no new states could be created during the Second Republic.

THE FUTILE CRUSADE FOR NEW STATES
IN THE SECOND REPUBLIC

Three major reasons account for the abortion of what President Shehu Shagari once described as the "holy crusade for new states" in the Second Republic, despite the enormous "amounts of time, energy, and wealth invested in the enterprise" in virtually every part of the country.[41] These reasons were the difficult constitutional provisions on state creation, the deep differences among the major parties on the issue, and the extravagant and institutionally unsupportable number of proposals for new states in the new republic.

Reflecting the expressed commitment of the departing Mohammed-Obasanjo administration to a "constitutional restriction" on further state creation, the 1979 Constitution included provisions on new states that were universally regarded as extremely stringent and virtually incomprehensible.[42] According to section 8(1):

> An Act of the National Assembly for the purpose of creating a new state shall only be passed if—
> (a) a request, supported by at least two-thirds majority of members (representing the area demanding the creation of the new state) in each of the following, namely—
>> (i) the Senate and House of Representatives,
>> (ii) the House of Assembly in respect of the area, and
>> (iii) the local government councils in respect of the area, is received by the National Assembly;
> (b) a proposal for the creation of the state is thereafter approved in a referendum by at least two-thirds majority of the people of the area where the demand for creation of the state originated;
> (c) the result of the referendum is then approved by a simple majority of all the states of the Federation supported by a simple majority of members of the Houses of Assembly; and
> (d) the proposal is approved by a resolution passed by two-thirds majority of members of each House of the National Assembly.

As James Reed put it, "if the draftsman was instructed to produce a section which would effectively prevent any future tampering with the present states, then he has succeeded admirably."[43] Among the specific legal difficulties and procedural obstacles that stymied the attempts to create new states in the Second Republic were the following:

❖ The sheer demographic impossibility of getting "two-thirds" of the "people" (not electorate!) of an area demanding a new state to endorse the request in a referendum.

❖ The absence of any constitutional provisions specifying the body to conduct referendums for the purpose of state creation.

❖ The fuzzy and contradictory use of the words "request," "proposal," and "result of the referendum" to refer to different stages of statehood demands.

❖ The complications regarding the role of local councils (governing bodies for Local Government Areas, or LGAs) in the state creation process given the absence of local council elections since December 1976 and the dissolution and proliferation of local councils and areas after October 1979.

❖ The absence of any regulations defining the implications of state creation for the tenure or status of state governors, judges, and other key state-level functionaries.

❖ The issue of the implications for state creation of section 3(1) of the constitution, which specifically enumerated and institutionalized the existing nineteen states of the federation.

The opinion in most informed circles was that new states could not be created without an elaborate process of constitutional amendment. However, the requirements for amending section 8(1) in particular were so stringent that this option became singularly unattractive to most state advocates and the National Party of Nigeria. Instead, the NPN established an interparty committee, under the chairmanship of Vice President Alex Ekwueme, to streamline the procedures and delineate the principles for the creation of new states. The Ekwueme Committee produced a draft bill "for an Act to regulate the procedure for the creation of new states and for matters connected therewith."[44]

The proposed bill gave short shrift to the difficult constitutional provisions on state creation. Among other things, the draft law provided that a proposal for a new state needed to be approved only by a two-thirds majority of the people of the relevant area who actually voted in a referendum on the issue; gave the Federal Electoral Commission (FEDECO) the general powers to organize and supervise referenda on state creation; and did not make the conduct of fresh local government elections a precondition for the participation of local councils in the presentation of state requests. Following the statutory approval of the draft bill's main features by the National Assembly, President Shagari gave his assent to it on November 15, 1982 as the "Creation of States and Boundary Adjustments (Procedure) Act of 1982."[45]

Yet the constitutionality of the State Creation Act was widely considered to be suspect. According to one observer, "The Act contains at least fifteen provisions which contravene sections . . . of the 1979 Constitution."[46] It was widely believed that the implementation of the law could only lead to the creation of several new illegal states and the development of legal challenges to the new structure of states by unsuccessful aspirants for new states.

Among the more consistent and vociferous critics of the State Creation Act was the NPN's key rival, the Unity Party of Nigeria (UPN). UPN members in the National Assembly denounced the State Creation Act as a "dangerous fraud" and an attempt to "overthrow the constitution," and insisted that no new states could be created without an amendment to the constitution and the conduct of new local government elections.[47] But this position invariably implied a longer gestation period for new states than was anticipated by the NPN, which wanted new states created before or immediately after the July–August 1983 elections. Indeed, according to the UPN leader, Chief Obafemi Awolowo, the most realistic period for the inauguration of new states would be 1987. Such a time frame, according to Awolowo, was necessary to give ample time for amendment of the constitution and to afford incumbent state governors a fair opportunity to serve out their maximum two four-year terms without having to preside over a fraction of their initial jurisdictions.[48]

The UPN's legal puritanism was probably sectionally and politically inspired. Its Yoruba supporters were generally regarded as the main beneficiaries of the nineteen-state structure and, specifically, of the Mohammed-Obasanjo administration's decision to reject the recommendation of the Irikefe Panel that Lagos be merged with Ogun state. More important, though, the UPN—along with the other major opposition party, the Nigerian People's Party (NPP)—was haunted by the suspicion that elements within the NPN were attempting to use the issue of new states not only to consolidate electoral support for the Shagari administration but also to destabilize key opposition state governments. Thus, both the UPN and the NPP boycotted the interparty summit convened by President Shagari in February 1982 as a follow-up to an earlier interparty effort in July 1980 to fashion a political consensus on the issue of new states. Both parties also declined to participate in the deliberations of the Ekwueme Committee.

Given the support of the officially recognized factions of the Great Nigerian People's Party (GNPP) and the People's Redemption Party (PRP) for the state-creation project and the overwhelming political dominance of the NPN after the 1983 elections, perhaps new states might have been created had the Second Republic not collapsed at the end of 1983. Even then, a serious complication stood in the way: the "melodramatic profusion" and unsupportable deluge of demands for new states in the republic.[49] Indeed, by 1983 the number of demands for new states had reached fifty, several of which were mutually inconsistent or spearheaded by rival sectional or partisan interests, or both.

Despite the concerted efforts of the Shagari government, neither the parties nor the National Assembly could agree on a "shortlist" or even a manageable number of proposals for new states. In their memorandums to the president after the July 1980 interparty meeting, for instance, the GNPP, NPN, PRP, and NPP had proposed the creation of 27, 25, 24, and 21 new states, respectively. As the Ekwueme Committee observed, the parties' proposals reflected largely the "number of states for which requests had been made to the National Assembly as at the time their memoranda were submitted . . . [as] no political party appears to be willing to oppose any requests for creation of any new state."[50]

The National Assembly's role in the ratification of state requests was equally pathetic. After a protracted, contradictory, and dramatic series of deliberations and resolutions on the issue by a succession of state creation committees in both houses of the federal legislature, the assembly eventually resolved in 1983 to approve twenty-nine new state demands for referendums. Yet it was obvious to all dispassionate observers that the nation's economy (already reeling under the impact of an unprecedented crisis precipitated by the collapse in international oil prices) could not sustain the establishment of almost thirty additional state administrations. This anxiety over the economic implications of too many new states, coupled with the suspicion that the constitution was being subverted to satisfy state advocates, led many to conclude that the states issue had been trivialized and overpoliticized by the politicians of the Second Republic. Not surprisingly, one of the initial actions of the Buhari junta, which replaced the Shagari administration at the end of 1983, was to foreclose any further consideration of the states issue and confiscate the properties of all state creation movements.

FROM NINETEEN TO TWENTY-ONE TO THIRTY: STATE REORGANIZATIONS UNDER THE BABANGIDA ADMINISTRATION

With the removal of the Buhari administration in August 1985 and the proclamation of a program of recivilianization by the new Babangida government, the debate on the shape and number of federal constituent units was once again revived in the Nigerian federation.

The seventeen-member Political Bureau, which was appointed in January 1986 to coordinate the debate on the country's future, was presented with specific requests and general suggestions for new states. The body extensively discussed the matter in its report as one of the more contentious or "special" issues in Nigerian politics.[51] Although it acknowledged the suggestions by some Nigerians that the nineteen-state structure be retained, or that the states be consolidated into more viable units or even abolished altogether, the Political Bureau observed that "the more dominant view is that a few more states (or provinces) should be created in the country."[52]

The bureau was, however, presented with different, if familiar, views on the modalities for the creation of states in Nigeria.[53] One proposal called for the reconstitution of the country along the boundaries of the twenty-four to thirty colonial-era provinces. But the bureau, like the Irikefe Panel before it, argued that the provincial boundaries lacked stability and any substantive political rationale; therefore, they should be used only when they were not contradicted by other principles or considerations. A second proposal, which the bureau dismissed as idealistic, suggested the transformation of the country into an organic federation based on ecological or functional constituent units. Yet another proposal, which the bureau also considered as potentially sectionally divisive, urged the establishment of a thirty-two-state structure, with the states being distributed "in such a way as to achieve a near-balance in terms of the number of states between the component ethnic units in the country."[54] A final, and apparently vague, viewpoint suggested the creation of additional states within the broad framework of such previously enunciated criteria as the expressed wishes of the people, development needs, geographical compactness, and adequate population base.

The bureau itself was polarized between those members who supported the retention of the nineteen-state structure and those who wanted to see a few additional states created. The latter group was, in turn, divided between members who endorsed the creation of only Katsina and Akwa Ibom states and those who supported the creation of Katsina and Akwa Ibom, as well as Delta, Kogi, Sardauna, and Wawa states.[55]

The support by many bureau members for the establishment of Katsina and Akwa Ibom derived from the sheer intensity and longevity of the two demands and the belief of these members that the Mohammed-Obasanjo administration had erred in not creating both states in 1976. Members of the bureau who wanted the creation of Delta, Kogi, Sardauna, and Wawa states invoked the need to promote interethnic justice and balanced development within the existing federal structure. Contrary to the impression conveyed by the government's white paper on the report of the Political Bureau, the bureau did not recommend the creation of six additional states in the country.[56] Rather, the "contending positions" within the bureau were elaborately presented in its report in order to "assist the government in disposing of this matter in the larger interests of the country."[57]

In a nationwide broadcast on September 23, 1987, President Babangida dismissed most of the arguments for additional states as "untenable" and "politically motivated," but nevertheless announced the creation of Katsina and Akwa Ibom in the "national interest."[58] The precise justification for the government's decision to approve only the two oldest state demands centered on the increasing cost of running state governments and the perception of a revitalized local government system as a more reasonable answer to the demands of communities for basic development. Aware of the disaffection that the government's decision would generate among many state agitators, Babangida warned against any "further comments or petition" on the issue by self-seeking political aspirants or communal activists. "For this Administration," he vowed, "the number of states . . . shall remain twenty-one . . . [as] we cannot continue to dissipate our energy over the creation of more units or states in Nigeria."[59]

Yet on August 27, 1991, the sixth anniversary of his administration and barely four years after inaugurating the twenty-one-state structure, Babangida announced the creation of nine additional states in the country: Abia from Imo state, Anambra from Enugu or the old Anambra state, Delta from Edo or the old Bendel state, Kebbi from Sokoto, Kogi from Benue and Kwara, Osun from Oyo, Taraba from Adamawa or old Gongola state, Jigawa from Kano, and Yobe from Borno.

Babangida argued that the reorganizations were designed to advance the principles of social justice, even development and interethnic balance. The territorial changes were also portrayed by the government as necessary to prevent a further politicization of the issue and save the Third Republic from being overwhelmed, like its predecessor, by aggrieved state agitators.

Apart from the official reasons, at least three other factors may have induced the government into undertaking the lavish reorganizations of 1991. The first was Babangida's apparent intention to win some legitimacy for his government and possibly prolong his stay in power.[60] Indeed, the 1991 reorganizations invariably led not only to an extension of the recivilianization program but also to fulsome praise for Babangida and an intensification of the campaign for him to remain in power beyond his proposed handover in October 1992.

A second factor was the abortive coup of April 22, 1990, which poignantly highlighted the existence of profound sectional divisions and alienation in the Nigerian federation. The coup plotters, who included several elements from the oil-rich Delta area, vehemently condemned inequities in the ethnoregional distribution of power and privilege in the country and sought to expel the politically dominant Muslim North from the federation. Some four months after the coup attempt,

Babangida acknowledged that "recent events" had underscored the existence of deep and pervasive fears of sectional "domination and deprivation" in the country. He therefore reiterated the commitment of his government to the implementation of policies that could mitigate some of the "social costs arising from the national question."[61] The creation of nine new states, including the Delta state, underscored this commitment.

A final influence on the decision to establish new states in 1991 was the massive campaign for new Igbo states that was launched by the major ethnic group's intelligentsia and political leadership during late 1990 and early 1991. The highpoint of this campaign was the publication in April 1991 of a memorandum to the president and members of the Armed Forces Ruling Council (AFRC) by ten noted Igbo leaders. Invoking the long-standing view that the Igbo had been consistently "discriminated against in the state-creation exercise," the memorandum urged the government "to favourably consider the urgent creation of three new Igbo states," namely Enugu or Wawa from Anambra, Abia from Imo, and Anioma from Igbo-speaking areas of Bendel state.[62] Not only were the requests for Enugu and Abia subsequently granted by the government, but Asaba (the seat of the proposed Anioma state) was made the capital of Delta state. As Babangida himself admitted at the end of 1991, "creation of states came about largely because of the petitions we . . . received from prominent Igbo citizens."[63]

Any hopes that the inauguration of the thirty-state structure would finally put an end to further statehood demands, however, were rudely dashed by the renewed agitations, and even violent and fatal protests, by protagonists of such unfulfilled statehood proposals as Zamfara, Hadejia-Gumel, Apa, Port Harcourt, Abayelsa, Oil Rivers, Upland Rivers, Ebonyi, Gombe, Ekiti, New Ondo, New Oyo, Ibadan/Ibarapa, Oke-Ogun, and Real Delta.

FROM THIRTY TO THIRTY-SIX STATES:
GENERAL ABACHA AND THE 1996 REORGANIZATIONS

With the Babangida administration's trivialization and overpoliticization of the state-creation project, the stage was effectively set for further manipulation of the issue by Babangida's immediate military successor,

General Sani Abacha. Specifically, the continued politicization of the issue of new states seemed inevitable, given the unresolved protests and pressures emanating from the 1991 reorganizations, the contentious circumstances surrounding General Abacha's rise to power, the general's thinly veiled civilian-presidential ambition, and the attendant need for him to secure some basis of support and legitimacy for his administration.

The issue of new states figured prominently at the 1994–95 National Constitutional Conference, which received a total of about forty-five requests for new states (see table 3). Two consecutive committees of the conference, headed by Peter Odili and Paul Unongo, respectively, were established to examine the issue. Yet both committees failed to produce acceptable recommendations regarding the precise number, composition, governmental seats, and distribution of new states. Consequently, the conference resolved to entrust the matter to the Abacha administration.

In December 1995, General Abacha inaugurated a committee, under the leadership of Chief Arthur Mbanefoh, on the creation of states and local governments. The committee claimed it received a total of seventy-two requests for new states; however, its specific recommendations for new states and localities were not officially published. Nonetheless, on the occasion of Nigeria's thirty-sixth independence anniversary on October 1, 1996, General Abacha announced the creation of six new states:

- ❖ Bayelsa (with the capital at Yenagoa) was created out of Rivers state.
- ❖ Ebonyi (with the capital at Abakaliki) was formed from parts of Abia and Enugu states.
- ❖ Ekiti (with the capital at Ado-Ekiti) emerged from Ondo state.
- ❖ Gombe (with the capital at Gombe) was excised from Bauchi state.
- ❖ Nasarawa (with the capital at Lafia) was formed out of Plateau state.
- ❖ Zamfara (with the capital at Gusau) emerged from Sokoto state.

Abacha justified these reorganizations on four interrelated grounds. First, he argued that the creation of new states, although economically and politically disruptive, had become a periodic and accepted feature of the country's politics. Abacha also claimed his administration could not ignore the popular demands for new territorial units because some of the requests were apparently "genuine and [were] capable of improving the administrative machinery of government."[64] In addition, Abacha alluded to both the broad support for new states at the NCC and to the decision of the conference to entrust his administration with the matter. Finally, Abacha claimed that his administration's action on the issue of new states would help minimize the volume of contentious matters that could "impede the stability of a democratically elected government" in the future.[65]

Regarding the precise rationale for the ratification of the six new statehood proposals out of the seventy-two reported requests, Abacha explained that it had been informed by the need to "ensure a fair spread and balancing within the geopolitical zones of the country, applying such criteria as population and land mass, among others."[66] Accordingly, the country's six informal geographic zones got one state each as follows: North-West (Zamfara), North-East (Gombe), North-Central (Nasarawa), South-West (Ekiti), South-East (Ebonyi), and South-South (Bayelsa).

Although they were apparently less arbitrary (and therefore provoked fewer misgivings) than the 1991 exercise, the 1996 reorganizations did not end the persistence of politically significant pressures for new states in the country. Thus, following the reorganizations, lobbying continued for the creation of several additional new states, including Ogoni from Rivers state, Ijebu from Ogun, Kachia or Kaduna South from Kaduna, Apa from Benue, Okun or Oya from Kogi, Oke Ogun or New Oyo from Oyo, Anioma and Real Delta from Delta state, Itai from Akwa Ibom, Hadejia from Jigawa, and Sardauna from Adamawa and Taraba states. Yet, reflecting the mounting national concern about the proliferation and emasculation of the extant Nigerian states, such statehood demands were accompanied by countervailing pressures for the restructuring of the existing states into bigger, fewer, and more viable geopolitical units.

One of the ways by which successive military administrations sought to manage or assuage the unrelenting pressures for new states was through the reform and reorganization of the local government

Table 3. The Forty-Five Requests for New States Received by the 1994–95 National Constitutional Conference

Present State	Proposed States	Proposed Capital
Abia	(1) Aba	Aba
Adamawa/Taraba	(2) Sardauna	Mubi
Akwa Ibom	(3) Itai	Ikot Ekpene
	(4) Atlantic	Oron
Anambra	(5) Ezu	Awka
Bauchi	(6) Gombe	Gombe
	(7) Katagum	Azare
Benue	(8) Apa	Otukpo
	(9) Katsina-Ala	Zaki-Ibiam
Cross-River	(10) Ogoja	Ikom/Ogoja
Delta	(11) Anioma	Asaba
	(12) Toru-Ebe	Patani
Edo	(13) Afemesa	Auchi
Enugu/Abia	(14) Ebonyi	Abakaliki
Imo	(15) Njaba	Okigwe
Jigawa	(16) Hadejia	Hadejia
	(17) Lautai	N/A
	(18) Bayajida	Daura, Kazaure, or Gumel
Kaduna	(19) Gurara	Zonkwa or Kanfanchan
Kano	(20) Tiga	N/A
	(21) Gari	N/A
	(22) Tigari	Gwarzo
Katsina	(23) Karadua	N/A

Present State	Proposed States	Proposed Capital
Kogi	(24) Okura	Anyigba
	(25) Okun	Kabba
Kwara	(26) Oya	Kabba
	(27) Yoruba/Ekiti	Ilorin
Niger/Kebbi	(28) Kainji	Kontagora
	(29) Ndaduma (Nupe)	Bida
Ogun	(30) Ijebu-Remo	Odogbolu or Ijebu-Ode
Ondo	(31) Ekiti	Ado-Ekiti
Osun	(32) Oduduwa	Ile-Ife or Ilesha
Oyo	(33) New Oyo	Ogbomosho
	(34) Oke-Ogun	Shaki, Iseyin, or Igboho
	(35) Ibadan	Ibadan
Plateau	(36) Nasarawa	Akwanga
Rivers	(37) Bayelsa/Niger Delta	Yenagoa, Brass, or Sagbama
	(38) Orashi	Ahoada
	(39) Ogoni/Rivers East	Bori
	(40) Port Harcourt	Port Harcourt
	(41) New Rivers	South Port Harcourt
	(42) Oloibiri	Ogbia or Nembe
Sokoto	(43) Zamfara	Gusau
	(44) New Sokoto/Sakkwato	N/A
Taraba	(45) Mambila	N/A

Source: Adapted from Federal Republic of Nigeria, *Report of the Constitutional Conference,* vol. 2 (Abuja: National Assembly Press, 1995), Appendix 1.

system. Unfortunately, the politics of local government reorganizations in Nigeria have simply replicated the contradictions and conflicts of the state-creation process.

THE POLITICS OF LOCAL GOVERNMENT REORGANIZATIONS

A major impact of Babangida's strategy of promoting the political and financial "empowerment" of the localities was to completely entangle these governments in the communal struggles for distributive advantage in the Nigerian federation. In particular, the increase from 10 to 20 percent of the proportion of the Federation Account allocated to the localities, the proposed direct disbursement of central revenues to local councils, the extension of the presidential system to the local government level, and the simultaneous use of local areas as state and federal electoral constituencies all combined to unleash unprecedentedly vigorous pressures for the establishment of new LGAs throughout the federation. As with the demands for new states, pressures for additional localities have been enormously exacerbated by the heavy reliance on the standard of interunit equality in resource devolutions to LGAs. At the same time, the need to ensure some per capita equity in local access to central resources has significantly heightened official concern with minimizing extreme disparities in the population of the localities.

Thus, under the local government structure instituted following the historic 1976 reforms, the 301 localities were required to fall within a population range of 150,000 to 800,000 persons. Following the inception of the Second Republic in 1979, however, the number of localities in the federation increased almost threefold as a result of state governors' deliberate gerrymandering. On assuming power in 1984, the Buhari junta dismantled all the localities established by the civilian politicians, thereby reinstating the pre-1979 301–local government structure.

Pressures for the fragmentation of some of the larger localities, or for a better population balance among the local governments, remained intense. The Babangida administration responded to these pressures by asking the state governments to make recommendations regarding the creation of new areas in their respective jurisdictions. Such recommendations were to be guided by the need to ensure some correspondence between the local government structure and the number and distribution of the nation's demographically equivalent federal electoral constituencies. In May 1989, the federal government announced the creation of 149 new LGAs in the country, thereby bringing the number of such areas in the country to 450, including a mayoralty for Abuja.

Like the creation of new states, however, each reorganization of the local government system has simply fueled pressures for further reform. Thus proclaiming the establishment of nine new states in August 1991, Babangida also announced the creation of an additional forty-seven LGAs. But faced with even more strident demands for new localities after the announcement, the Babangida government established another set of eighty-nine new LGAs the following September. Finally, when the decree delineating the nation's new territorial structure was published in October 1991, it included one additional LGA each for Katsina, Kwara, Osun, and Plateau states. All of this brought the total number of localities in the Nigerian federation to 589, excluding the four area councils earmarked for the new Federal Capital Territory and mayoralty of Abuja.[67]

What stood out most about the 1991 local government reorganizations in Nigeria was their arbitrariness, contentiousness, and inconclusiveness. In the past, the creation of new localities was usually informed by such well-publicized criteria as population, relative viability, and the expressed preferences of the state governments and local communities involved. In creating new localities in 1991, however, the government only invoked, without necessarily applying, such omnibus and mutually inconsistent principles as the existence of a minimum of ten localities in each state, ecological peculiarities, historical affinities, popularity or intensity of demands, and the promotion of grassroots participation in decision making. The government's brazen equivocations on the number, location, designation, and administrative seats of the new localities further underscored its arbitrary management of the reorganizations. Indeed, if there was any single overriding logic to the 1991 local government reorganizations, it is that they were largely the result of the concerted manipulation of the distribution and configuration of the new localities to favor those of the administration's key members, advisers, supporters, or lobbyists.

To be sure, the 1991 local government reorganizations were the most controversial in the nation's history. In virtually every state of the federation, they provoked vicious protests, leading to tens of fatalities and the virtual paralysis of a number of local administrations in at least two states.[68] Although the Babangida administration sought to contain the uprisings by committing itself to further reorganizations, this strategy was ultimately sidetracked by the overwhelming number of demands for new localities.

Indeed, at the 1994–95 National Constitutional Conference, as many as 1,002 requests were received for new LGAs. The number increased to 2,369 during the sitting of the Mbanefoh Committee on the creation of new states and localities. Consequently, in proclaiming the creation of six new states in October 1996, General Abacha also announced "a 30 percent increase" in the "existing number of local governments in each of the states of the Federation."[69] Based largely on this announcement, the number of localities in the Nigerian federation increased from 593 in 1991 to 774 during 1996–97.

The 1996 local government reorganizations, and their subsequent modifications or adjustments, replicated the contentiousness and arbitrariness of the 1991 exercise. As in 1991, several communities were embittered by the failure of the Abacha government to name their areas as the seats of the new local councils, by its surreptitious imposition or arbitrary alteration of the administrative headquarters of some of the new localities, or by its failure to accede to the overwhelming majority of requests for new localities. The rancor became particularly intense—and, in some cases, violent—in states like Delta, Osun, Ondo, Akwa Ibom, Ekiti and Taraba, where the reorganizations inflamed pre-existing intercommunal tensions over access to economic and political resources. The role of the 1996 local government reorganizations in deepening and extending the internecine conflicts between the Ife and the Modakeke communities in Osun state and among the Urhobo, Ijaw, and Itsekiri communities in Delta state was especially tragic.

If the imbroglio over local government reorganizations convey a lesson for Nigeria, it is that the pressures for new localities in the country are bound to remain insatiable and intractable as long as they are linked to the communal struggle for access to an expanded share of central resources, opportunities, and representation rather than to the quest for local self-governance and self-reliance.

CONCLUSIONS

Although initially decisive in promoting the stability and enhancing the coherence of the federal system, the reorganizations of state and local governments have increasingly operated to accentuate disruptive and destructive distributive conflicts in the Nigerian federation. In concluding this chapter, five basic elements of these types of conflicts may be highlighted.[70]

First, the increasing emphasis on the distributive, rather than the linguistic, imperatives of territorial reforms has alienated many of Nigeria's smaller ethnic groups, whose representatives have condemned a situation in which the three big ethnic groups now dominate about twenty-two of the country's thirty-six states; most ethnic minority populations, including those in several of the oil-producing communities, "have been corralled into unitary . . . multiethnic states."[71] Ethnic minority communities like the Arogbo-Ijaws of Ondo state alleged a similar rigging of the local government structure.

Second, it is becoming increasingly obvious that political decentralization and financial devolution can only be impeded by the strategy of fragmenting the country into smaller and increasingly unviable states and localities with the proliferation of inefficient state and local bureaucracies that accompanies such fragmentation. This reality is underscored by the growing campaign, since the 1990s, for the territorial restructuring of the federation through the consolidation of the states. Moreover, as the discussion of NRMAFC in chapter 3 demonstrates, the proliferation of states is threatening to make a mockery of the federal character standard for national appointments, because with so many new states it becomes cumbersome or impossible to insist on the representation of every state.

Third, with the continuing implementation by state and local governments of educational and employment policies that discriminate against so-called non-indigenes, the proliferation of new states and localities is a recipe for more sectional discrimination. The sheer brazenness and divisiveness of this discrimination was poignantly conveyed by the wave of abrupt dismissals and expulsions from state and local bureaucracies that followed the August–September 1991 reorganizations. Far from ensuring or consolidating the unity of the federation, the creation of new states and localities may be undermining or eroding it.

Fourth, it is apparent that the territorial fragmentation of each of the three major ethnic groups has not made them significantly less cohesive in national politics. Indeed, despite the development of bitter intraethnic conflicts within and among major-group states over local and regional issues, each of the three major groups continues to demonstrate remarkable solidarity as it competes with the others in bidding for power and resources at the national level. The collective mobilization of pan-Igbo sentiments behind the movement for Igbo states clearly demonstrates that state-based identities and tribal chauvinism are not necessarily mutually inconsistent. In essence, "the creation of states and the development of 'statism' have added—and not substituted—new patterns of cleavages to the pre-existing ones."[72]

Fifth, it is now obvious that under the present system and practice of federalism, the constant reorganizations of the states and localities can never ease the pressures for still more constituent units. Rather, such reorganizations are likely to succeed only in producing new ethnic or subethnic minorities, fresh political animosities, and renewed distributive pressures, leading to continued agitations for more and more units of state and local government. Unless some structural or fundamental means can be found to discourage the process, the creation of new states and localities may become, in Olusegun Obasanjo's opinion, "an endless joke which will continue to reduce the viability of our federalism."[73]

5

THE "FEDERAL CHARACTER" PRINCIPLE

I N AN IMPORTANT SENSE, the "federal character" principle has come
to epitomize many of the controversies, anxieties, and complexities
associated with the Nigerian system of federalism. The principle's
basic rationale is to promote national loyalty, integration, and a "sense
of belonging" among the Nigerian citizenry, and it is supposed to
accomplish this through provisions for the accommodation of the
country's federal or pluralistic character in the composition and conduct of public institutions throughout the federation. But the interpretation, operationalization, and implementation of this seemingly
pious and innocuous principle has provoked some of the most virulent
debates and violent struggles in the Nigerian federation. Celebrated by
some as the "cornerstone of ethnic justice and fair government in
Nigeria," the federal character principle has also been denounced by
others as a euphemism for federal discrimination at best, or "geographical apartheid" at worst.[1]

SOURCES AND ELEMENTS OF THE FEDERAL CHARACTER

Although for long an informal norm of the country's federal praxis, the
federal character principle did not become a formal nostrum of constitutional policy and public practice in Nigeria until the inauguration of

the 1979 Constitution for the Second Republic. In his widely cited address in October 1975 to the inaugural session of the fifty-member Constitution Drafting Committee that produced the initial draft of the 1979 Constitution, Brigadier Murtala Mohammed had proposed a number of broad principles for the country's political future, among them the suggestion that Nigeria should adopt an "executive presidential system of government" in which the election of the president and the vice president and the choice of members of the cabinet would be done in "such a manner so to reflect the federal character of the country."[2] In the subsequent deliberations of the CDC, the phrase "federal character" was accepted as a convenient conceptual construct for reconciling the sharply divergent perspectives that had developed in the committee regarding the appropriate constitutional modalities for promoting equitable interethnic integration and representation in Nigeria. Consequently, the CDC adopted the following provisions on federal character, which were subsequently embodied in these two sections of the 1979 Constitution:

> 14 (3) The composition of the government of the federation or any of its agencies and the conduct of its affairs shall be carried out in such manner as to reflect the federal character of Nigeria and the need to promote national unity, and also to command national loyalty, thereby ensuring that there shall be no predominance of persons from a few states or from a few ethnic or other sectional groups in that government or in any of its agencies.
>
> 14 (4) The composition of the government of a state, a local government council, or any of the agencies of such government or council, and the conduct of the affairs of the government or council or such agencies shall be carried out in such manner as to recognize the diversity of the peoples within its area of authority and the need to promote a sense of belonging and loyalty among all the peoples of the federation.

A supplementary clause of the constitution went on to define the "federal character" as involving "the distinctive desire of the peoples of Nigeria to promote national unity, foster national loyalty, and give every citizen of Nigeria a sense of belonging to the nation."[3]

Apart from these broad, and essentially nonjusticiable, formulations and definitions, the 1979 Constitution also incorporated the following specific, and apparently justiciable, regulations or provisions for actualizing the federal character principle.

❖ The president of the Federal Republic shall appoint at least one minister from among the indigenes of each state of the federation (section 135).

❖ The president shall accord due regard to the federal character of the country in appointing persons to such offices as those of the secretary to the federal government; ambassadors, high commissioners, or other principal representatives of Nigeria abroad; permanent secretaries or other chief executives of federal ministries or departments; and any office on the personal staff of the president (section 157).

❖ The composition of the Nigerian armed forces shall reflect the federal character of the country, and the National Assembly shall establish a body to enforce this requirement (sections 197–199).

❖ The Federal Electoral Commission and the National Population Commission shall, respectively, have one member from each state of the federation (Part 1, Third Schedule).

❖ Each state shall be represented by its governor in the National Economic Council. Composition of the former will also include another one person from each state appointed by the Council of Chiefs of that state (Part 1, Third Schedule).

❖ The composition of the executive or governing council of a political party shall include members from two-thirds of the states in the federation, and the name, motto, or emblem of the party must not give the appearance that its activities "are confined to a part only of the geographical area called Nigeria" (section 202).

❖ To be elected directly as president of the Federal Republic, a candidate must obtain at least a quarter of the votes in each of at least two-thirds of the states in the Federation. Candidates for state governor must win a quarter of the votes in two-thirds of the state's LGAs (sections 125–126, 164).

❖ Finally, in exercising his powers to appoint persons to the offices of commissioner in a state, secretary to the government of the state, head of the state's Civil Service, permanent secretary or other chief executive positions in the state's bureaucracy, and any office on his personal staff, "the governor shall have regard to the diversity of people within the state" (sections 173 and 188).

These provisions have remained the basic institutional require-ments for the practice of federal character in Nigeria. The constitu-tional arrangements and agreements approved for Nigeria's Third and Fourth Republics, however, extended or redefined the federal character provisions of the 1979 Constitution in a number of ways. For instance, under the Third Republic's 1989 Constitution, the threshold require-ment for the election of the president and governors was modified to conform more closely to the realities of the imposed, two-party system. Candidates for these offices were, therefore, required to obtain a major-ity (not a simple plurality) of votes cast, as well as one-third (rather than one-quarter) of votes in two-thirds of the states or localities.[4]

The 1989 Constitution also included several new bodies under the specific purview of the federal character: NRMAFC, the Public Complaints Commission, and the boards or governing councils of "statutory corporations" (state-controlled companies), universities, col-leges, and other institutions of higher learning.[5] For its part, the 1995 draft constitution provided not only for the rotation of the federal pres-idency, but also for a Federal Character Commission (FCC) to moni-tor, improve, and enforce the application of the federal character in all public institutions.[6] Although the final 1999 Constitution for the Fourth Republic did not include a provision for a rotational presiden-cy, it retained the FCC as an important federal executive body.

Since its establishment by the Abacha administration in 1996, the FCC itself has proposed a number of guidelines for actualizing the norm of equity among various segments of Nigeria's populace. The guidelines, which have yet to be codified or enforced, include the following:

❖ On the basis of strict interstate equality, the indigenes of each of the thirty-six states in the federation ideally should account for only 2.75 percent of positions in the federal public service, after reserv-ing 1 percent for Abuja. To allow for flexibility, however, the norm of interstate equality should be modified such that indigenes of each state would be required to constitute not less than 2.5 percent and not more than 3 percent of officers in the federal bureaucracy.

❖ In those instances in which the available positions are too few to go around all the states, sharing should be done on the basis of a more or less equal distribution of opportunities either among the federation's six geographic zones or between the northern and southern regions, as appropriate.

❖ The indigenes of each of the six geographic zones should occupy not less than 15 percent and not more than 18 percent of positions in the federal public service.

❖ When a state cannot utilize fully its assigned quota of federal positions, the unused slots should go to indigenes of states in the same zone or region as the defaulting state.

❖ LGAs and Senatorial Districts are the most appropriate units for equitable representation or distribution at the state level, while the ward (an administrative subunit of an LGA) should be used for reflecting the federal character at the local level.

❖ In all cases, individuals should not be appointed to "offices for which they are unqualified, in the name of balanced representation." Consequently, the successful application of the federal character principle would require the equalization of educational opportunities in the federation through massive "investment in education . . . in the educationally backward states."

❖ The federal character principle should apply not only to the distribution of "jobs and posts," but also to the location of socioeconomic amenities and infrastructures.[7]

In spite of these extensive regulations and provisions, the federal character principle has remained a profoundly nebulous and contentious concept. In particular, critics have denounced the Nigerian constitution's rather unhelpful and somewhat tautological definition of the federal character as a "distinctive desire" of the citizenry; the inordinate emphasis on the states, as distinct from other "sectional groups," as the units for reflecting the federal character; the tendency to confuse interstate equality with interstate, interethnic, or interregional equity; the absence of any definitive or widely accepted criteria for identifying and correcting "the predominance of persons from a few states, ethnic or other sectional groups" in public agencies; the apparent or potential contradictions between the requirements of federal character, on the one hand, and the need to sustain professional or meritocratic standards, as well as the constitutional prohibition of discrimination on sectional grounds, on the other hand; the tensions inherent in the dual nature of the federal character as a nonjusticiable objective of state policy and as a justiciable constitutional requirement; and the apparent vulnerability of the federal character to manipulation by politically privileged groups or individuals.[8]

Such faultfinding stands apart from radical academic criticism, especially canvassed by some elements in the CDC, regarding the futility or counterproductiveness of the attempt to use the federal character principle to promote integration through the recognition and representation, rather than the sublimation or downgrading, of sectional loyalties or identities.[9] As will be shown, these reservations and criticisms have been borne out by the politics surrounding the federal character principle and by its application.

The Politics and Practice of Federal Character

The politics and practice of federal character are best examined in an overview of the implementation of the principle in the following critical institutional settings: the federal political executive, the federal bureaucracy, the military, the educational sector, and the states and localities. In addition, this section will document the increasingly important impact of the religious factor on the politics of federal character.

The federal political executive

To many observers in general, and for Nigerian political parties and politicians in particular, the federal character principle is synonymous with federal executive power sharing. Accordingly, some of the most heated debates and struggles over the federal character have involved the application of the principle at this level. At least four main areas of contention and concern can be identified in this regard.

In the first place, the federal character rules regulating the election of the president and the formation of political parties have been shown to be unduly restrictive or potentially counterproductive, or both. Indeed, the rules for the presidential election were the source of a near-disastrous controversy during the 1979 elections, involving legal-cum-mathematical disputes over precisely what constituted two-thirds of the then nineteen states in the federation and whether the leading presidential candidate in the elections had actually secured the required support in the prescribed proportion of the federation's states.[10] Given the largely contentious manner by which this controversy was resolved by the Supreme Court in 1979, a more manifestly political solution to the issue has been implemented since the 1987 state-creation exercise. This has involved a consistent, and more or less explicit, effort to ensure that the number of states in the federation is exactly divisible by three. In addition, Nigerian politicians have sought to respond to the requirements of the presidential election rule by forming very large, but often structurally and ideologically incoherent, multiethnic parties that can muster enough federal character to win the presidency easily. Examples include the NPN after the 1979 elections, the Social Democratic Party (SDP) and National Republican Convention (NRC) in the aborted Third Republic, and the PDP in the Fourth Republic.

The federal character rules guiding the formation of political parties have, however, posed enduring problems. Many observers have doubted whether parties established under these rules can lay claim to a truly national character. Harsher critics have denounced these rules for their delegitimization or demonization of associations with legitimate ethnic or regional agendas. For many critics, the requirement that all parties be national in character has severely inhibited the effective articulation of the diversities that define the Nigerian federation.[11]

In the second place, the requirement that each state must be represented in key federal institutions, including the cabinet, is unwieldy and impracticable simply because of the increasingly large number of states. Thus, in an attempt to fulfill this requirement during the Second Republic, President Shagari was compelled to assemble an unduly large federal cabinet, which reinforced popular images about his government's profligate character.[12] A similar tendency to proliferate or fragment ministerial positions and appointments in order to fulfill the mandate of federal character has been visible under the post-Shagari military and civilian administrations.[13] Besides its practical difficulties, there has also been considerable opposition to the norm of equal state representation. In 1991, NRMAFC chairman T. Y. Danjuma criticized the provision for the representation of every state in the commission, claiming the requirement could overpoliticize and cripple NRMAFC's work.[14] Under Babangida, the composition of two federal commissions, the National Population Commission (NPC) and the National Electoral Commission (NEC), was actually amended to exclude the requirement of full state representation. Indeed, many federal agencies now utilize zones or regions, incorporating several states, as the most viable units for reflecting the federal character in their operations or composition.[15]

In the third place, existing rules on federal character allegedly have not prevented the sectional domination or monopolization of strategic ministries or branches of government. Prior to the inauguration of Obasanjo's civilian administration in May 1999, the southern intelligentsia and political leadership, for example, repeatedly denounced the northerners' virtual monopolization of the top political echelons of such sensitive federal bodies as Defense, Internal Affairs, National Security, and the national police.[16] With the advent of the Obasanjo administration, however, elements from the North denounced what they described as Yoruba domination of some of these strategic positions. In essence, the constitutional provisions on the distribution of ministerial and other presidential appointments have been relatively ineffective in removing or reducing actual or perceived sectional control of the country's most important public positions.

Finally, until the informal interregional political compromise that ushered in the Obasanjo presidency in May 1999, the practice of federal character could not allay southern alienation and frustration over the seeming northern stranglehold on the position of the federation's political chief executive. It should be noted that in the more than thirty-eight years of Nigeria's postindependence history, from October 1960 to May 1999, northerners headed the federal government for thirty-four years and southerners for only a little more than four. Indeed, between October 1979 and May 1999, all the country's heads of government (save for one dubious and fleeting exception) were Muslims from the North.[17] Furthermore, the South's apparent hysteria and paranoia about northern political hegemony was reinforced by the annulment of the June 1993 presidential election, which would have put a southerner at the head of an elected federal government for the first time in the nation's history. Yet within the South itself, the Igbos and the ethnic minorities evidently have suffered greater political marginalization than the Yorubas, who have headed three of the four southern-led federal governments since independence. Consequently, there have been radical proposals for a more ethnically equitable structure of access to the apex of the Nigerian federal political executive. The more popular of these proposals are discussed in the final chapter of this work.[18]

Suffice it to say that the idea of rotation, and the accompanying principle of zoning, has been the most widely canvassed of these proposals. The idea was initially mooted by a subcommittee of the 1975–76 CDC, but was rejected by the plenary body as unwieldy and divisive.[19] It was subsequently introduced and popularized as a "convention" of ethnoregional power sharing by the NPN in the Second Republic.[20] Zoning was also explicitly, if somewhat more flexibly, practiced by the two state-sponsored parties of the Third Republic—namely, the SDP and the NRC;[21] it was an important, common feature of the PDP, APP, and AD in the Fourth Republic. Zoning was also endorsed by the 1994–95 National Constitutional Conference, which incorporated a provision for the rotation of the presidency between North and South in the 1995 draft constitution.[22]

Most important, however, General Abacha announced in October 1995 plans for a thirty-year power-sharing scheme in which the offices of the president, vice president, prime minister, deputy prime minister, Senate president, and speaker of the House of Representatives would be rotated among the country's six geographic zones.[23] Presumably, a nonrenewable five-year tenure for the affected incumbents would ensure the rotation of the designated key offices among all six zones by the end of the thirty-year period.

While speaking to deep-seated sectional anxieties about the structure of interregional access to federal power in Nigeria, the idea of zoning and rotation carries very profound contradictions and limitations of its own. One major limitation is the proposal's conscious ethnicization, fragmentation, and, by implication, devaluation of the ostensibly integrative office of the presidency. Moreover, the attempt to formally entrench zoning rotation in the Nigerian Constitution detracts from the proven ability of Nigerian parties and politicians to experiment with creative formulas of ethnic power sharing autonomously, informally, and flexibly. This last reason was largely responsible for the decision to drop the provision for a rotational presidency from the 1999 Constitution.

Federal character and the bureaucracy

The application of the federal character to the federal civil service has been extremely contentious for several reasons. First, the very notion of ethnic or regional representativeness as a norm of bureaucratic recruitment or advancement is generally regarded to be inconsistent with the universal norm of meritocratic placement. Consequently, proponents of federal character in the bureaucracy have had to contend with stiff opposition from technocratic and politico-regional forces that favor, or benefit from, the notion of an exclusively merit-based bureaucracy.

Second, largely because of the differential impact of Western cultural penetration and colonial administration, the Nigerian sociopolitical landscape has been characterized by an uneven interregional distribution of educational and bureaucratic competence in favor of the South; historically, therefore, the South has been disproportionately represented in the federal bureaucracy. In such a way, then, the federal character's application in the bureaucracy has tended to be more of an ethnoregional campaign by the North to use political considerations to dislodge qualified southerners from, or inject less qualified northerners into, the bureaucracy.

Third, and related to the above, the historic tension between the regional locus of political power in the North and the geographical basis of bureaucratic privilege in the South has raised the political stakes of the federal character.[24] Southern administrative power is perceived, and indeed deployed, by many southerners as a counterpoise to northern political dominance. But dominant northern political interests have exhibited considerable unease at the region's lack of an effective and reliable administrative undergirding for its political clout. Consequently, these interests perceive the federal character as an instrument for achieving a fusion of political and administrative power. Predictably, the induction of a southern-led administration in May 1999 further complicated the pre-existing ethnoregional configuration of political and bureaucratic power, leading to northern fears of political displacement and of the erosion of the region's modest gains from the enforcement of federal character in the bureaucracy.

Fourth, the political complications arising from the uneven regional distribution of bureaucratic competence have been compounded by the ethnogeographical implications of the location and relocation of the federation's administrative capital. The location of the Yoruba-dominated coastal city of Lagos as the country's federal capital from 1914 to 1991 has resulted in the disproportionate placement of westerners in general, and Yorubas in particular, in the federal bureaucracy. This imbalance has provoked the chagrin not only of northerners but also of most southerners from the Eastern Region. These elements see the relocation of the federal capital to the more centrally located Abuja in northern Nigeria as a means to achieve greater regional representativeness, or federal character, in the federal bureaucracy. At the same time, concerned Yorubas have bemoaned the tendency to use the relocation to settle long-standing ethnoregional scores in the federal bureaucracy.

Finally, given the pervasive influence and presence of the Nigerian state in the country's socioeconomic life and the relative paucity of employment opportunities outside the public sector, the civil bureaucracy has had to bear an inordinate amount of the pressures by sectional elites and their constituents for career placement and advancement. The federal character principle has proved to be a veritable lightning rod for these pressures.

Having identified some of the factors that have rendered the issue of federal character an especially sensitive problem in the bureaucracy, it is now appropriate to outline the precise mechanisms or procedures by which the federal character principle has been implemented in the bureaucracy. Three broad guidelines regulate the attempts to apply the principle in Nigeria's civil service.

First, in the case of federal government agencies located in the states or outside the federal capital, the relevant recruiting authority is required to reserve low cadre positions (Grade Levels, or GL, 01–07) to indigenes of the states in which such agencies are located.[25]

Second, "suitably qualified" indigenes of states that are relatively underrepresented in the middle and upper middle ranks (GL 08–15) of the civil service are consciously encouraged to take up appointments in the service. Accordingly, not only are new graduates from such states consciously encouraged by the Federal Civil Service Commission

(FCSC) to begin a career in the federal service, but civil servants from these areas are also encouraged to transfer their services from their respective states to the federal civil service: "As a general rule, transfers are on a lateral basis, that is, from one grade level to an equivalent grade level, unless the officer is being offered transfer on promotion. Transfers occur at all grade levels, but the optimum levels are the entry grades, GL 08–09, and the training grades for senior management levels, GL 12–13."[26]

Third, it is the deliberate policy of the federal government to enforce the norm of geographical equity, if not equality, in the distribution of the highest administrative position in federal ministries or agencies—namely, the office of permanent secretary or director-general. For instance, under the Shagari administration in the Second Republic, federal policy stipulated that there be at least one permanent secretary from each state of the federation. Consequently, some eight states that did not have a permanent secretary as of 1979 had their indigenes appointed to this position.[27] Moreover, with the inception of the 1988 Civil Service Reforms, the position of permanent secretary (which was redesignated as the office of director-general) was formally politicized and effectively made subject to the imperatives of the federal character. The bureaucratic career structure now peaked at the level of director. But the director-general (effectively the deputy minister) not only became a political appointee of the president but was also expected to relinquish his office at the expiration of the president's tenure.[28]

In general, the 1988 Civil Service Reforms sought (rather spuriously) to reconcile the practice of federal character with the requirements of professionalism in the federal bureaucracy. The reforms gave the FCSC the authority to appoint and recruit staff into GL 7–10. Such appointments were to be undertaken on the basis of the federal character principle's strict application—that is, on the basis of equal state representation. Each ministry, however, was given the power to appoint and promote officers from GL 11 and above on the basis of "the universally accepted principle of experience, performance, (and) relevant qualification."[29] Nevertheless, such appointments and promotions were expected to conform to general "guidelines" from the FCSC, which remains the key agency for promoting federal character in the bureaucracy.[30] Moreover, these appointments and promotions were to be undertaken by an Internal Personnel Management Board whose membership was required to "as far as practicable, reflect the federal character principle."[31]

Predictably, the actual practice of federal character in the bureaucracy has proved to be extremely invidious, contentious, and onerous in ethnoregional and political terms. For many southerners, the application of the federal character principle has involved numerous abuses that have compromised the integrity, unity, efficiency, identity, and future of Nigeria's federal bureaucracy. The more widely cited abuses include the rejection of many qualified southern applicants for federal civil service jobs on the grounds that they come from states that are already overrepresented in the civil service; the use of periodic retrenchment exercises (which invariably have relatively high southern casualties) to create vacancies for northerners, or curtail southern representation, in the federal bureaucracy; the injection or transfer of relatively young or inexperienced functionaries from the northern states into the federal civil service as seniors or equivalents of older and far more experienced southern bureaucrats; the victimization, frustration, or premature retirement of senior southern bureaucrats who resist or question the undue introduction of political considerations to appointments or promotions in the federal service; the manipulation of federal establishments' relocation from Lagos to Abuja to advance northern bureaucratic interests; and the appointments of northerners as executive political heads of virtually all major federal agencies or parastatals, including such southern-based bodies as the ports, customs, and petroleum agencies.

The following editorial comments by two of the country's more influential Lagos-based newspapers aptly capture the intensity of southern disenchantment with the practice of federal character in the federal bureaucracy:

> [The] present practice is to encourage young graduates from the "disadvantaged states," which is a euphemism for the northern states, to refuse appointment into the federal civil service until they have first served four or five years in the civil service of their home states, by which time the most promising of them, already distinguished with double promotions, are sought by the "Federal Character" scouts . . . and installed in the topmost posts . . . [as] bosses to Southerners who are ten to twenty years

their senior in the public service and who are themselves not lacking in excellence. Predictably, what follows is resentment, a sag in morale, sometimes stonewalling and sabotage. In the end, what is achieved is not national integration or federal character, but a mockery of it. . . .[32]

Many critics also point to the appointment of Northerners as chief executives in charge of almost all major parastatals in the country. These include the National Electric Power Authority (NEPA), Nigerian Telecommunications (NITEL), Nigerian National Petroleum Corporation (NNPC), Nigerian Maritime Authority (NMA), Nigerian Ports Authority (NPA), Nigerian Airways, National Fertilizer Company (NAFCON), Nigerian Television Authority (NTA) (and) Federal Radio Corporation of Nigeria (FRCN), among others.[33]

Yet for most northerners, these criticisms are largely self-serving attempts by southerners to maintain the South's bureaucratic hegemony. They complain of various attempts by southern bureaucrats to exclude northerners from the civil service and see both the rigorous application of federal character and the movement to Abuja as essential to the creation of a truly national bureaucracy.[34]

It should be stated here that a major source of the controversy over the practical role of the federal character principle in the bureaucracy involves the question of whether its application should take place at the entry grades or at more senior or professional levels of Nigeria's civil service. Existing guidelines and practices tend to combine and confuse both approaches. Yet evidence suggests that while the practice of federal character has secured several visible, high-level bureaucratic positions for northerners, the main body of the service still remains regionally imbalanced in favor of the South. Thus FCC data indicate that, although officially the North contains a majority of the federation's population and constituent states, the region accounted for only 33.3 percent of federal officials at GL 8 to GL 14 as of 1996 (see table 4).

The best represented northern states were in the North-Central zone, which encompasses the Federal Capital Territory of Abuja. The zone provided 16.6 percent of federal officials at the aforementioned levels, as opposed to only 9.2 percent and 7.5 percent by the North-Western and North-Eastern zones, respectively. The six states of the Yoruba South-West were the best represented bloc of states nationally; these states provided 27.8 percent of the GL 8–14 federal officials, as opposed to 20.4 percent by the states of the South-South and 18.5

Table 4. Distribution of Federal Officials (GL 8–14) as of 1996

Geographic Zone	Component States	% of National Population (per 1991 Census)	Number of Officials	% of Officials
North-West	Jigawa, Kaduna, Kano, Katsina, Kebbi, Sokoto, Zamfara	25.75	5,876	9.2
North-East	Adamawa, Bauchi, Borno, Gombe, Taraba, Yobe	13.37	4,790	7.5
North-Central (*Lower North*)	Benue, FCT (Abuja), Kogi, Kwara, Nasarawa, Niger, Plateau	14.11	10,602	16.6
South-West	Ekiti, Lagos, Ogun, Ondo, Osun, Oyo	19.61	17,755	27.8
South-East	Abia, Anambra, Ebonyi, Enugu, Imo	12.11	11,815	18.5
South-South	Akwa Ibom, Bayelsa, Cross River, Delta, Edo, Rivers	15.05	13,029	20.4
TOTALS	36 states and the FCT	100	63,867	100

Source: Adapted from Federal Character Commission, "Press Briefing on the Activities of the Commission," Abuja, August 19, 1999, 6.

percent by the South-Eastern Igbo states. In essence, the seventeen southern states, with officially only about 47 percent of the national population, accounted for 66.7 percent of GL 8–14 federal officials as of 1996.

Northern representation at the top management cadre (GL 15 and above) of the federal civil service was slightly better at almost 40 percent in 1996 (see table 5). The Yoruba South-Western states remained the best represented of the six zones with almost 30 percent of the federation's top public positions. How to redress this continuing regional imbalance without inflicting further damage to the stability and efficiency of the federal bureaucracy remains a key political and policy challenge in Nigeria.

Federal character and the military

The military is the institution with the longest history of federal character engineering in the Nigerian federation. It is a commonplace observation that a regional recruitment quota was introduced for the enlisted ranks of the army in 1958 and for the officer corps in 1961.[35] The 1958 quota sought to correct the underrepresentation of southerners in the ranks of noncommissioned officers in general, and the infantry in particular, while the 1961 quota sought to enhance the representation of northerners in the officer corps. This military quota system gave 50 percent of army recruitment to the North and 25 percent each to the Eastern and Western Regions. (The Mid-West was assigned four percentage points from the Western Region's quota when the new region was created in 1963.) By the end of the First Republic in 1966, the military quota system was barely effective in removing the inherited disparities in the regional composition of the army, which continued to have a fairly ethnically mixed upper officer corps but an Igbo-dominated middle officer corps and northern-dominated enlisted ranks.[36] Yet the introduction of the military quota system did provoke enough institutional politicization, interpersonal suspicion, and inter-regional polarization to contribute to the bloody coups of January and July 1966 and the outbreak of civil war in 1967.[37]

Following both the start of the war and the dissolution of the four-region structure in 1967, the regional quota system fell into disuse. For much of the duration of the war, recruitment into the military was governed purely by the exigencies of the war effort. After the war, however, conflicting perspectives did develop in and outside the military regarding the relative appropriateness of a purely meritocratic or a revised quota-based recruitment policy for this critical national organization. By 1979, a consensus had emerged (effectively reinforced by the provisions of the 1979 Constitution) that recruitment into the military must consciously and faithfully conform to the imperatives of geographical representativeness, or federal character. This requirement was interpreted by the relevant military and political authorities to mean the use of state-equality quotas (as distinct from the population-based regional quotas

Table 5. Geographical Distribution of Top Management Positions (GL 15 and above) in the Federal Civil Service as of 1996

Geographic Zone	Number of Officials	% of Officials
North-West	339	12.2
North-East	291	10.5
North-Central	456	16.4
South-West	820	29.6
South-East	437	15.8
South-South	429	15.5
TOTALS	2,772	100

Sources: Federal Republic of Nigeria, *Federal Civil Service Manpower Statistics 1996*. Publication No. 2 (Abuja: Federal Character Commission, n.d.), 5; compare with Federal Character Commission, "Press Briefing on the Activities of the Commission," 6–7.

of the First Republic) in recruitment for the officer corps and ranks of the Nigerian military.[38]

The consensus on this new military quota system has been significantly sustained by the relatively low educational requirements for a military career (and the concomitant absence of any significant pressures for reverse discrimination in favor of the educationally backward North) and by a broad awareness of the dangers of a sectionally dominated military. Yet, despite its apparently faithful implementation, broad acceptability, and relative success, the practice of federal character in the military has provoked at least three broad criticisms.

First, the policy of state-equality quotas has engendered several predictable and familiar problems, including the inequitable treatment of the larger or more ethnically heterogeneous units; the inevitable discrimination against states with many more qualified applicants than can be accepted into military training schools under the state-equality quota system; the periodic modification and destabilization of the state-based quotas as a result of repeated changes in the boundaries and number of states; and the general perception of a regional bias in the use of equal state quotas because of the greater number of northern than southern states since the 1976 reorganizations.

Also, the enduring political interventionism of the Nigerian military appears to have distorted and eroded whatever interregional equitability could have resulted from the use of federal character in the composition of the military. Military coups everywhere are almost always executed by sectional, conspiratorial cliques whose members invariably dominate the government and military power structure after a successful takeover. In the Nigerian case, virtually all successful military coups, and the governments established therefrom, have been northern-based. This has given military officers from the North a political visibility and hegemony that appears to be out of proportion to their actual representation in the main ranks of the military. Thus Muslim northerners headed all four military governments between 1984 and 1999. Officers from the North also dominate strategic military positions, especially the office of the army's chief of staff. All this has tended to create the image of a military that is heavily dominated politically by the North. In the words of one of the few southern officers to have ever occupied the position of army chief of staff, Major General David Ejoor (ret.),

> the North has maintained absolute control of the army. . . . Southern officers have been gradually eliminated by posting and retirement from competing for the highest positions available. The control of the federal government and the armed forces has enabled the North (in civilian as in military regimes) to gradually dominate and exploit all other aspects of national life.[39]

The military's commitment to federal character has also not been reflected in the distribution of strategic military institutions and installations in the country, because these bodies are overwhelmingly concentrated in the northern part of the country. Examples include the Nigerian Defense Academy, Kaduna; the Command and Staff College, Jaji, Kaduna; the Nigerian Defense Industries Corporation, Kaduna; the Nigerian Military Training School, Zaria; the Nigerian Air Force Base, Makurdi; and the Nigerian Institute of Policy and Strategic Studies—the equivalent of the British Royal College of Defense Studies—in Kuru, near Jos.

Federal character and educational institutions

As in the military, the application of federal character to educational institutions predates the inauguration of the 1979 Constitution. Nigerian governments have long recognized the need to redress the historical regional educational imbalance in the country through the equitable distribution of educational opportunities and facilities throughout the federation. The promotion of federal character in the educational sector has involved the following initiatives:

1. The extensive involvement of the federal government in the design and funding of primary education throughout the federation through such instruments as the 1973 Universal Primary Education scheme, the 1989–90 National Primary Education Commission, the 1999 Universal Basic Education scheme, and the use of inverse and actual primary school enrollment figures in the allocation of federal revenues to the states and localities. The primary objective and visible achievement of these interventions have been to reduce the considerable North-South imbalance in access to primary schooling.[40]

2. The establishment of at least two "unity" secondary schools in each state of the federation and the formulation of appropriate admission guidelines to ensure equitable interstate enrollment in these institutions. Specifically, admission into practically all of these schools is on the basis of a quota formula that assigns 50 percent of places on an equal basis among all the states (excluding the state of location), 30 percent to the state of location, and 20 percent on national merit.[41]

3. The establishment in different parts of the country of several tertiary functional-cum-vocational institutions, including schools of arts and science, advanced teachers' colleges, and polytechnics. Eighty percent of places in these institutions is allocated equally among the states, while the balance is allocated on the basis of "national merit."[42]

4. The equitable interregional or interstate distribution of federal universities and of admission into them. Specifically, each of Nigeria's thirty-six states is expected to have a federal university, and admission into them is guided by the following criteria: merit, 40 percent; catchment area, 30 percent; educationally less developed states, 20 percent; and discretion, 10 percent.[43]

The catchment area of each university is defined to include mainly the states in the immediate vicinity of the university, although one or two other states from outside the vicinity are often included in the "catchment" category to promote national integration. The universities of Ibadan and Lagos, however, have the entire country as their "catchment area," while the Ahmadu Bello University, Zaria, has all the northern states as its area.[44]

The educationally less developed states are defined to include not only all the northern states, except Kwara and Kogi, but also Lagos, Rivers, Bayelsa, and Cross River in southern Nigeria. The inclusion of these southern states in the category of the "educationally disadvantaged" is presumably because they are less educationally advanced than other southern states and also because of an apparent official desire to "reflect" federal character even in the selection of educationally backward states![45]

Nevertheless, the pervasive use of various forms of preferential quotas in federal postprimary educational institutions has provoked some of the most emotive debates and struggles over the federal character principle. It is widely believed that a major impact of these quotas has been to deprive many qualified southern candidates of places in federal educational institutions in order to accommodate less qualified candidates from the educationally disadvantaged North. One of the more widely reported instances of such discrimination involved Yinka Badejo from Ogun state. Badejo had scored 73.25 percent in the 1988–89 national unity schools' entrance examinations. She was not shortlisted for the required admission interviews, however, because Ogun State's share of the quota for interview places—defined as the best five hundred candidates from each state—had been filled. Yet several northern candidates who had scored less than 50 percent (and sometimes as low as 37.75 percent) in the same examinations were shortlisted for the interviews. In an unsuccessful legal suit she instituted to challenge her exclusion from the interviews, Badejo averred that "national merit should be given preference in the issue of admission because the colleges into which admission is sought are national institutions established to promote national unity and not discrimination on the grounds of state-of-origin."[46]

At the university level, virtually all of the southern states, and at least one of the more educationally developed northern states, have been constrained to establish their own universities to accommodate qualified indigenes who cannot get places in federal universities because of the quota system. Predictably, however, most northerners remain resolutely supportive of the federal character in education, which they see as indispensable for rectifying the huge enduring imbalance between South and North in postprimary education.[47]

The states and localities

Quite unlike the kind of intense debates swirling around the principle at the federal level, there have been relatively few discussions of the application of federal character, or the diversity principle, at the state and local levels. Yet the available evidence suggests that struggles over federal character also have been extremely pervasive and emotive at the subnational level. Indeed, because the constitutional guidelines on its application are more nebulous at state and local levels, federal character has tended to be even more contentious in these subnational arenas than at the federal level. For instance, while the states have emerged as the pre-eminent and most convenient units for reflecting the principle at the federal level, the relevant units at the state level have ranged from senatorial and federal house of representatives' constituencies through the localities to distinct communal, religious, ethnogeographical, or subethnic blocs of the population.

A few of the more widely reported instances of interethnic or subethnic struggles for the distribution of public resources at the state level may now be briefly highlighted. In Benue state, for example, a recurrent source of political turbulence has involved the opposition of the non-Tiv section, especially the Idoma community, to alleged Tiv domination of the distribution of political appointments, deployments to key ministries, and location of vital commercial and industrial projects and educational institutions.[48] The state government has responded to these strictures by publishing detailed statistics that not only show an equitable distribution of opportunities between the Tiv and non-Tiv blocs but also suggest that, in some instances, the Idoma are overrepresented in per capita terms in the composition of key institutions.[49] The crux of Benue's ethnic problem would appear to be the disenchantment of the Idoma with their location and continued retention in a state in which the Tiv group accounts for some two-thirds of the population and local government areas.

In Akwa Ibom, the Annang minority alleges victimization, persecution, and discriminatory domination by the Ibibio majority in such areas as the provision and rehabilitation of educational infrastructures, appointments to the civil service, the selection and deployment of directors-general, and the choice of Ibibio as the sole indigenous language for news translations (from English) in the state electronic media.[50] The charge of Ibibio linguistic domination was particularly emotive and widely documented. Following the intervention of the federal government, however, seven other "dialects"—Annang, Oron, Mbo, Okobo, Itu, Mbanuso, and Ibeno were officially recognized, along with Ibibio, for news translations by the Akwa Ibom Broadcasting Corporation in 1991.[51]

In Delta state, the Itsekiri minority in June 1992 expressed apprehension at a situation in which the state had an Urhobo governor, Urhobo government secretary, Urhobo chief judge, and Urhobo legislative majority leader.[52]

In Borno, indigenes of southern Borno have alleged that they have been marginalized by the Kanuri-Shuwa group of northern and central Borno in the allocation not only of key positions in the state's public service but also of the state's share of federal appointments.[53] Similar allegations of the monopolization of state-channeled federal patronage have been made by Adamawa's numerous minorities against the Fulani majority:

> During the Babangida administration, a total of thirty-eight indigenes of [Adamawa] were appointed into Federal boards and parastatals. While twenty-one out of these came from Yola Local Government alone, another eleven came from the same [Fulani] ethnic group in two neighboring local governments. . . . Also out of ten ambassadorial appointments [from the state] since independence, seven went to this same ethnic group while only three were shared by the remaining ninety-nine tribes.[54]

Analogous recriminations over the distribution of public resources, amenities, and positions are evident between the Nupes and Gwaris in Niger state, the Igala and non-Igala (Ebiras, Okuns, Bassa, Nupes, and others) in Kogi state, and the Ijaws and non-Ijaws in the old Rivers state, among others. Moreover, such recriminations have also figured prominently, even if less explosively, in several of the relatively homogeneous Yoruba, Igbo, or Hausa states, including Ondo, Ogun, Enugu, Anambra, Abia, Bauchi, and Sokoto. The favored approach of most communities to their alleged marginalization at state and local levels is to agitate for the creation of independent states or local councils of their own. Yet, as discussed previously, no sooner are such new units created than fresh allegations of marginalization, and demands for new political authorities, erupt among otherwise politically united or culturally interrelated communities.

The religious dimension

Despite periodic controversies over the status of Shari'a law, religion was never explicitly recognized as a politically salient element of Nigeria's federal character until relatively recently. Accordingly, for much of the postindependence period, relations between Nigeria's large Christian and Muslim communities remained relatively amicable, if occasionally unpredictable. Perhaps the simplistic duality and territorial discontinuity of the Christian-Muslim cleavage could not capture the intensity and complexity of Nigeria's diversities, which remained largely ethnic, linguistic, and regional in character. Moreover, Nigeria's political leaders appeared consciously to have de-emphasized the religious aspect of Nigeria's plurality to avoid the devastating experiences of religious polarization in countries like Lebanon and Sudan.

However, developments following the surreptitious enlistment of Nigeria in the Organization of Islamic Conference in 1986, including the particularly incendiary conflicts over Shari'a law since 1999, suggest that Nigeria has dramatically transformed from a religiously peaceable to a religiously polarized federation. An immediate consequence of this degeneration is an upsurge in demands for interreligious balance in the composition of public agencies throughout the federation. Hence, the noted Yoruba Muslim chief, M. K. O. Abiola, in a 1988 "advertorial," explicitly called for a reinterpretation of federal character in religious terms. Contending that public policies and institutions had not given due regard to the interests of the "largest body of Nigerians, (who) are Muslims," Abiola said he would like federal character "to be interpreted to include religious beliefs so that in the formulation of public policy, due regard shall be given to the religious beliefs of the constituent people of Nigeria."[55] A similar case for the explicit recognition of religion as an element of Nigeria's federal character was made by Ambassador Jolly Tanko Yusuf of the Christian Association of Nigeria (CAN). According to Yusuf, "if a Muslim was appointed Minister of External Affairs, a Christian should be made Minister of Petroleum Resources, and if the President was a Muslim, a Christian should be the Minister of Defense."[56]

Indeed, a major concern of Nigerian Christians in the immediate aftermath of the announcement of the country's OIC membership involved the perception that Nigeria's effective participation in the summits of the OIC heads of government and foreign ministers may require reserving these two key political offices for Muslims. Subsequent developments under the Babangida administration appeared to have confirmed Christian fears about a growing Muslim stranglehold on key national political appointments. Specifically, Christians complained of (1) a "gradual but meticulous" replacement of Christians by Muslims in key ministries such as Defense, Petroleum, and Foreign Affairs; (2) Muslims' monopolization of command positions in the military; (3) the victimization or removal of Christian political appointees who had opposed the government's pro-Islamic policies, such as chief of staff Ebitu Ukiwe and Foreign Minister Bolaji Akinyemi; and (4) the arbitrary imposition of Muslims as heads of virtually all key federal agencies, including the southern-based Nigerian National Petroleum Corporation.[57] Such complaints reached a frenzied climax in January 1990, when Christian groups staged large street demonstrations in some of the country's major cities to denounce new federal cabinet appointments that appeared to favor Muslims heavily.

Yet under Babangida, many Muslims criticized the Christian-dominated leaderships of various transition agencies—the Political Bureau, the NEC, the Constituent Assembly, and the Mass Mobilization for Self-Reliance, among them—claiming that such lopsidedness created the impression "that Muslims do not exist or are incompetent to handle crucial matters."[58]

The restoration of civilian rule in 1999, under an elected southern Christian head of government for the first time in the nation's history, was accompanied by even more complaints about the marginalization of the core Muslim North. In an April 2000 communiqué, the Council of Ulama of Nigeria, for example, denounced "the imbalance" allegedly perpetuated by the new administration's "systematic relegation of Muslims within the ranks of the armed forces and federal establishments."[59] Similarly, Ibrahim Datti Ahmed, a noted Kano politician and Muslim scholar, accused the Obasanjo administration of openly pursuing a "Christian agenda" by "removing Northerners and Muslims from positions and replacing them with Christians."[60] A widely cited instance of such alleged regional and religious discrimination involved the retirement of Alhaji U. K. Umar, a Kano indigene and acting comptroller-general of Nigerian Immigration Services. Denouncing this particular decision in April 2000, the governor of Kano state, Rabiu Kwakwanso, declared: ". . . our son was schemed out for inexplicable reasons. This wrong decision is highly objectionable to the people of Kano state, and we condemn it in the strongest terms. We will not forget the great injustice done to our son by the federal authorities."[61]

Yet allegations and counterallegations of religious or ethnoreligious domination have probably been more turbulent in some of the states than at the federal level. For instance, Christian groups in the northern states, including the northern branch of CAN and the Northern Christian Elders forum, have inveighed against alleged political domination of many of these states by Muslims. Specifically, they have condemned the vesting of the permanent leadership of northern traditional rulers' summits in the sultan of Sokoto; the continuing imposition of emirate authority or Shari'a law on the non-Muslim populations of the Middle Belt; the marginalization of Christian police officers in the appointment of police commissioners in the northern states; and the suppression of Christian broadcasts, as well as Christian religious curricula and other educational privileges, in state-owned electronic media and schools in the North.[62]

The introduction or planned application of strict Shari'a law in the Muslim North after May 1999 reinforced the political marginality and insecurity of the region's Christian population. The full introduction of Shari'a law was defended by the northern Muslim elite, including ex-heads of state Alhaji Shehu Shagari and General Muhammadu Buhari, on several grounds: the overwhelmingly Muslim composition and culture of the North; the popularity of Shari'a law especially among youths and the intelligentsia, for whom the Islamic code represents a potential weapon for the reorientation of a morally decadent and materially dislocated northern society; the recognition, under the 1999 Constitution, of collective religious rights, as well as the rights of the states to establish and define the jurisdiction of the Shari'a Court of Appeal; the fact that the constitutionally prescribed legislative procedure was carefully observed in Zamfara, Sokoto, Kano, and other states where the Shari'a system had been, or was in the process of being, established; and the recognition, under the new Shari'a regime, of the fundamental rights of non-Muslims, who will be largely exempted from the purview of Islamic law.

Even as non-Muslims throughout the federation were denouncing the imposition of strict Shari'a law as a violation of the constitutional prohibition of a state religion, however, Christians in the North contended that the extension of Shari'a law would effectively relegate them to the status of "second-class citizens."[63] The CAN branch in Yobe, for instance, linked the planned introduction of full Shari'a law to the political and economic marginalization of the state's Christians.[64] Similarly, in both Zamfara and Katsina states, Christian groups condemned the decision of the state governments to establish religious affairs ministries for Muslims only.[65]

In Niger, a state with a much more substantial indigenous Christian population than Yobe, Zamfara, or Katsina, the CAN branch in an open letter to the governor in January 2000 denounced the government for pursuing the "Shari'a . . . agenda." It also complained that the religious plurality of the state "sadly . . . has not been reflected in appointments to positions of authority. The Christians have never had it so bad under any of the past governments in Niger state."[66]

The most violent opposition to the planned introduction of strict Shari'a law took place in Kaduna, where hundreds of lives were lost in horrific riots over the issue during February and May 2000. The riots occurred precisely because the proposed extension of Shari'a law in the state inflamed the long-standing antipathy between the predominantly Christian southern Kaduna minority tribes and the Muslim Hausa-Fulani, "who are in total control of government machinery and resources in the state."[67] Indeed, according to the report of an ad hoc panel of the Nigerian Senate on the Shari'a crisis in Kaduna, "the setting up of an eleven-man, all Muslim, committee by the state House of Assembly to explore the desirability or otherwise of implementing the

Shari'a legal system in Kaduna state . . . turned out to be the single most insensitive action by an Assembly composed of twenty-one Muslims and thirteen Christians in a state without an overwhelming Muslim majority."[68]

The Shari'a crisis of 1999–2000 barely resonated in the religiously bicommunal Yoruba South-West. But the wave of religious polarization and agitation that developed in the immediate aftermath of the OIC debacle did not spare the Yoruba states, which hitherto had been famous for the exceptionally peaceful coexistence between their Muslim and Christian communities.[69] In February 1986, for instance, the Lagos-based Muslim Council criticized the appointment of only six Muslims to the seventeen-member cabinet of Lagos state.[70] In 1990, it was the turn of Lagos's Christians to protest the occupation of the state's two highest political positions (governor and deputy governor) by Muslims.[71] In Oyo, during 1989 and 1990, the National Council of Muslim Youth Organizations and the League of Imams and Alfas condemned, respectively, the inclusion of only three Muslims in the state's eleven-member cabinet and Christian domination of the governing council of the Oyo State University of Technology.[72] In November 1991, a spokesperson for the Osun state Muslim Council, Alhaji Yisa Yagboyaju, condemned a "situation whereby sensitive . . . political appointments in the state were tilted in favor of Christians."[73] To be sure, the OIC controversy highlighted the relative political insecurity of Muslims in the Yoruba states, and the result was a more conscious effort by the Yoruba political leadership to enhance the political representation of Muslims in order to reduce the susceptibility of the entire ethnic community to a potentially self-destructive polarization along religious lines.

Indeed, such was the intensity and popularity of the pressures for religious balancing in state cabinets that, in naming a new executive council in 1988, the military governor of Kwara was compelled to lament: "I consider it a very sad commentary on the state of affairs of our dear country that there are many who will analyze this kind of appointment from the point of view of the numerical representation of the major religious groups."[74] Yet in the wake of the religious hysteria generated throughout the federation since the OIC debacle in particular, such representation was generally considered to be crucial preventing the core interests of either of the two major religions from being violated by functionaries of the rival denomination.

CONCLUSIONS

Several points emerge from this analysis of Nigeria's federal character debate. First, although the federal character principle was intended to promote national integration, its politics have proved to be extremely divisive in regional, ethnic, and religious terms. The absence of any definitive, comprehensive, and widely accepted guidelines for actualizing the federal character and the intensity of sectionally based distributive pressures on public offices and resources have combined to ensure that the federal character has operated more to expose and exacerbate Nigeria's divisions than to contain them. To use Kirk-Greene's apt description, the federal character has turned out to be more of a bone of sectional contention than a boon of contentment.[75]

Second, the struggles over the federal character have served to demonstrate and reinforce the country's debilitating "cake-sharing" psychosis. Federal character, in the words of Peter Ekeh, focuses exclusively

> on the sharing of the privileges and benefits that come with participation in government. It has no conception of the need for the units which will be the recognized beneficiaries from the operation of "Federal Character" to reciprocate by making contributions to the overall common good of the nation. . . . Seen in these terms, "Federal Character" is . . . concerned with that age-long game of Nigerian politics: the sharing of the national cake.[76]

Third, the contending arguments and perspectives on the federal character appear to be largely opportunistic in nature. The positions adopted on federal character have been shaped not by any clear or consistent principles but by the pursuit of sectional advantage. Most southerners have supported the effective use of federal character to contain the North's political hegemony, but they have also opposed the use of the principle in the educational and bureaucratic sectors, ostensibly because of its incompatibility with meritocratic and professional standards. In reality, such opposition is informed by the realization that, while federal character could advance southern political aspirations, the principle has hurt the region's privileges and advantages in education and the civil service. A similar opportunism is evident in the attitudes of northerners who endorse the use of quotas in bureaucratic and educational placement but oppose the zoning or rotation of political offices.

Fourth, the current practice of federal character has been extremely elitist in nature. The country suffers from an excessive preoccupation with the sharing of positions and offices among sectional elites and relatively little consideration for the equitable distribution of public developmental undertakings among broad geographical blocs or regions of the population. Thus, as currently conceptualized and practiced, the federal character cannot address the huge regional disparities in Nigeria, generally to the disadvantage of the North, in such basic social indicators as infant and maternal mortality, health care, and female education.[77] And with such neglect of mass-based regional concerns, it is doubtful whether the federal character can promote national integration and equity in any genuine or enduring fashion. Certainly, the popular pressures for the introduction of strict Shari'a law in the Muslim North, as well as the hardening of elite attitudes in the region on the issue, cannot be dissociated completely from the North's general feeling of alienation over the region's continuing socioeconomic backwardness, coupled with its more recent political displacement with regard to the South.

Fifth, some of the tensions associated with federal character reflect a profound contradiction between the goal of nondomination and the objective of nondiscrimination, and between the idea of group rights and the value of individual rights. The federal character seeks to ensure that ethnic or regional collectivities are equitably treated. In doing so, it has often violated the rights of individuals to equal treatment. This is particularly the case in the use of state-based quotas in educational institutions. The answer to this dilemma is not to denigrate group rights on the grounds of meritocracy or equality before the law, but to creatively expand and channel socioeconomic opportunities in a manner that may minimize the tension between the two sets of rights.

Sixth, and finally, in spite of the passionate controversies that have been spawned by the politics and practice of federal character, very few Nigerians have actually opposed the idea of interethnic or interregional equity or proportionality in the composition and conduct of governmental affairs. On the contrary, whatever its shortcomings in practice, the idea of federal character is widely accepted as a potentially effective antidote to the country's ubiquitous "monster of marginalization," to use ex-governor Samuel Mbakwe's apt terminology.[78] Disagreements have focused on the policies and practices by which this noble idea has been promoted. Perhaps, if imaginatively and astutely interpreted and fairly and sensibly implemented, federal character may become not only less invidious and obnoxious but also more effective in promoting national integration. Crafting such imaginative guidelines for defining and upholding the principle of intersegmental equity will be a continuing challenge for the Federal Character Commission in particular and for Nigeria's political leadership in general.

6

THE

POLITICS OF

POPULATION COUNTS

No ANALYSES OF CONFLICT AND FEDERALISM in Nigeria would be complete without a discussion of the intersegmental and interregional struggles over the true size and geopolitical distribution of the country's population. It is almost axiomatic to say that national censuses in Nigeria have invariably degenerated into intersectional contests for numerical superiority and for the enormous politico-distributive advantages of such superiority in the Nigerian context. Consequently, the succession of national censuses in Nigeria since 1954, and especially after independence in 1960, have provoked disintegrative ethnopolitical tension, suspicion, and recriminations.

This chapter discusses the political explosiveness and ethnoregional sensitivity of population counts in Nigeria. The first section probes the underlying sources and the features of the competitive and distributive pressures that are associated with the ethnopolitics of population counts in Nigeria. The second and third sections of the chapter are devoted to a recapitulation of the imbroglio that ensued from Nigeria's initial postindependence censuses in 1962–63 and 1973, respectively. The fourth section provides an extensive and original discussion of the politics of the country's 1991 census, whose final results were released only in 1997. The final section is devoted to some concluding observations and reflections on the politics, problems, and prospects of Nigeria's population counts.

DEMOGRAPHIC POLITICS AND THE
PATHOLOGIES OF NIGERIAN FEDERALISM

The political problems that have come to be associated with Nigeria's censuses attest to (1) the primacy and tenacity of ethnic identities and interests in the country; (2) the attendant fragility of civic or national loyalties; (3) the heavy dependence of ethnoterritorial constituencies on the public sector for socioeconomic advancement and political security; and (4) the official reliance on raw population data not only for the demarcation of the country's internal electoral and geopolitical boundaries but also for the distribution of developmental patronage and other public benefits among the country's constituent governments and segments of the population. In essence, craving political control and its enormous advantages, and lacking any autonomous capacity for resource generation and socioeconomic development, Nigeria's subnational segments and governments have relied on favorable returns from national censuses to establish claims to political power and to the proportional devolution or disposition of centrally controlled public resources. Reflecting its own technical incapacity and ethnopolitical biases, the federal government has promoted and entrenched the population principle as the pre-eminent standard of ethnic entitlement. The following public policies and practices underscore the enormous political and distributive importance of population data in Nigeria.

The relative population of constituent units has been an important factor in the allocation of federal statutory revenues and discretionary grants to the country's financially weak states and localities. Following the military government's transformation of regional federalism into a multistate system in 1967, the population principle was explicitly endorsed officially as a neutral, equitable, and convenient criterion for dividing federally collected revenues among the subnational governments. Indeed, to reiterate, in the period from 1970 to 1980, 50 percent of federal financial devolutions to the states (and the localities) was shared among these governments on the basis of their relative population, with the balance being shared on the basis of interunit equality. Between 1981 and 1990, the weight for the population factor in horizontal revenue sharing was reduced to 40 percent. Since 1990, the population factor has been assigned a 30 percent weight in federal statutory financial devolutions.[1] The declining weights (from 50 percent in 1970 to 40 in 1981 and 30 in 1990) ascribed to demography in revenue allocation reflect a growing official desire to reverse or de-emphasize the distributive importance and political sensitivity of population data in Nigeria. Nevertheless, the population principle not only remains the second most important factor (after the standard of interunit equality) in Nigeria's horizontal revenue-sharing policies, it has continued to figure quite prominently in other distributive strategies and policies of the Nigerian state.

Relative population size has been widely invoked in the recurring popular demands for new (centrally funded) states and localities. Indeed, although the principle of intergovernmental equality is often officially portrayed as an alternative distributive criterion to the population factor, it has virtually become a proxy for the population factor, given the official commitment to establishing constituent units of roughly equivalent populations. Thus, in explaining the rationale for the state reorganizations of 1976, the government's White Paper claimed that "states are to be created only where demand has been long, strong and widely articulated, and where the population (size) and the land (area) justify such an action."[2] In establishing a new set of states and localities in 1991, Babangida claimed the reorganizations were guided by the "need to achieve a measure of relative balance in population and resource distribution."[3] Similarly, in inaugurating new states and localities in 1996, General Abacha explained that the "principle adopted for the creation of states and local governments was to ensure (their) fair spread . . . within the geopolitical zones of the country, applying such criteria as population and land mass, among others."[4]

The ethnopolitical sensitivity of population data in Nigeria has arisen partly from the public perception that such data are important in putting together new constituent governmental units, which in turn could enhance access by territorial communities to federal financial devolutions and developmental undertakings. Moreover, the relative population sizes of towns or cities could be an important consideration in the determination of which areas would be named as the administrative seats of new states and localities.

Governments at all levels in Nigeria have emphasized the importance of the relative population sizes of cities, towns, or areas in dispensing a wide range of services, including schools, clinics, water, electricity, and roads. Indeed, the Third National Development Plan (1975–80) affirmed that the provision of medical services, primary and secondary schools, and related public facilities should be "based on population distribution, district by district, community by community, throughout the country."[5] Such official policy has invariably both reinforced the popular perception "of an association between sizes of communities and the delivery of welfare" and created a strong inducement to manipulate population data as a means of "swaying official decisions on development."[6]

Finally, the ethnopolitical sensitivity of censuses in Nigeria reflects the importance of population data in constituency delimitation and political representation. Given this linkage, along with the ethnic basis of partisan loyalties and the enormous role of state power in shaping the fortunes of ethnic and other collective interest groups in Nigeria, it was inevitable that population counts would become an instrument in the electoral struggle among the country's ethnic political elites. Indeed, the historical source of Nigeria's census problems has involved the competition between northern and southern ethnoregional power groups for the control of the federal government. This mobilization of population data behind the interregional struggle for national power has been replicated at regional, state, and local levels as various ethnic or subethnic communal blocs jostle for effective political representation or domination even as they vehemently resist marginalization or domination by other groups.

Nigeria's census debacle, therefore, has its roots in the value of population data for attaining sectional political and socioeconomic advantage in a context of intense ethnic pluralism, extreme economic statism, and perverse distributive federalism, as well as an abiding popular and official commitment to "proportionality" as a rule of collective entitlement. But how has the ethnopolitical sensitivity of population data actually led to the manipulation and politicization of censuses in the country? Three basic trends are discernible in this regard. First, as the discussion of Nigeria's census operations in subsequent sections should illustrate, there is copious evidence of attempts by sectionally oriented political elites and officials to manipulate the population figures of their areas through multiple enumeration or the outright inclusion of fictitious persons, households, and even whole villages in the census register.

Second, there is the notorious phenomenon of census migration, in which persons or groups relocate during census exercises from their normal places of residence to their home communities in order to enhance the demographic weight and relative sociopolitical power of the latter. In one extremely perverse expression of this trend, some migrant ethnic groups are known to prepare lists of their members for inclusion in the enumerated population of their home communities. As has been rightly observed:

> The major negative implication of census migration is the distortion of figures of the actual number of people resident, enjoying and needing facilities in a given area. . . . [However] those who migrate . . . [do] . . . so because they have no traditional attachment to the place where they live. They are also aware that if they require anything of benefit they might be referred to their states of origin.[7]

The third trend in distorting census data for political reasons in Nigeria involves the subjective dimension, in which widespread communal suspicions of "population manipulation" invariably serve to tarnish or undermine the acceptability of census outcomes, even when such results are reasonably reliable.[8] As Isiaka Yahaya and Mannir Dan-Ali have observed:

> Every community believed that the other had cheated and that the figures released for each community was more as a result of their ingenuity in manipulating [the] census exercise rather than real enumeration. [This] . . . automatically provided a real . . . excuse for communities not favored [by census outcomes] to complain.[9]

Thus population data in Nigeria are subject not only to the test of accuracy or reliability but also to the test of politico-communal acceptability. Clearly, the two may not be mutually consistent.

This section has highlighted the financial, infrastructural, electoral, and political-territorial advantages communities stand to reap from favorable (that is, relatively large) population figures in Nigeria. It has also identified the actual strategies by which communities, particularly elites within such communities, have sought to manipulate or distort demographic information. The rest of this chapter is devoted mainly to a discussion of the role of this census rivalry and politicization in engendering the controversies over Nigeria's postindependence censuses in 1962–63, 1973, and 1991.

ETHNOREGIONALISM AND THE 1962–63 CENSUSES

The 1962–63 census operations were the first in the country's history to be undertaken by an independent Nigerian government and the second to aim at a comprehensive national coverage. Prior to Nigeria's independence in 1960, a decennial enumeration of the population of Lagos was made between 1871 and 1931. In addition, estimates or enumerations of the population of several other areas of the country began in 1901 and continued until 1931, after which the decennial census was suspended because of World War II.[10] These colonial enumerations and estimations were flawed in many respects. Among other shortcomings, these censuses never truly covered the entire country, were often conducted in a perfunctory manner, suffered from the shortage of competent administrative and technical staff, were obstructed or evaded by a suspicious or superstitious local population, and, consequently, often produced contradictory, unreliable, or implausible results.[11]

The last colonial census, and the first truly national enumeration, took place in Nigeria during 1952–53 (see table 6). Although it was "a real house-to-house census covering the whole country," the 1952–53 census suffered from three fundamental problems.[12] First, it was conducted at different times throughout the country. Consequently, the census lacked an essential ingredient of an accurate count, namely, simultaneity. Also, it was not free from the suspicion and superstition that led to popular evasion of and gross underenumeration in previous censuses. Most important, though, the 1952–53 census results were retrospectively, but progressively, linked to the interregional struggle for the control of the Nigerian federation, reflecting the country's growing political ethnoregionalism in the 1950s. In particular, many southern politicians disbelieved the attribution to the North of some 55 percent

Table 6. Regional Population Figures (in millions) According to the 1952–53, 1962, and 1963 Censuses

Region	1952–53	1962	1963
North	16.84	22.01	29.78
East	7.22	12.33	12.39
West	4.60	8.10	10.28
Mid-West	1.49	2.40	2.53
Lagos	0.27	0.45	0.68
TOTALS	30.42	45.29	55.66

Source: Reuben K. Udo, "Geography and Population Censuses in Nigeria," in *Fifty Years of Geography in Nigeria: The Ibadan Story,* ed. Olusegun Areola and Stanley I. Okafor (Ibadan: Ibadan University Press, 1998), 356.

of the country's reported population of 30.42 million. To these politicians, the North's reported population majority was part of a British ploy to entrench the political hegemony of the conservative pro-British elites of northern Nigeria. Southern elites hoped that a future census would expose the alleged perfidy of the British by showing the South to be more populous than the North. This southern angst, and the concomitant northern determination to preserve its political-demographic majority, served to make the imbroglio over the 1962–63 censuses largely inevitable and predictable.

The fiasco over the 1962–63 censuses has been extensively documented.[13] Consequently, it would suffice here simply to highlight five key features or consequences of the counts.

To begin, the results of the 1962–63 censuses were extensively and brazenly manipulated. To be sure, two separate censuses were conducted during 1962–63. The results of the initial census exercise in 1962 were canceled by the federal government, following outrageously inflated returns from the Eastern and Western Regions and the consequent attempt by the North, under the guise of verification checks, to inflate its own returns in order to maintain the region's threatened population majority. Although the product of much more vigorous monitoring, the second census exercise in 1963 appeared to have merely legitimized the manipulations of the 1962 exercise. The final 1963 census figure of 55.66 million (which was administratively pruned down from allegedly inflated field returns of more than 60 million) was generally considered to be unreliable. The figure implied an implausible increase of 83 percent in the national population in the ten years since the 1953 census, with the Western Region reporting a more than 100 percent increase during this period.

Indeed, I. I. Ekanem has judged the 1963 census outcome to be demographically incredible. Observing a number of apparent incongruities in the age-sex, ethnic group, urban-rural, religious, and labor force data as reported in the 1963 census, as well as the glaring inconsistencies between the 1953 and 1963 census data, Ekanem argued that the "total Nigerian population in 1963 should have been in the range of 39 to 43 million."[14] He concluded that "the 1963 Nigerian census was manipulated by politicians," and that this manipulation took the form of "overcounting the numbers of young adult males."[15]

A second feature of the 1962–63 census crisis is that it involved a direct ethnoregional power struggle between the dominant parties and politicians of the Hausa-Fulani–dominated North and the Igbo-led East. The East's bid to end the North's population majority was effectively frustrated by the federal government's cancellation of the 1962 census exercise. On the other hand, acceptance of the 1963 census outcome, which preserved the North's population majority at 53.5 percent of the national total, was facilitated by the North's control of the federal government, the pro-northern stance of the vulnerable Yoruba western government, and the eventual decision of the Mid-West government to acquiesce in the final 1963 census results. The census crisis left the East truly embittered and, in pitting the region against the North, sharpened the ethnopolitical fault line that would snap into a ghastly civil war four years later.

Third, the 1962–63 census debacle underscored the veracity of the popular observation that census outcomes in Nigeria are often the result not of statistical enumeration but of political negotiation. The 1962 census returns were not officially approved because they were actively supported by the Eastern Region only and were opposed by the politically dominant North. The final 1963 census figures were upheld because they were acceptable both to the northern-dominated central government and to three of the four regions. The North endorsed the figures because they restored its population majority. The West did the same because it recorded the highest rates of increase and its unpopular government was particularly dependent on the northern-dominated center. Despite its ethnic and political linkages with the East, the newly created Mid-West region also ultimately accepted the census results both because it felt opposition to the results was futile and because it was unwilling to lose crucial institutional and developmental support by antagonizing the central authorities. Thus the Eastern Region was isolated in its opposition to the 1963 census figures. Although the East sought annulment of the figures in the Supreme Court, the court ruled that it had no jurisdiction over the matter.[16]

Fourth, the 1962–63 census imbroglio arose not simply from the interregional struggles to control the federation but also from intercommunal rivalries within regions. As Larry Diamond has noted:

> the census conflict was not simply a competition between regions but between communities within regions. The message of mobilization was that power and resources depended on numbers. It took little political acumen to realize that if population figures would determine which regions would get what, they would also be the basis for determining within each region the distribution of money for water, schools, paved roads, medical clinics, and the like.[17]

Fifth, the 1962–63 census problems did not arise solely from the politicization and manipulation of the census for regional, ethnic, or communal advantage, and it would be misleading to argue such because the crisis was also the result of administrative shortcomings and technical difficulties: the lack of adequate maps; the attendant inefficient or incomprehensive demarcation of enumeration areas; the shortage of competent enumerators; poor transportation and communication facilities, compounded by the near-inaccessibility of certain areas and groups, including the riverine areas and itinerant farm laborers and nomads; the bureaucratic inefficiency and delay in processing the census results, thereby fueling widespread suspicion about attempts to manipulate them; the inadequate or ineffective provisions for the enumeration of Muslim women in purdah (that is, in seclusion from public observation); and the weak coordination or integration of the central and regional census agencies.[18] Some of these administrative and technical limitations were undoubtedly exacerbated, and sometimes partly induced, by the ethnoregional politics of the census. Nevertheless, imperfections in the census organization and logistics were an important and independent source of the 1962–63 census crisis. In all, the 1962–63 censuses set a pattern of ethnopolitical polarization and administrative-technical confusion that was to haunt future attempts at enumerating the Nigerian population.

THE 1973 CENSUS AND THE REAFFIRMATION OF REGIONALISM

The 1973 census operation in Nigeria has been described as a "nightmare rerun of the 1962–63 show."[19] Indeed, if observers "had accepted the 1963 census results with dazed disbelief, those of 1973 were received with total incredulity."[20] Not only did the 1973 census figures of 79.79 million represent a marked increase from the reportedly inflated 1963 figure of 55.66 million, the new figures implied that the North had grown from about 54 percent of the population in 1963 to almost 65 percent in 1973 (see table 7). To be sure, it was this interregional distribution of the census figures—and the attendant exacerbation of southern paranoia about northern hegemonic domination—rather than the reported total size of the national population that transformed the 1973 census exercise into such a huge fiasco. Using the line of analysis pursued in discussing the 1962–63 censuses, the following key features of the 1973 census may now be highlighted.

The 1973 census results were demonstrably manipulated. The chairman of the census board, Adetokunbo Ademola, revealed that the body "had been let down by some elements in different parts of the country who had played foul during the head count by inflating the census figures."[21] These census malpractices, however, were not perpetrated by the general public, which showed little inclination to "intentionally mislead the enumerators or to defraud."[22] Rather, the fraud arose from "deliberate cheating by (local census) officials backed by the administrative leadership of the states," including some military governors.[23] The gross inflation of the census figures, according to the official census report, "took place in at least one-third of all the enumeration areas."[24] The report discovered various fraudulent devices for

Table 7. State Population Figures (in millions) and Growth Rates According to the 1963 and 1973 Censuses

State	1963	1973	Annual Intercensal Growth Rate % (1963–73)
NORTHERN STATES			
North-East	7.79	15.38	6.8
Kano	5.77	10.90	6.4
North-West	5.73	8.50	3.9
North-Central	4.10	6.79	5.1
Benue Plateau	4.01	5.17	2.5
Kwara	2.40	4.64	6.6
SOUTHERN STATES			
Western	9.49	8.92	−0.62
East-Central	7.23	8.06	1.1
South-Eastern	3.62	3.46	−0.51
Mid-Western	2.54	3.24	2.5
Rivers	1.54	2.23	3.7
Lagos	1.44	2.47	5.4
TOTALS/AVERAGE	55.66	79.76	3.57

Sources: Ian Campbell, "The Nigerian Census: An Essay in Civil-Military Relations," *Journal of Commonwealth and Comparative Politics* 14, no. 3 (1976), 247; Aderanti Adepoju, "Military Rule and Population Issues in Nigeria," *African Affairs* 80, no. 318 (1981): 33.

manipulating the census, including the inclusion of "ghost" households and the inflation of the number of persons within existing households by "filling vacant rows of the census questionnaire" with fictitious names.[25] Moreover, according to Ademola, "Rolls and rolls of paper bearing the same name(s) and same address(es) were discovered during the counting."[26]

If the 1962–63 censuses involved a direct confrontation between the North and the Igbo South-East, the 1973 operation pitted the North against the Yoruba South-West. Indeed, the ethnoregional implications of the 1973 census were most stridently emphasized by the Yoruba leader Chief Awolowo. In his words:

> . . . during the intercensal periods of 1931 to 1953 and 1953 to 1963 . . . the South was gaining (population) steadily at the expense of the North. . . . The 1973 provisional census figures have, however, shown a complete and sharp reversal of this normal trend. . . . [The] figures have revived, with greater vividness and starker reality, the erstwhile fear of permanent domination of one group of Nigerians by another.[27]

Yet, while Chief Awolowo and many other southerners were denouncing the 1973 figures as "absolutely unreliable," General Yakubu Gowon, along with most northern politicians and military governors, defended the census as "probably the most thorough head count of human beings by human beings anywhere in the world."[28] Indeed, Gowon's decision to release the 1973 census figures was opposed by the southern-dominated census board and reflected his vulnerability "to pressures from military officers and politicians from the northern states."[29]

Also, apart from reviving the ethnoregional schism between North and South, the 1973 census was also buffeted by complex intraregional, subethnic, or communal political rivalries. In particular, the intercommunal competition over new proposals for the creation of more units of state governments created a strong incentive for census manipulation at the local level, which was somewhat independent of the politico-demographic struggle between North and South.

Additionally, the ultimate decision to annul the 1973 census results, as well as to revert to the 1963 figures, was basically politically inspired. This very decision was canvassed by Chief Awolowo, who, after denouncing the 1973 figures and rejecting any proposals for a recount, had argued that the country

> should go back and stick to the 1963 census figures; not because they are accurate—of course they are not, but because: (1) they represent a mutual compromise among the entire people of this country at the time they were produced or concocted; (2) they had stood us in good stead in the past and can with necessary expert adjustments . . . continue to avail us in the future; and (3) they are . . . the least bad, the least ugly, and, therefore, the most acceptable of all our bad, ugly, and disputable census results from 1931 to 1973.[30]

Because the 1963 census results were especially advantageous to his western Yoruba political base, Awolowo's position was clearly not free from ethnopolitical bias. Nevertheless, in sheer geopolitical terms, the 1963 census outcome clearly posed fewer risks to national unity and interregional relations than the 1973 results. In other words, the more symmetrical interregional demographics of the 1963 census were less politically disintegrative or unacceptable than the huge northern demographic preponderance reported in 1973.

The decision to revert to the 1963 figures, however, could not be made by the Gowon administration, which, according to Obasanjo, "seemed to have been hell bent on selling a false idea to the nation that the census was a success."[31] Rather, this decision was announced by Gowon's successors in 1975. According to them, the 1973 figures had been "politicized beyond repairs," published "against all expert advice," and, therefore, would "not command general acceptance throughout the country."[32]

Finally, the 1973 census exercise, like its colonial and postcolonial predecessors, was plagued by an inefficient administrative machinery and weak technical logistics. To be sure, the 1973 census benefited from a more vastly improved organization, more thorough planning, and better techniques than previous censuses. Nevertheless, there were profound flaws in the 1973 census organization. A primary administrative weakness involved the fragmentation of the census organization between the center, which coordinated and exercised final responsibility for the census, and the states, which exercised responsibility for both the actual head count and the safe return of the completed census forms to Lagos. As it turned out, many of the state-level officers involved in the census not only lacked the necessary administrative expertise and technical competence but also perceived and prosecuted the census as an operation in communal, ethnic, or regional competition.[33]

Other administrative and technical shortcomings of the 1973 census included the absence of adequate maps for about 30 percent of the area of the country; the skewed composition of the national technical and administrative teams for the census, which provoked complaints of underrepresentation from the northern states; a five-month gap between the scheduled and the actual date the results were announced, thereby fueling accusations of covert manipulation; and the ill-advised composition and brazen partisanship of the so-called Census Review Committee, which was headed by Ukpabi Asika, the East-Central administrator and a noted "supporter" of the controversial census results.[34]

Despite a lag of ten years since the controversial 1962–63 censuses, the reality of centralized military rule, the replacement of the big ethnoregional bastions with smaller states, the chastening experience of the civil war, and a vastly improved administrative and technical framework for the enumeration exercise, the 1973 census essentially ended in total failure. So poignant was this failure—and so profound and pervasive was the fear of another unsuccessful or contentious count—that the decennial census scheduled for 1983 was skipped by the political leaders of the Second Republic (1979–83). Nevertheless, the return of "reformist" military rulers in 1983 and the logistics of transition to a Third Republic served to nudge the country into another census in 1991.

THE 1991 CENSUS: CHANGE OR CONTINUITY?

It is often noted that the 1991 census was the least politically contentious and demographically outrageous of Nigeria's postindependence censuses. This is partly because, apart from being relatively well organized and executed, the census put the country's total population at a demographically modest 88.9 million (the provisional figure was 88.5 million) and the northern proportion of this population at a politically tolerable 53 percent (see tables 8 and 9, respectively). Yet the 1991 census also engendered a great deal of contention. Indeed, although they were officially accepted, the 1991 census results were rejected by the 1994–95 National Constitutional Conference. According to the conference, the long delay in releasing the final census figures and the numerous complaints by communities and state and local governments over the conduct and outcome of the census exercise had effectively eroded the credibility of the count.

The following pages will, first, examine the political-administrative framework that was put in place to depoliticize the 1991 census operation and, second, discuss the geoethnic ramifications of and responses to the census.

Table 8. State Population Figures According to the 1991 Census (Provisional and Final Figures)

State	Provisional	Final	Provisional Rank	Final Rank
Lagos	5685781	5725116	1	2
Kano	5632040	5810470	2	1
Sokoto (and Zamfara)	4392391	4470176	3	3
Bauchi (and Gombe)	4294413	4351007	4	4
Rivers (and Bayelsa)	3983857	4309557	5	5
Kaduna	3969252	3935618	6	6
Ondo (and Ekiti)	3884485	3785338	7	7
Katsina	3878344	3753133	8	8
Oyo	3488789	3452720	9	9
Plateau (and Nasarawa)	3283704	3312412	10	10
Enugu (and parts of Ebonyi)	3161295	3154380	11	11
Jigawa	2829929	2875525	12	12
Benue	2780398	2753077	13	14
Anambra	2767903	2796475	14	13
Borno	2596589	2536003	15	16
Delta	2570181	2590491	16	15
Imo	2485499	2485635	17	17
Niger	2482367	2421581	18	18
Akwa Ibom	2359736	2409613	19	19
Ogun	2338570	2333726	20	21
Abia (and parts of Ebonyi)	2297978	2338487	21	20
Osun	2203016	2158143	22	23
Edo	2159848	2172005	23	22
Adamawa	2124049	2102053	24	25
Kogi	2099046	2147756	25	24
Kebbi	2062226	2068490	26	26
Cross River	1865604	1911297	27	27
Kwara	1566469	1548412	28	28
Taraba	1480590	1512163	29	29
Yobe	1411481	1399687	30	30
Abuja (FCT)	378671	371674	31	31
TOTAL	88514501	88992220		

Source: Adapted from I. A. Yahaya and M. A. Dan-Ali, *Breaking the Myth: Shehu Musa and the 1991 Census* (Ibadan: Spectrum Books, 1997), 133–34.

Administration of the 1991 census and the quest for depoliticization

Beginning with the establishment of the National Population Commission in 1988, several measures were taken by the federal military government as well as the NPC itself to promote the depoliticization of the census in Nigeria.[35]

• The NPC was established as a permanent national, but nonpolitical, agency. Such a designation was intended to insulate the commission from the vagaries of intergovernmental politics and the institutional uncertainties associated with ad hoc agencies. Moreover, the three-year period between the inception of the NPC and the conduct of the 1991 census was expected to give it ample time to design and execute the census, thereby avoiding the difficulties that arose from the relatively hasty execution of previous censuses.

• In appointing members of the NPC, the government avoided the political norm of equal ethnic or state representativeness in the constitution of sensitive national agencies. Rather, the NPC's chairman and seven commissioners were appointed on primarily meritocratic grounds, but without ignoring the norm of broad geographical or zonal (not state or ethnic) representativeness.

• All key census functionaries (excepting the actual enumerators, who were expected to be local indigenes or residents) were assigned to areas other than their local governments, states, or regions. For instance, the seven NPC commissioners were assigned to zones with which they had no familial or marital affiliations; supervisors from the northern states were posted to the southern states and vice versa; and state directors and local government comptrollers were deployed, respectively, to states and local governments other than their own. This scheme would ensure the neutrality of, and remove suspicion about, the census operation. As explained by the NPC chairman in 1993:

> In order to ensure that census functionaries were free from social and political pressures emanating from their areas of operation, a policy of deploying these functionaries from their areas of origin was adopted. This guaranteed that they could not do anything to favor their communities in the discharge of their duties. It also made it possible for them to resist pressures from their communities of operations, which would have been difficult if they had originated from there.[36]

• The state and local governments were explicitly excluded from direct involvement in the census operation. Rather, NPC offices were established at zonal, state, and local levels to enable the commission to assume full and direct responsibility for the census operation.

• All census functionaries, including the temporary staff of enumerators, were also directly recruited and remunerated by the NPC, rather than by the state or local governments, to ensure full loyalty of these functionaries to the commission, rather than to state or local authorities.

• Severe penalties were stipulated for a wide range of census offenses, including the evasion or obstruction of enumeration and the falsification of census figures.

• Private Nigerian and international experts and observers were apparently involved in the census operation to enhance public confidence in the conduct and outcome of the count.

• On the recommendation of the NPC, the federal government approved the establishment of census tribunals as a "conflict resolution mechanism" that would investigate communal complaints against the census exercise and, where necessary, recommend new enumerations in the aggrieved localities.[37] This device was expected to mitigate tension arising from the census.

• Questions on ethnicity and religion were excluded from the 1991 census questionnaire. As the NPC chairman explained:

> Having identified tribal considerations as one of the primordial issues that the elites have used to promote distrust among Nigerians on common issues like population census, and [in] cognizance of the rising tide of religious intolerance with instances of violent clashes across the nation, the National Population Commission [concluded] that the 1991 census could do without the error-generating and acceptance-inhibiting factors of religion and ethnicity. The findings indicated that the nation stood a better chance of obtaining acceptable census figures if these two controversial indices were left out.[38]

• The NPC's seven administrative zones, apart from being headed by nonindigenous commissioners, were deliberately constituted in such a way as to crosscut the country's ethnoregional boundaries and "break (the) traditional political affinity and alliance of (the) states."[39]

• To further curb what was regarded as the excessive and obstructive influence of state or regional loyalties, the Local Government Areas (and not the states) were established as the primary unit of census operations for purposes of logistics, publicity, and execution.

• The NPC embarked on a massive publicity campaign that was designed to forge a "national consensus" on the 1991 census.[40] This campaign, and indeed the whole census exercise, was enormously supported by the availability of new or improved facilities, expertise, and insights that were unavailable or underutilized in previous census operations.

Apart from these administrative reforms, the government implemented three more general, and explicitly political, decisions to attenuate the linkages between population data, on the one hand, and revenue allocation, political representation, and state creation, on the other hand: In 1990, the federal government reduced the weight for relative population size in the horizontal revenue-sharing formula from 40 to 30 percent. In August 1991, it announced that LGAs, rather than constituencies comprising ostensibly equivalent populations, would serve as the units for election into state assemblies and the federal House of Representatives. Finally, President Babangida's decision to create nine new states and more than four hundred new localities immediately before, rather than after, the 1991 census helped to reduce the incentives for the manipulation of the count among the advocates for new states or localities.

All of this is not to suggest that the political-administrative arrangements for the 1991 census were flawless. On the contrary, some aspects of these arrangements generally were considered to be inimical to an accurate census. In the first place, there was criticism of the constitutional and statutory provision that empowered the president, acting on the advice of the Council of State or the Armed Forces Ruling Council, to pass judgment on a census report.[41] Such official purview appeared to both underscore and reinforce the political character of the census project in Nigeria.

In the second place, the appointment of Alhaji Shehu Musa as the first chairman of the NPC in 1988 was considered by many observers to be inappropriate. Musa, an indigene of Babangida's Niger state in the lower North (Middle Belt), was the secretary to the federal government during the infamous Second Republic. According to the radical Yoruba lawyer Chief Gani Fawehinmi, Alhaji Musa "is a member of the Kaduna Mafia with the agenda to suppress the south to the advantage of the north."[42] More important, Alhaji Musa was considered to be a politician with covert presidential ambitions. Indeed, following the announcement of the provisional 1991 census results in March 1992, Musa promptly (even abruptly) resigned from the NPC to join the National Republican Convention, in which he unsuccessfully sought the party's presidential nomination.

In the third place, the organization of the 1991 census was not unaffected by the twists and turns in Babangida's notoriously tortuous and ultimately unsuccessful transition program. Thus, although originally scheduled for the first quarter of 1991, the census had to be moved to November 1991 following unanticipated alterations in the transition program. What is more, the creation of new states and localities on the eve of the census threw the NPC into confusion as it had to realign its administrative and enumeration units with the new structure of constituent subnational administrations. Ultimately, in several instances, the NPC could release census figures only for the old localities. In addition, communal disputes over some arbitrarily instituted local government boundaries actually obstructed enumeration in many areas.

Finally, despite enjoying much better facilities and resources than its predecessors, the NPC was still constrained by many technical, logistical, or administrative problems, including insufficient or belated governmental funding of the census operation; inadequate transportation, communication, and storage facilities; fraudulent, negligent, or incompetent enumerators; and problems arising from the improper mapping of several remote or expansive areas of the country. Because of these and related constraints, the enumeration exercise, which was scheduled to take place November 27–29, 1991, was not completed in most parts of the country until November 30. Moreover, although the provisional census figures were promptly released in March 1992, the final results and full tabulation of the count were presented only in February 1997, about four years behind schedule.

The 1991 census results and the politics of communalism

Three broad tendencies typified the political responses to the 1991 census results in Nigeria. First, the 1991 census exercise and results were vigorously endorsed, applauded, and defended by the federal government. While conceding that the 1991 census may have understated the

Nigerian population by at least 10 percent, many experts and independent observers also broadly acknowledged that the exercise was more credible and reliable than the postindependence censuses in 1962, 1963, and 1973. Second, most members of the southern intelligentsia and political leadership rejected or disbelieved the 1991 census results, apparently because the figures failed to fulfill the long-standing southern aspiration for an end to the North's political-demographic dominance. Third, several subnational authorities and local communities spread across the six geoethnic axes of the Nigerian federation rejected the census results for allegedly understating their populations. Many of these communities and authorities succeeded in having their complaints upheld by the census tribunals amidst resolute opposition from the NPC, which insisted on the total accuracy of the census results.

The 1991 provisional and final census results were accepted by the military administrations of Generals Ibrahim Babangida and Sani Abacha, respectively. On the presentation of the provisional census results in March 1992, the Babangida administration promptly accepted and released the results. His administration subsequently used the figures to discredit the extant inflated voter register and to compile a new one. In his words, "We are satisfied with the conduct of the census and hereby confirm that the population of Nigeria is 88,514,501."[43]

General Sani Abacha was even more fulsome in his praise of the NPC's work and in his endorsement of the census results. Receiving the final census figures in February 1997, Abacha described the presentation of the results as a "milestone" and a "major breakthrough" in "the history of national population censuses in Nigeria":

> We have had a dismal history of unsuccessful census exercises in the country. Previous exercises were bedeviled by allegations and counter-allegations of unfair advantages and unhealthy manipulations by interest and ethnic groups. . . . The resultant disillusionment has led cynics to the unfortunate conclusion that it is futile to attempt to conduct censuses in Nigeria. . . . I am very happy that we have finally broken the myth of the unworkability of a national population census in the country. . . . It is my prayer that the lesson and legacy of the 1991 census would sink into our national psyche and lift the country from an era of conflict and rancor to consensus and cooperation.[44]

Endorsement of the census results also came from such independent observers as Samuel Aluko, a professor of economics and noted writer on Nigeria's census problems; Adetokunbo Ademola, the chairman of the 1973 National Census Board; Alfonso Macdonald, the director in Nigeria of the United Nations Fund for Population Activities; and Frank Hobbs of the United States Bureau of the Census.[45] Revealing that the 1963 and 1991 census results are demographically inconsistent, Hobbs, for instance, argued that this "incomparability" was more likely to be the result of gross overcounting in 1963 than gross undercounting in 1991.[46] Like many other experts, however, he concedes that there is a great deal of uncertainty about Nigeria's actual population size. Yet an even greater degree of mystery and controversy surrounds the issue of the true ethnopolitical distribution of the Nigerian population.

Thus for the southern intelligentsia and political leadership, the North's continuing demographic majority, as reported in the 1991 census, was dubious. Such southern critics of the census included noted Yoruba and Igbo public figures like Akinola Aguda, Bola Ige, Ebenezer Babatope, Arthur Nwankwo, Christian Onoh, and Emeka Odumegwu-Ojukwu, as well as writers in the Lagos-Ibadan axis newspapers like *The Guardian* and the *Nigerian Tribune*.[47] These critics provided no concrete evidence against the accuracy of the census figures, however, beyond invoking the general argument that the much higher levels of urbanization, population concentration, and primary school enrolment in the coastal and forest regions of the South should ordinarily translate into a higher population for the area vis-à-vis the apparently arid and drought-prone North. But they ignored the fact that the 1991 census figures, like all previous censuses, actually showed the South to be more densely populated than the geographically expansive North, which has a land mass of 730,885 square kilometers against 192,883 for the South.[48]

An ostensibly more compelling critique of the North-South population ratios in the 1991 census was provided by Samuel Adamu, a professor of statistics and the sole administrator of the Federal Office of Statistics during the census exercise. Adamu argued that the improper construction and inefficient utilization of enumeration areas by the NPC during the 1991 census led to the underestimation of the population of "certain areas of the country that are thickly populated urban conurbations, like the Yoruba cities of the

South-West," and the overestimation of the population in "areas that are sparsely populated, mostly in the northern part of the country."[49] Yet Adamu was unable to show that such under- or overestimation actually led to underenumeration of the South or overenumeration of the North during the count proper, which the NPC reportedly conducted on a de facto basis (that is, enumerating only those physically seen during the census). Indeed, for Andrew Obeya, a northerner and former federal chief census officer, "any credible population census . . . will put the population of the old North as being larger than that of the old South. . . . The reason is not just because of the disparities in size (between the North and the South) but also the disparities in the sizes of the habitable areas of the two parts of the country."[50]

Obeya, however, argued that the 1991 census significantly understated the country's population. This position was apparently confirmed by proceedings of the two census tribunals, which upheld several complaints of nonenumeration of whole communities or settlements during the census. More generally, the following facts emerged from the proceedings of the tribunals:

The belief that population figures are the sine qua non for obtaining adequate socioeconomic welfare and political advantage was still widely and deeply held by Nigerian communities. The census tribunals were repeatedly told by aggrieved communities that the NPC had understated their populations, and that such understatement would inflict grave socioeconomic costs on the affected communities. Thus, in challenging the 1991 census figures for Kukawa and Nganzai LGAs of Borno state, the chairmen of the two local councils claimed that the NPC's underenumeration of the areas "has meant losses for citizens of Kukawa/Nganzai Local Government Areas in terms of inappropriate allocation of social amenities and reduced remittance from the Federal Accounts, both of which are based on population."[51] In a similar vein, the Gwer-West LGA of Benue state argued that "the low population figure released" for the area, which actually "falls below the 1963 figure," "has adversely affected, and will adversely affect, its developmental, social, political and other fortunes."[52]

The primarily distributive pressures associated with the communal responses to the 1991 census outcome were exacerbated by plain political rivalries among neighboring ethnic communities. In Kogi and Ondo states, for example, the census figures produced much sectional contention and litigation because they reversed the assumed (1963 census-based) political-demographic majorities of the Igala-Bassa and Ekiti ethnic blocs in these states, respectively. Consequently, the Igala-Bassa bloc sought to challenge the census figures for the bloc primarily because they lagged behind the reported population growth "of neighboring localities," while the political tensions in Ondo over the results were relieved only by the establishment of the aggrieved Ekiti bloc as a separate state in 1996.[53]

In a similar case of primarily political sectional rivalry over the census, leaders of Ogbomosho town condemned the census organization and outcome for the town "in comparison to Oyo, Iseyin, Iwo (and) Ejigbo."[54] This comparison is not unrelated to the fact that Ogbomosho has been in contention with Oyo and Iseyin, in particular, to be named as the seat of a proposed new state to be carved out of Oyo state.

Because of these distributive and political pressures, many Nigerian communities (or, more accurately, the elite within these communities) apparently made vigorous attempts to manipulate, inflate, or otherwise influence the 1991 census results. For instance, the NPC had "vetted all the booklets used for the enumeration throughout the country and a common feature discovered was the incidence of multiple thumb-printing by some unscrupulous persons to inflate the population" of their communities.[55]

More important, the census tribunals themselves found that several nonenumeration complaints against the NPC by communal groups or leaders were fraudulent or spurious. In Ogun, Kwara, and Ondo states, for instance, the census tribunals not only found that the witnesses for some of the complainants were "not truthful" and "very unreliable," but also that some persons, households, or settlements that "swore" they "were not counted were indeed counted," and listed on the relevant NPC enumeration forms.[56]

In challenging the census figures, most state and local governments referred to data from primary school enrollment, local government birth registration records, the 1963 census, tax assessment records, number of officially registered buildings, voter registers, and voter turnout, all of which suggested that such states and localities had been underenumerated. Yet a lot of these data were suspect, misleading, or simply self-serving. School enrollment figures, for example, were unreliable because "in many states two lists are often compiled: (a) the authentic record which contains the actual number of school children and (b) an inflated record used for collecting revenue" from the federal government.[57]

Some of the judgments of the census tribunals effectively contradicted the claims of the NPC that it had demarcated and enumerated "every inch of Nigerian soil." Indeed, many complaints of nonenumeration of whole settlements, wards, villages, or towns were successfully proved at the tribunals. These included the nonenumeration of tens of wards and villages in the Damboa, Dikwa, Kaga, Konduga, Kukawa, Magumeri, Maiduguri, Mafa, Ngala, and Nganzai LGAs of Borno state; eight villages in the former Warri North LGA of Delta state; twelve villages in Epe LGA of Lagos state; and three villages and seven enumeration areas in the Asari-Toru LGA of Rivers state.

Other local governments whose census figures were voided by the census tribunals on account of the nonenumeration of some of their constituent parts included Guyuk LGA in Adamawa state; Alkaleri, Bauchi, and Dass LGAs in Bauchi state; Okpokwu LGA in Benue state; Akure, Ijero, and Owo LGAs in Ondo state; Biriniwa, Gwiwa, and Kazaure LGAs of Jigawa state; Jema'a, Kachia, Kaura, and Zangon-Kataf LGAs in Kaduna state; Bakori, Jibia, Kaita, Kankara, Matazu, and Safana LGAs of Katsina state; Wukari LGA of Taraba state; and Bursari, Geidam, Machina, and Yusufari LGAs of Yobe state. In Rivers state, in what the second census tribunal described as a "major lapse," it was found that parts of Abonemma town and twenty-seven of the town's satellite settlements were neither demarcated nor enumerated by the NPC.[58]

These and related instances of nonenumeration largely reflected inadequacies in the administrative and technical capacity of the NPC. Specifically, the problems in the counts often arose from the improper demarcation of some areas of the country; weak transportation and communication facilities and the attendant inability of the NPC to reach some areas with difficult terrain, lack of good roads, floods, and other obstacles; too few enumerators and enumeration materials; incompetent enumerators; and the dislocation ensuing from intercommunal conflicts and clashes, especially over interlocal boundaries.

It is noteworthy that the census tribunals upheld only glaring cases of nonenumeration but dismissed virtually all complaints of partial enumeration or underenumeration. From the tribunals' standpoint, "undercounting is . . . difficult to prove or disprove in the absence of any existing authentic population figure for comparison."[59] Had the tribunals been more responsive to complaints of undercounting, the volume of cases lost by the NPC at the tribunals (twenty-three out of seventy-seven cases) would have been significantly higher.

A major source of communal opposition to the census figures involved complaints of wrongful allocation of the figures between neighboring communities, localities, or states. Such complaints directly arose from the country's ubiquitous interlocal and interstate boundary problems, which gravely undermined the work of the NPC. Areas where the census figures became disputed on account of such boundary problems included Okrika Obu, Umuadabele, and Umuigboeze in Abia/Akwa Ibom states; Shelleng and Song in Adamawa state; Onuko, Urue Offong, and Oron in Akwa Ibom state; Idemili and Onitsha in Anambra state; Gwer West and Otukpo in Benue state; Ethiope and Warri in Delta state; Adavi and Okehi in Kogi state; Andoni/Opobo, Asari-Toru, Brass, Degema, Khana, Okrika, and Oyigbo in Rivers state; and Ibi and Wukari in Taraba state.

The census tribunals argued that their task was "to determine whether people were counted or not." Accordingly, they claimed they had no "jurisdiction . . . to determine to which state or local government any particular locality belongs."[60] Boundary problems, the tribunals concluded, could be settled administratively or by the regular courts. Yet, in a suit instituted by Wukari LGA (in Taraba state) against the NPC, the census tribunal was constrained by the sheer weight of the evidence to uphold the complaints of the Wukari authority that the census figures for four administrative areas (Bantaji, Jibu, Gindin Darowa, and Chediya) had been wrongfully credited to the neighboring Ibi LGA rather than to Wukari.[61]

In one striking revelation, the census tribunal found that the NPC had arbitrarily reduced the population figure of a major southern state. In Oyo state, the tribunal confirmed that "the field figure of 123,488 obtained for Oorelope Local Government Area was reduced to 82,555."[62] The tribunal rejected as an afterthought a claim by the NPC that the reduction was made on the basis of demographic tests and checks that eliminated "fraudulent entries and double counting."[63] Indeed, no evidence of such fraudulent entries and double-counting in Oorelope was presented by the NPC to the tribunal. The embittered leaders of Oyo state claimed that "what the National Population Commission did in respect of Oorelope Local Government was done in respect of every other Local Government in Oyo State."[64] In May 2000, the Oyo state governor, Alhaji Lam Adesina, not only reiterated the state government's rejection of the 1991 census results, but also called on all localities in the state to "mobilize" for the next census.[65]

The NPC's approach to criticisms, complaints, or even the official judicial decisions against the conduct and outcome of the census was basically "dogmatic."[66] Alhaji Shehu Musa spuriously claimed that the NPC enumerated "about 99.7 percent of all the people in the country during the census period."[67] His successor as NPC chairman, Chris Ugokwe, dismissed all criticisms of the census as motivated by sectional prejudice and political mischief.[68] Indeed, reflecting its bureaucratic hubris, the commission neglected the reports of the "independent" observers it had appointed for the census, failed to make relevant documents available to most complainants at the census tribunals, threatened to prosecute members of its staff who gave evidence against the commission at the tribunals, and generally treated all independent census researchers with suspicion and disdain.[69]

Not surprisingly, the final 1991 census figures were not adjusted to "accommodate the complaints against the census or the judgments for recounts ordered by the two census tribunals."[70] Statutorily, such recounts could be authorized only by the head of state after the judicial process had run its full course. Yet the NPC, and several of the complainants themselves, appealed at the appropriate appellate courts against some of the judgments of the tribunals. As of 2001, none of these cases has been resolved. In essence, despite its official endorsement and the unresolved issues in anticipation of the next census, the 1991 census exercise remains politically inconclusive.

CONCLUSIONS

Nigeria's 1991 national population count reflected both change and continuity in the country's contentious census history. The change involved the manner in which key reforms in the design and administration of the census operation helped to contain not so much the incentives or pressures as the capacity or opportunity to manipulate the count for sectional advantage. The continuity was reflected in the relentless sectional perceptions of the census as an instrument of communal socioeconomic and political advantage, in the administrative shortcomings and constitutional vulnerability of the National Population Commission, and in the development of significant political opposition to the 1991 census figures.

Three basic conclusions regarding the 1991 census in particular, and Nigeria's censuses in general, emerge from this chapter. The first relates to the possibility that manipulation and inflation of census figures can occur in tandem with the underenumeration of the population. All of Nigeria's postindependence censuses, including the 1991 exercise, were the objects of vigorous, sectionally inspired attempts at manipulation through the falsification or inflation of population data. At the same time, the country's censuses have never succeeded in enumerating the entire population, largely because of technical and administrative weaknesses in the census organization. The attendant phenomenon of under- or nonenumeration has led some observers to dismiss charges of inflation in Nigeria's censuses as unfounded.[71] To be sure, the manipulation of population figures may compensate for some shortfalls arising from underenumeration; yet, because inflation is unlikely to occur evenly across the nation's demographic and geopolitical constituencies, its more likely effect is to detract from the accuracy and reliability of the country's demographic data.[72]

The second observation relates to the abiding primacy of the North-South fault line in the politics of Nigeria's censuses, despite the fragmentation of the two regions into numerous zones, states, and ethnic groups (see tables 9 and 10). Nevertheless, this political bipolarization should not obscure the more diffuse, complicated, and distributively oriented competition over the census among ethnoterritorial constituencies at the subregional, state, and local levels. The North-South census rivalry has been sustained by Nigeria's established national political figures, mainly from the three ethnic majority groups. Local politicians, on the other hand, have been more concerned with the implications of the census figures for resource sharing and political bargaining within specific states or localities.

Table 9. Composition and 1991 Population of Nigeria's Six Geographic Zones

Geographic Zone	States	Predominant ethnic composition	Population size	% of Total population
North-West	Kano, Sokoto, Kaduna, Katsina, Jigawa, Kebbi, Zamfara	Hausa-Fulani	22,913,412	25.75
North-East	Bauchi, Borno, Adamawa, Taraba, Yobe, Gombe	Hausa-Fulani and Northern minorities	11,900,913	13.37
Middle Belt (Lower North)	Plateau, Benue, Niger, Kogi, Kwara, Nasarawa, and FCT	Northern minorities	12,554,912	14.11
South-West	Lagos, Ondo, Oyo, Ogun, Osun, Ekiti	Yoruba	17,455,043	19.61
South-East	Enugu, Anambra, Imo, Abia, and Ebonyi	Igbo	10,774,977	12.11
South-South	Rivers, Delta, Akwa Ibom, Edo, Cross River, Bayelsa	Southern minorities	13,392,963	15.05

Source: Computed on the basis of the 1991 final census figures. For the zonal distribution of the states, see *The Guardian* (Lagos), November 16, 1996, 12–13 and March 24, 1997, 15.

The third observation concerns the explanation for the relatively limited political controversy over the 1991 census figures and their resolute official acceptance. This outcome could be related to the fact that the 1991 census did not alter the extant political-demographic balance of power between the North and the South. Moreover, in electoral terms, the figures suggest that no single ethnic or geopolitical group can dominate the federation unilaterally. As Samuel Aluko has noted, "Even a candidate from the far North (i.e., the North-West and North-East zones) has not much . . . chance of winning the presidency unless he can win support from other . . . blocs in the Middle Belt, the Western and the Eastern areas."[73]

It is unlikely that a census outcome that ends the demographic advantage of the North (as reportedly happened in 1962) or that indicates

Table 10. Distribution of the Nigerian Population (in millions) on a North-South Basis, 1911–1991

Region	1911 Census		1921 Census		1931 Census		'52–'53 Census	
	M	%	M	%	M	%	M	%
North	8.12	50.60	10.56	56.41	11.44	57.03	16.84	55.36
South	7.93	49.40	8.16	43.59	8.62	42.97	13.58	44.64
TOTAL	16.05	100	18.72	100	20.06	100	30.42	100

Region	1962 Census		1963 Census		1973 Census		1991 Census	
	M	%	M	%	M	%	M	%
North	22.01	48.60	29.78	53.50	51.38	64.42	47.37	53.23
South	23.28	51.40	25.88	46.50	28.38	35.58	41.62	46.77
TOTAL	45.29	100	55.66	100	79.76	100	88.99	100

Source: Adapted from Reuben K. Udo, "Geography and Population Censuses in Nigeria," in *Fifty Years of Geography in Nigeria: The Ibadan Story,* ed. Olusegun Areola and Stanley I. Okafor (Ibadan: Ibadan University Press, 1998), 356.

a dramatic expansion in the demographic power of one regional group (as happened in 1973) would survive in Nigeria. Political acceptability, rather than statistical accuracy or demographic reliability, clearly remains the most important determinant of the fate of the census in Nigeria. As such, it is a sad commentary on the continuing ethnopoliticization of basic demographic information in the country.

How, then, may Nigeria transcend its census problems? Like several other Nigerians, Adetokunbo Ademola contends that "a good head count in this country is hardly possible as long as the allocation of revenue and the representation in parliament are tied to census figures."[74] Yet, despite the modest measures that have been taken to reduce the weight of population in resource allocation and power distribution, the principle of proportionality apparently still enjoys overwhelming political popularity in Nigeria. Moreover, Babangida's policy of de-emphasizing population in constituting the aborted Third Republic's legislative chambers resulted in glaring inequities, anomalies, and controversies. Rather than diverting attention from the geopolitical distribution of the country's population, these results ultimately refocused it. Most important, the modest downward adjustments in the proportionality rule under Babangida did not appear to have significantly reduced the incentives to falsify the census for sectional advantage. Such sectional pressures to manipulate the census were arguably restrained only by the innovations and reforms in the 1991 census organization, not by the government's half-hearted downgrading of the proportionality principle.

To be sure, adjustments in the rules for allocating national power and resources, coupled with cumulative improvements in census administration, may contribute to the depoliticization and administrative routinization of census taking in Nigeria. Yet Nigeria's census problems are primarily rooted in a pervasive culture of ethnic "cake-sharing" and an entrenched structure of centralized distributive federalism. Consequently, the efforts to assuage these problems will also need to focus on strategies for the decentralization of the political economy of Nigerian federalism and for the expansion of opportunities and incentives for economic self-governance at the subnational level.

The challenge of such reform in Nigerian federalism is the focus of the next and final chapter of this work.

7

ISSUES
IN THE REFORM OF
THE NIGERIAN
FEDERAL SYSTEM

I F THERE IS A SINGLE, FUNDAMENTAL THEME OF THIS WORK, it is the
insidiously distributive and conflictual nature of the Nigerian system of federalism. The country's intergovernmental and intersegmental relations have been dominated by the unproductive, divisive,
and ultimately destructive competition for the powers and resources of
an overweening central state apparatus. The perverse conflicts generated by this competition have been documented in the preceding discussions of Nigeria's four staple distributive arenas—namely, revenue
allocation, territorial reorganizations, the "federal character" policy, and
population censuses.

Contrary to popular interpretations, the past and prospect of prolonged military rule per se may not be the basic or only source of
federal instability in Nigeria. Rather, the problem may lie in a monolithic, statist, and centrist political economy that would require several years
of rigorous and broad-based decentralized economic development to
overcome. Nevertheless, by dramatically enlarging the powers of the center and precluding potential institutional options for decentralized democratic development, the military has significantly deepened and exacerbated the irregularities, pathologies, and conflicts that have come to be
associated with Nigeria's centralized ethno-distributive federalism.
Particularly during the second phase of military rule, from 1984 to 1999,

the Nigerian federation was vexed by such perversities as the center's relentless emasculation and immiseration of subnational governments, the monopolization of power by an ethno-military oligarchy, the wanton violation of civil and communal rights, and the attendant mobilization and intensification of disintegrative ethnoregional resentments. Despite the euphoria that accompanied the restoration of civilian rule in May 1999, the country still faces fundamental and unresolved problems of federalism that arise not only from the legacy of prolonged hypercentralized military rule but also from the distortions inherent in the monolithic, oil-based, ethno-distributive political economy.

The pathologies of Nigerian federalism have produced strident criticisms about the country's political failings, profound cynicism about the federation's structural viability, and vigorous debates about alternative political futures for the Nigerian state. According to the maverick Nigerian party leader Tunji Braithwaite, the Nigerian system of federalism amounts to "a hollow federation" and represents "the worst form of federalism anywhere in the world."[1] The same sentiments are expressed by Nobel laureate Wole Soyinka, who dismisses the Nigerian federal experiment as a "cracked model" of federalism. In his words:

> Nigeria serves . . . as a prime example of the failed federation, but perhaps failure is the wrong word, for it implies that an attempt has been made in the first place, one that unfortunately ended in failure. The truth is that, beyond the first four years of independence, the federal principle was simply thrown overboard. A deliberate subversion of the rational relations of the states to the center was embarked upon, upsetting the balance between federal authority, the states, and even local government.[2]

The flip side to this ritual bemoaning of Nigeria's federal decline is, of course, the burgeoning debate on alternative strategies for reforming or recrafting the Nigerian federation. This discourse has been dominated by the following themes:

- ❖ The need for the intergovernmental decentralization of constitutional powers and responsibilities.
- ❖ The reform of the revenue allocation system.
- ❖ The institution of effective mechanisms for promoting or enforcing equitable power sharing among Nigeria's diverse ethnic and regional groups.

❖ The rebuilding and consolidation of Nigeria's fragile and fledgling democratic institutions.

❖ The issue of the viability or legitimacy of the very idea of a single, multiethnic, Nigerian state.

What follows, then, is an elaboration on these themes in a wide-ranging discourse that documents the complexity and diversity of the ongoing debates on the nature and future of Nigerian federalism and suggests options to ameliorate its pathologies.

INTERGOVERNMENTAL RELATIONS: RETRENCHING THE HYPERCENTRALIZED STATE

The most widely lamented feature of the Nigerian federation involves the massive, relentless, and comparatively unprecedented accumulation of powers by the center at the expense of the states and the localities. According to Dele Olowu, "The pattern which centralization has followed in Nigeria is not the familiar one of swings of the pendulum between centripetal and centrifugal forces, but a tendency, effectively, to move toward abrogating the country's federal status."[3]

The process of hypercentralization in Nigeria, which roughly began with the first phase of military rule between 1966 and 1979, was legitimized by the 1979 constitutional framework for the Second Republic (1979–83) and was subsequently perpetuated and extended under the second phase of military rule (1984–99). Despite the retreat of the military in May 1999, the center's political hegemony has been virtually preserved by the imposition of a barely modified version of the 1979 Constitution as the framework for Nigeria's Fourth Republic.

Broadly speaking, functional centralization in Nigeria has featured several basic processes. First, some residual powers exercised by the states during the pre-military era—such as primary education, basic health services, housing, and, most important, local government—have fallen within the purview of concurrent federal-state jurisdiction, with federal competency being paramount in cases of conflict.

Federal intervention in local government matters, in particular, expanded dramatically in the wake of the 1976 nationwide local government reform. Since then, such intervention has involved the imposition of a uniform, single-tiered structure of local government throughout the federation; organization of local government elections; creation and dissolution of local government units; abolition of state-controlled local government ministries and services (personnel) commissions; enunciation of an approved scheme of service for local government employees; ratification of key local government personnel appointments and dismissals; direct transfer of federal statutory revenues to local authorities; regulation of local government budgets or expenditures; and, in 1993, the creation of a federal Ministry of State and Local Government Affairs with the explicit authority to monitor and enhance executive capacity at the local level. Although the 1999 Constitution restored partial responsibility for the conduct of local elections and the creation of new localities to the states, it preserved the structural and fiscal centralization of the local government system.

These measures were ostensibly designed to both establish local government as an effective third tier of the Nigerian federal system and shield the localities from manipulative domination or exploitative depredation by the states. Yet, by almost universal acknowledgement, federal intervention in the localities did not lead to a significant strengthening of the local government structure. Instead, it produced a number of disastrous consequences, including fatally violent communal strife over arbitrary, centrally directed reorganizations of local territories.

The second basic feature of functional centralization has involved the exclusive assignment to the center of several matters that were previously under concurrent federal-state jurisdiction: the police (including native police), elections, constitutions, arms, prisons, bankruptcy, traffic on federal roads, industrial relations, and topographic surveys. Whereas the regions of the First Republic could both establish their own constitutions and exercise considerable control over native police units in their territories, the states have been formally divested of these powers since the Second Republic.

Also, entirely novel powers and functions have been added to the already expansive repertoire of the center's exclusive powers. For example, since the 1979 Constitution, the federal government has been empowered exclusively to establish and regulate authorities throughout the federation in order to promote a comprehensive set of public goals defined as "fundamental objectives and directive principles of state policy."[4] Underscored by developments during the Second Republic, this specific power would enable the federal government to intervene in practically every matter of public importance, including areas of residual jurisdiction formally belonging to the states.[5] The federal prerogative to promote the "objectives and principles of state policy" effectively perpetuates, under a constitutional democratic dispensation, the antifederalist powers of the Nigerian federal military government "to make laws for the peace, order, and good government of Nigeria or any part thereof, with respect to any matter whatsoever."[6]

Predictably, this sweeping centralization has been widely denounced as making a mockery of Nigerian federalism. It has also inspired many proposals for the decentralization of the country's intergovernmental relations. Even with the repressive Abacha government came official recognition of these anticentralist pressures through the innovative inclusion of a list of exclusive state powers (as distinct from previous unspecified residual powers) in the 1995 draft constitution and through the government's establishment of a committee on the devolution of powers from the federal to the state and local governments.[7] Unfortunately, both initiatives died with the Abacha administration.

Nevertheless, broad areas of consensus may be isolated from recent debates and proposals regarding the need for political decentralization in Nigeria. One such area is that "the direct functions of the federal government ought to be limited principally to . . . clear areas of national activities," such as defense, external affairs, currency, customs, common citizenship laws, and macroeconomic management for broad-based economic development.[8] Outside these areas, the federal government should limit its public interventions to setting minimum national standards for socioeconomic development and nurturing an appropriate enabling environment for wealth creation and welfare delivery by private-sector and local-level institutions.

Another area of consensus is that the states should be constitutionally empowered to actualize their putative status as a coordinate, rather than subordinate, order of government. Thus, "each of the current states should be allowed, and required, to have their own constitutions, in addition to, and consistent with, a federal constitution."[9] Moreover, there is a need for the "decentralization of policing functions that will respect the needs of different levels of governments in a federal system."[10] Specifically, what must be avoided is a rerun of the situation in the Second Republic, when the executive capacity of state administrations was undermined by the state-level commissioners of the unitary Nigeria Police Force. Particularly in the states controlled by parties other than the center's ruling party, these commissioners "defied and ignored elected governors, and instead flaunted their allegiance and loyalty to the inspector-general of police and the president of the Federal Republic of Nigeria."[11]

There is also broad consensus that the system of local government administration, like other largely local issues in a federation, should be determined by state administrations and local populations. In Anthony Enahoro's view, "the needless imposition of a uniform local government system on the country is an antifederalist arrangement because local government should ideally be an expression or function of the character and individuality of the federating units."[12] Consequently, to cite a 1986 memorandum by a group of northern emirs and chiefs, "in conformity with the principle of federalism, each state should be allowed to evolve its own system of local administration which would suit the peculiarities of such a state."[13]

The same argument for the transfer of powers and responsibilities from the center to the states requires the latter, in turn, to devolve more functions to the localities. Indeed, the idea of a viable local government system should enrich—not enfeeble—Nigerian federalism. And this federalist process would be further deepened if the local government units themselves would support and stimulate the developmental activities of town, village, district, or community associations or unions within the localities.

Also, overriding recognition should be accorded to the principle of subsidiarity in the intergovernmental distribution of functions. This rule would discourage a higher level of government from continuing its intervention in, or assuming responsibility for, tasks that could be undertaken successfully by a lower level of government.

Finally, it is obvious that the basis for the functional marginalization of subnational authorities and the political overexpansion of the center in Nigeria is as political as it is fiscal. Essentially, Nigeria's states and localities have lacked the autonomous resources that are necessary to resist marginalization or domination by the center and to sustain a system of noncentralized intergovernmental relations. Accordingly, most interested observers recognize that the devolution of powers and responsibilities in Nigeria can be effective only if it is underpinned by a commensurate decentralization of resource control and revenue sharing.

REVENUE ALLOCATION: BEYOND CENTRALIZED "CAKE SHARING"

Undoubtedly, the issue of revenue allocation lies at the very heart of the crisis of Nigerian federalism. As already detailed in chapter 3, the basic pathologies of the Nigerian revenue allocation system involve (1) the monocentric structure of the country's political economy, stemming from the fact that federally collected oil revenues account for some 80 percent of all government revenues; (2) the predictable concentration of financial resources in the central government; (3) the attendant immiseration of the states and the localities; (4) the heavy reliance on the political criteria of interunit equality and population in disbursing national revenues to the subfederal tiers of government; (5) the relatively negligible weights assigned to less explicitly political factors like internal revenue generation and the social development index in horizontal revenue sharing; (6) the brazen neglect of the needs and demands of Nigeria's ethnic minorities in the Niger Delta's oil-bearing communities; and (7) the absence of a transparent and broadly acceptable process for the administration of intergovernmental financial relations. The maladministration and manipulation of the revenue-sharing process, in particular, deprived the states and the localities of huge amounts of revenue due to them under the revenue allocation formula.[14]

The struggle for a more decentralized system of revenue allocation in Nigeria would involve more than a faithful implementation of revenue-sharing laws, however. It would also require a downward adjustment of the center's statutory share of federal revenues and perhaps the devolution of more taxing powers to the states and localities. Indeed, a growing tide of popular and expert opinion in Nigeria has called not only for the reduction of the center's share of current federally collected revenues to not more than 40 percent but also for the redesignation as state taxes of such current federal taxes as business tax, value-added tax, and mining rents.[15] Apart from promoting a more balanced system of fiscal federalism, the decentralization of revenues and revenue jurisdictions could induce the states to improve and rationalize their administrative capacities, enhance the delivery of socioeconomic welfare by subfederal entities to their largely impoverished constituents, reduce waste and corruption at the federal level, and restrain the destructive competition for economic opportunities at the center. The devolution of more tax jurisdictions (as distinct from tax revenues) to the subfederal levels, in particular, could soften the conflicts over horizontal revenue sharing (that is, the distribution of federally collected revenues among the states and among the localities).

Nevertheless, part of the immediate challenge of federal reform in Nigeria would be to transform the horizontal revenue sharing system from an instrument for strengthening a cake-sharing psychosis or dependency syndrome into a mechanism for promoting fiscal capacity and autonomy at the subfederal level.

As is generally acknowledged, the current horizontal revenue-sharing formula is a recipe for perverse, distributive conflicts. Yet several attempts to modify this scheme or reduce its domination by population and equality factors have foundered. In 1977, for example, the technical committee on revenue allocation led by Ojetunji Aboyade advocated a novel sharing formula that would utilize equality of access to development, national minimum standards, absorptive capacity, independent revenue or tax effort, and fiscal efficiency.[16] Similarly, in a minority report of the Commission on Revenue Allocation led by Pius Okigbo in 1980, Adedotun Phillips advocated an alternative horizontal-sharing scheme involving three basic principles: expenditure obligation, internal revenue effort, and fiscal equalization.[17]

Although the Aboyade scheme was partially adopted and implemented by the Obasanjo administration, it was widely denounced and promptly discarded by the politicians of the Second Republic. The Adedotun Phillips scheme, on the other hand, was simply ignored. Essentially, Nigerian politicians have consistently demonstrated a preference for explicitly political and technically unsophisticated factors of horizontal allocation. The population and equality factors, in particular, seem to satisfy Nigerian politicians' aversion for a sharing scheme in which large sums of central revenues would be disbursed on the basis of technical criteria that would be unintelligible to the average Nigerian citizen or politician. Yet the current sharing scheme will need to be modified significantly if "revenue allocation in Nigeria must supplement revenue generation, . . . guarantee equity, justice and fairness [and] . . . serve as [an] inducement to self-generating growth," as claimed by the report of the 1994–95 NCC's Revenue Allocation Committee.[18]

One immediate way to realize reform of the revenue allocation system would be to implement the Danjuma Committee's recommendation that a weight of 20 percent (rather than the current 10 percent) be assigned to the internal revenue generation criterion. This adjustment could be implemented by eliminating land mass/terrain as a substantive factor, as envisaged by the Danjuma Committee, or by reducing the weight for the equality factor from 40 to 30 percent.[19] In the longer term, Nigeria's decision makers could revisit the horizontal revenue-sharing scheme proposed by Phillips in 1980. This would assign a weight of 50 percent to the verified expenditure obligation of the states and a weight of 25 percent each to internal revenue generation effort and fiscal equalization. The scheme effectively eliminates the perverse principles of interunit equality and population, is less technically ponderous than the Aboyade formula, and seems to be directly geared toward actualizing and optimizing both equity and efficiency in the allocation of federal revenues.

The dual objectives of fiscal equity and efficiency would also be served by according greater recognition to the derivation principle. This factor is somewhat related to, but quite distinct from, the principle of internal revenue generation effort. While the internal revenue criterion is designed to reward the autonomous revenue generation effort of subunits, the derivation principle is aimed at accommodating the claims and rights of resource-endowed regions in the distribution of centrally collected revenues emanating from such regions. In the specific Nigerian context, the effective application of the derivation principle would serve both the goal of efficiency (by reducing the tendency for states from outside the oil-rich Delta to perceive the revenue allocation system as an easy source of unearned oil revenues) and the objective of equity (by giving greater resources to Nigeria's neglected and ecologically endangered Delta region).

An important achievement of the Fourth Republic would involve the satisfactory implementation of the constitutional provision "that the principle of derivation shall be constantly reflected in any approved formula as being not less than 13 percent of the revenue accruing to the Federation Account directly from any natural resources."[20] Nonetheless, there can be little doubt that the so-called 13 percent derivation formula still falls short of the expectations and demands of the oil-bearing areas.

For Tam David-West, a former petroleum minister from Rivers state, the 13 percent proposed for derivation "is meager; at least 20 percent is more acceptable."[21] Similarly, the late Ogoni ethnic minority activist, Ken Saro-Wiwa, felt the Ogoni and other oil-bearing communities should be allowed to retain "at least 50 percent" of their economic resources exclusively for their own development.[22] Saro-Wiwa's position is shared by Edet Akpan, who contends that "anything less than a 50 percent special allocation will amount to paying lip service to . . . the problems facing the oil producing areas . . . and postponing the process and imperatives of a true and holistic national reconciliation."[23]

The distribution of Nigeria's oil wealth is an extremely complex matter, but the conflicts over mineral revenue allocation can be disaggregated into three basic elements. The first involves the contradictions arising from Nigeria's centrist and statist constitutional structure, which vests complete ownership of all mineral resources not in the constituent states or individual or communal land owners, but exclusively in the federation's government.[24] Consequently, the only way by which the oil-rich areas may share in the funds (mineral rents, royalties, and oil company profits) emanating from their regions is by concession or redistribution by the federal government. This government, however, is dominated heavily by largely self-serving elites from outside the oil-rich regions. Yet, as the Okigbo Commission recognized, both the imperatives of equitable federalism and the realities of Nigeria's land-use law require that mineral rents, at least, should be vested completely in the mineral-rich states and not in the federal government.[25]

The second basic element in Nigeria's mineral revenue allocation conflicts involves the debates in an economically backward country over the feasibility and desirability of a derivation-based approach to the allocation of huge windfall revenues from mineral resources concentrated in a specific region. It is broadly recognized that the impact of the derivation principle in this context could be dramatically different from its impact in an agricultural economy, as Nigeria was in the 1950s and '60s.

Yet, alluding to the overriding role of the derivation principle in the pre-1970 era and attributing the progressive downgrading of the principle to the politics of minority oppression, many in the oil-rich states have called for the full restoration of the derivation rule. For the federal government, and many elements from outside the oil-rich areas, however, such a strategy would engender a huge undesirable and unsustainable gap between the revenues available to the oil-producing states, on the one hand, and those available to other states and, indeed, the federal government, on the other.

The challenge here is to fashion a truly federal compromise that would balance, as shrewdly as possible, the economic rights or claims of the oil-rich regions with the need to equalize socioeconomic opportunities throughout the federation. Although obviously difficult, such a compromise is not impossible to achieve: A goodly number of the leaders of the oil-rich states are not necessarily averse to the use of a significant proportion of oil wealth to support socioeconomic development in other parts of the country.[26] What they have found objectionable, though, particularly in every section of the Niger Delta region, is the brazen official neglect of the ecological problems arising largely from oil exploration and exploitation in the region.

The third element in oil revenue allocation debates in Nigeria thus involves the ecological problems of the oil-producing areas. Even in downgrading the derivation principle, the federal government has been constrained to acknowledge the urgency and legitimacy of the ecological problems and rights of the oil-producing areas. Yet such an acknowledgement has never really been acted upon. Rather, by all accounts, the Niger Delta is severely ecologically degraded, neglected, and endangered.[27] The predictable outcome of this injustice is the current rise of violent and militant ethnic agitation in the Delta region.

An allocation of 13 percent of mineral revenues in the Federation Account would seem to be too inadequate a response to both the special claims of the oil-rich areas to federal oil revenues on the grounds of derivation, and to the ecological problems of these areas. However, these fed-eralist and environmentalist imperatives are precisely the twin objectives that Nigerian central authorities expect the inaptly named "13 percent derivation formula" to satisfy. Not surprisingly, though, since May 1999, the governments and representatives of the oil-rich areas have sought both the full transfer of the 13 percent derivation revenues to the affected states and the establishment of an adequately funded federal commission (such as the NDDC) to assume responsibility for alleviating the ecolog-ical and developmental problems of the oil-rich communities. Clearly, an effective response to the problems of the Niger Delta will require greater recognition, discussion, and accommodation of the demands and needs of the country's oil-producing areas.

The multiple conflicts and high stakes that are associated with revenue allocation in Nigeria have been compounded by sheer admin-istrative disorganization, confusion, and manipulation. Elements of this administrative crisis include the absence of transparency in the pay-ment of centrally collected revenues into the Federation Account; the manipulation of and confusion over the administration of special funds; the invidious, multiple access of the Federal Capital Territory to the Federation Account via the territory's participation in the alloca-tions to the center, the states, the localities, and special funds; the absence of any viable institutional mechanism to protect the fiscal integrity of the localities; and the flawed method for constituting the NRMAFC.[28] Again, most of these problems were aggravated during military rule, when neither the subfederal tiers nor the courts could restrain the center from its self-serving maladministration of the rev-enue-sharing system. Yet, given the inadequacy of existing relevant con-stitutional provisions, some of these problems have persisted, and may even intensify, under civilian rule.

Broadly, the reform of intergovernmental revenue administration in Nigeria would need to (1) establish a procedure by which the sub-federal tiers could receive, from the federation's accountant-general or the Central Bank, a regular (possibly monthly) statement of all rev-enues paid into the Federation Account; (2) institute a substantive and self-enforcing mechanism to ensure the effective disbursement of the approved proportions of federal and state revenues statutorily assigned to the localities; (3) make specific provisions for the administration of all special funds in the Federation Account (these being funds not directly allocated to any of the three governmental tiers); (4) clarify the status of Abuja in the revenue-sharing system and, preferably, exclude the territory from partaking in the allocations to the states and special funds; (5) transform NRMAFC into a truly technical, independent, and intergovernmental (rather than purely presidential) commission; and (6) streamline the unwieldy composition of NRMAFC by removing the current constitutional requirement for the representation of every state and the FCT in the commission.

POWER SHARING AND THE SEARCH FOR A GENUINE FEDERAL CHARACTER

Perhaps the most emotive political issue in recent Nigerian history has involved the struggles for an ethnically equitable power-sharing formula. These struggles are inspired by a broad recognition that the constitutional provisions on federal character have neither been faithfully implemented nor truly effective in ensuring interethnic equity in the composition and conduct of the federal government. The following are some of the proposals that have been gleaned from the ongoing debate about an acceptable, equitable, and effective "power-sharing regime" in Nigeria:[29]

The institutionalization of an arrangement for rotating the presidency of the Federal Republic among some recognized geographic zones of the country. Known as "rotation" or "zoning," this proposal was broadly accepted and adopted by the dominant party of the Second Republic and by all the registered political parties of the Third and Fourth Republics. Reflecting the growing interregional recriminations in Nigeria over power sharing, however, there are mounting pressures for the transformation of zoning from a convention of the parties into an explicit and entrenched constitutional provision of the Nigerian state.

The prohibition of consecutive presidential terms, or the restriction of each elected president to a single, nonrenewable four- to six-year term. This proposal is often seen as an important operational adjunct to the rotary formula. In the words of Second Republic Vice President Alex Ekwueme, "with the introduction of rotation between zones . . . a single term at a time for each chief executive will ensure a faster rate of rotation."[30] The idea of single terms for political chief executives (at both

federal and subfederal levels), however, has the distinct additional potential value of preventing the violence and electoral-law violations that
invariably accompany the re-election bids of incumbents in Nigeria.

A multiple vice-presidential system. Under this arrangement, three or
more vice presidents, originating from different regions of the country,
will be elected along with the president. According to its proponents, this
arrangement would ensure the broad, effective, and simultaneous representation of all key geographic zones, including minority-populated
regions, in the federal executive. In some versions of this proposal, one of
the vice presidents would come from the same geographic zone as the
incumbent president. This would allow a zone to complete its presidential term, under a rotatory presidential scheme, in the event of the death
or removal of the incumbent president.

Whether this proposal is seen as an adjunct, or as an alternative,
to the rotational presidency, however, proponents of the multiple vice
presidency share the view that the arrangement could reduce widespread fears of ethnoregional marginalization by giving every major
regional group "a feeling of belonging and a sense of participation" in
the governance of the country.[31]

*A French-style presidential-parliamentary system in which the offices of
the president and prime minister would be constituted in such a way as to
vary, broaden, and balance the regional base of federal executive power.* A
variant of this proposal was actually partially implemented by the Babangida administration and officially touted under the Abacha government.
This sought to institute an ethno-institutional power-sharing scheme in
which the incumbent northern (Muslim) military president would be
complemented by a southern (Christian) civilian prime minister.

For many proponents of the presidential-parliamentary arrangement, the undiluted application of American-style presidentialism is
counterproductive in the Nigerian experience. The American presidential model, it is claimed, concentrates so much power in the hands of
one person that it invariably engenders a destructive competition for
the presidency among all politicians, parties, and ethnoregional groups.

*A full-fledged reversion to the First Republic's Westminster-style parlia-
mentary system.* Proponents of this view argue that the parliamentary system is more institutionally conducive to ethnic power sharing than the
pure presidential model. In Enahoro's opinion, "The parliamentary

system recommends itself because of its institutional safeguards, paramount among which is a collective presidency. The cabinet collectively (not the prime minister solely), as in a presidency, is the executive."[32]

The establishment of a Swiss-type federal collegiate council. In such an arrangement, federal executive powers would be collectively exercised by the representatives of the country's principal geographic zones, and the chairmanship or presidency of the council would be rotated annually among these representatives.

A national coalition or "unity" government in which all major parties (along with their ethnic constituencies) would be adequately and equitably represented in the executive. For instance, according to section 148(6) of the 1995 draft constitution, "Any political party which wins not less than 10 percent of the total number of seats in the National Assembly shall be entitled to representation in the cabinet in proportion to the number of seats won by that party in the National Assembly." However, this provision did not find its way into the 1999 Constitution. Nevertheless, the Obasanjo civilian government, shortly after its inauguration in May 1999, came under pressure from segments of the opposition to form a government of national unity that was supposed to undertake and consummate Nigeria's constitutional transformation from a postauthoritarian state into a stable and equitable federal democratic republic. Obasanjo's cabinet appointments during June–July 1999 eventually included elements from the opposition parties.

Yet many of the aforementioned proposals for ethnic power sharing, particularly the various formulas for geoethnic power rotation, appear to be fundamentally flawed or misplaced and potentially counterproductive. Many of these proposals involve ideas or arrangements that would detract from the putative role of Nigeria's presidential federalism as an integrative design, rather than as an instrument simply for projecting or reinforcing the country's inherent ethnic divisiveness or competitiveness. It was for this reason, for instance, that the Political Bureau in 1986 dismissed suggestions for a constitutional provision for rotation as "an acceptance of our inability to grow beyond ethnic or state loyalty."[33]

In addition, a system of rotational power sharing would perpetuate and exacerbate Nigeria's perverse ethnopatrimonial or prebendal political culture, thereby sustaining the mentality that public offices could (and, indeed, should) be competed for and then appropriated by sectional power groups and their constituents. Thus Julius Ihonvbere has denounced a rotational presidential arrangement as "a recipe for further corruption and ethnicization of Nigerian politics."[34] For Eskor Toyo, a rotational presidency is a "cake-sharers' presidency"; further, "[the] presidency of Nigeria must never be trivialized and desecrated by being reduced into a part of a cake to be shared by people who have the same mentality as armed robbers."[35] The same sentiments are expressed by the prominent journalist Peter Enahoro, who derides rotational power sharing as "a secret code for taking turns to seize possession of the keys to the treasury in order to brazenly divert a disproportionate level of development to one's ethnic area."[36]

Also, by actually paying relatively little attention to mass-based ethnic concerns, while giving such overriding consideration to the distribution of political offices among sectional elites, a goodly number of the Nigerian proposals for power sharing may serve more to consolidate elite domination and manipulation than to promote genuine interethnic unity and equity. Thus the vigorous debates about power sharing in Nigeria and several years of federal-character engineering in the country have done very little to address or redress the severe imbalances between the South and the North in such basic socioeconomic indicators as family planning, employment opportunities, health facilities, educational development, and gender equality.[37]

Moreover, it is quite obvious that the presidency cannot realistically be rotated among Nigeria's 250-odd ethnolinguistic groups. Hence, proponents of power rotation are constrained to reduce the country's extraordinary ethnic complexity into such popular, but largely contrived or simplistic, stratifications as North vs. South, Christian vs. Muslim, majorities vs. minorities, or competition among the country's six geographic zones. Yet, because these demarcations often submerge several divergent identities, a scheme for geoethnic rotational power sharing can never really guarantee justice for smaller groups. Rather, it could simply re-establish the hegemony of the bigger ethnicities. In denouncing the 1995 draft constitution's provision for the rotation of the presidency on a North-South basis, Eskor Toyo asked,

> Is it imaginable that the chauvinists among the Igbo and Yoruba will allow a minority . . . [politician] from . . . [the] South to become the president when it is the turn of the so-called South? Is it conceivable that

the "born-to-rule" chauvinists among the Hausa-Fulani will permit a . . . [politician] from one of the minorities in . . . [the] North to become president when it is the turn of the so-called North? If the answer is "no," as it is, then zoning is a way to ensure that no person of ethnic minority origin can become a president of Nigeria.[38]

This fundamental problem would not go away even in a six-zone power-sharing arrangement. Rather, this arrangement would tend simply "to reserve the highest offices for members of the largest ethnic group in each of the six electoral regions," as Richard Sklar concludes.[39]

As already indicated, the main source of the agitations for rotational power sharing is southern opposition to perceived northern political domination. Several northern politicians, however, have denounced these protests as both vindictive and selective in view of the continuing southern, especially Yoruba, domination of education, economy, and bureaucracy. As claimed by the first executive governor of Kano state, Abubakar Rimi, "the North is behind in education, economy, industry, and representation in [the] federal bureaucracy. . . . [I]f anybody is talking about power-shift, then those elements of power should be looked into."[40]

As should be evident from the diversity and inconsistency of the various proposals for power sharing, proponents of zoning and rotation in Nigeria often betray deep confusion and disagreement over several basic issues: the most appropriate demarcation of the geoethnic segments in the rotational scheme, the precise nature and number of the political offices to be rotated, the ethnoregional sequencing of the rotatory scheme, and whether or not such a scheme should be a transitional or a permanent feature of the Nigerian constitution.[41] The contradictory proposals for power sharing expressed in the 1994–95 National Constitutional Conference and by the Abacha government (which instituted the NCC) well illustrate this confusion and inconsistency.[42] Such contradiction, confusion, and manipulation tend to cast grave doubts on the viability and utility of Nigerian ethnic power-sharing proposals.

Above all, though, most of the proposals for power sharing tend to be undemocratic. In other words, they tend often to detract from the democratic autonomy and responsibility of parties and electorate to freely select or elect key political representatives. Perhaps the most compelling argument against many Nigerian power-sharing proposals is that they actually seek merely to "share positions."[43] That is because they hardly address the need to decentralize powers and resources effectively, or to undercut the massive, oppressive, divisive, and destructive hegemony of the Nigerian central state apparatus. As Wole Soyinka eloquently puts it, "once the relations of the parts to one another and to the center are consensually and equitably rearranged, once the arbitrary dictatorship and interference of the center in areas of regional competence and developmental priorities is abrogated, it would not matter in the slightest what part of the nation produces the leadership at the top, or how frequently."[44] Anthony Enahoro basically makes the same crucial point: "What is required in Nigeria is to erect power-sharing configurations, including equitable monitoring structures, rather than a mere transfer from one zone to another of the power to corrupt and misapply the instruments and organs of power."[45]

All of this is not to say that the debates about power sharing in Nigeria amount to no more than an "empty sop" and a "bewildering distraction," as Soyinka claims.[46] Particularly because the center will continue to play an overriding role in the Nigerian federation, questions about the equitable interethnic composition of the federal government will remain of some great moment. Nevertheless, the debates about power sharing in Nigeria need to be salvaged from their current seeming shallowness, contentiousness, and fuzziness. For instance, much of the emotion surrounding and confusion over the most appropriate formulas for the geoethnic distribution of key political offices could be avoided if the issue were allowed to remain more within the realm of potentially flexible political party platforms rather than a matter for rigid constitutional prescription. This much was recognized by Justice Nikki Tobi's constitutional debate coordinating committee of 1998, which was "persuaded by the argument that rotation as a modality for the distribution of power among geopolitical zones in the country should be left to political parties to operationalize."[47]

Nigerian proposals for power sharing would also become far more viable if issues of power sharing (shared central rule) are frankly acknowledged to constitute only one out of three normative institutional pillars of federalism, the other two pillars involving questions of self-rule (subfederal autonomy) and limited rule (constitutionalism, the rule of law, and a reasonably marketized economy). Debates about power sharing at the center are impoverished when they give little or no consideration to these other fundamental conditions of multiethnic federal equity and stability.

Also, there seems to be considerable merit in condemning the zero-sum ethnopolitical calculations or outcomes associated with pure presidentialism in the Nigerian experience. Clearly, much interethnic envy, anxiety, recrimination, and suspicion have suffused the country's political debates with the perception that such a singularly pre-eminent position is in, or could fall into, the hands of a member of a competing ethnic or regional group. Moreover, given the inherent centralization of the Nigerian economy and the relative underdevelopment of the country's civil society, the powers of the executive presidency could give it such overwhelming institutional dominance as to engender strong personal rule and endanger the countervailing federalist processes of shared rule, self-rule, and limited rule. Thus, short of voting for a return to the Westminster-style parliamentary system, future constitutional negotiations in Nigeria would need to involve, or reinforce, institutions for restraining the enormous powers of the presidency, especially its power to control key regulatory institutions like the judiciary and the electoral, revenue allocation, and population census commissions.

TERRITORIAL RESTRUCTURING AND THE QUEST FOR ADEQUATE SELF-RULE

Proponents of territorial restructuring in Nigeria contend that the country's current multistate internal territorial structure is fundamentally defective. There are at least two radically different versions of this position.

Claiming that the states have become sources of economically wasteful administrative patronage and politically baneful state-consciousness, the first position calls for the replacement of the multistate federal system with a new territorial structure consisting of the central government and development-oriented localities only. This ostensibly developmentalist, but fundamentally unitarist, proposal has been canvassed not only by key elements within successive Nigerian military governments, but also by such respected independent public figures as Balarabe Musa, Jubril Aminu, Tekena Tamuno, Ukpabi Asika, and Ahmed Joda.[48]

Briefly, this position may be dismissed as fundamentally flawed. Among other inadequacies, it downplays the pathologies associated with the current Nigerian local government system; it detracts from the significant national consensus on the need for "true federalism" in the country; it appears to overlook the violent reactions that followed Aguiyi-Ironsi's flirtations with a unitary political framework in 1966; and it seems to be oblivious to the disastrous consequences of hyper-centralization in Nigeria's more recent history.

The following discussion of territorial restructuring will be devoted to the second, more popular, critique of Nigeria's current multistate territorial structure. This critique calls for a drastic reduction in the number of the Nigerian states through the consolidation of some of the more economically unviable or ethnopolitically superfluous states or through the aggregation of all the states into bigger zones or regions. There are obviously different, often complex and contradictory, strands of this second version of the argument for territorial restructuring in Nigeria. Broadly speaking, however, most proponents of this position call for the reconstitution of Nigeria into a balanced or loose federation, or even confederation, of between about six and ten geoethnic zones. In essence, while proponents of territorial restructuring often express some general commitment to a form of true federalism in the country, three tendencies are actually evident within the group: balanced federalist, loose federalist, and explicitly confederalist.

The case for a restructuring of Nigeria into a more balanced federation of bigger constituent units was articulated by Obasanjo in 1994 in the following terms:

> With the atomization of Nigeria by means of state creation almost to the point of rendering the constituent units prostrate, I find the concept of zones as the basis of our federation worth examining. At this stage of our development, we cannot abandon the federal system, but perhaps the federating units should be zones rather than the existing states. Each zone should be large enough to be viable, and [should be] made up of local governments. [Under this structure] we may be able to save costs on administration for development.[49]

Obasanjo's somewhat tentative support for restructuring, which he effectively abandoned on assuming the presidency of the federation in May 1999, may be carefully contrasted with Alex Ekwueme's more definitive advocacy of territorial reconfiguration as a blueprint for balanced federalism. According to Ekwueme,

> The federation as it existed at independence had only two major pitfalls;
> first, that one region was larger than the other two regions put together
> and, secondly, that each region had a majority ethnic group in control as
> well as minority ethnic groups which, quite naturally, felt threatened by
> the majority. Otherwise, the regions were large enough to function effec-
> tively and viably as constituent units in a federal structure.[50]

Alluding to growing official support for central power sharing on the basis of the six geographic zones, Ekwueme concluded that "what is now left is for the . . . zones to be nurtured to maturity and . . . transformed in due course to full-fledged regions which will be the federating units in a free, united, strong, prosperous, and stable Federal Republic of Nigeria anchored on equality, equity, justice, and fair play for all Nigerians irrespective of creed or ethnic origin."[51]

Yet, although obviously a liberal federalist, Ekwueme is sometimes associated with a more extremist or centrifugal Igbo campaign for territorial restructuring that involves proposals for the territorial regionalization of the armed forces, the police, and security services, as well as effective regional control of key economic resources or the full application of the derivation principle.[52] It is to the Yoruba leader, Chief Abraham Adesanya, that the analyst must turn for a succinct statement of the "loose federalist" position:

> We [the Yoruba leadership] support (the) widespread demands for the
> restructuring of Nigeria . . . into six or more zones or regions for admin-
> istrative and political purpose(s). We fully endorse proposals regarding
> the formation of zonal or regional armies as well as police. . . . Each . . .
> zonal army and police will have its own territorial command. Equally,
> the operational command of the joint territorial armies should devolve
> on a National Security Council to be constituted by the zones.[53]

Economically, advocates of loose federalism support the enthronement of derivation or the funding of the central authority by "agreed contributions" from the federating zones. As former senator Patrick Ani put it, "If Nigeria is a federation of six zones, . . . each zone would be in control of the funds in the zone, sharing revenue from such resources among [its] member states according to level of production and paying an agreed percentage in revenue to the federal government."[54] It is, therefore, the specific recommendation for the regionalization of the military structure, plus some assumption of virtual regional economic sovereignty, that distinguishes the proponents of "loose federalism" from the advocates of balanced federalism.

Unlike the confederalists, however, the proponents of "loose federalism" assume that their proposed arrangement is feasible within the framework of a single, united federal democratic republic. The confederalists, on the other hand, envisage the dissolution of the single Nigerian federation into a union of six or more federations. For instance, in 1992, the Movement for National Reformation (MNR), led by Anthony Enahoro, called for the transformation of Nigeria into eight ethnic-based federations:[55]

- ❖ Western federation—the Yoruba states of Lagos, Ogun, Oyo, Osun, Ondo, and Ekiti.
- ❖ South-Central federation—the ethnic minority–populated states of Edo and Delta (the former Mid-West Region).
- ❖ South-Eastern federation—the ethnic minority states of Akwa Ibom, Bayelsa, Cross River, and Rivers.
- ❖ East-Central federation—the Igbo states of Abia, Anambra, Ebonyi, Enugu, and Imo.
- ❖ Central federation—the ethnically mixed states of Bauchi, Benue, Kaduna, Plateau, and Nasarawa.
- ❖ West-Central federation—the lower Middle Belt states of Kwara, Kogi, and Niger.
- ❖ North-Eastern federation—the ethnically mixed states of Adamawa, Borno, Taraba, and Yobe.
- ❖ Northern federation—the Hausa-Fulani states of Jigawa, Kano, Katsina, Kebbi, Sokoto, and Zamfara.

As envisaged by the MNR, these federations would enshrine the rights of their ethnic or subethnic constituents to internal self-government, decentralize as many functions and responsibilities as possible to their constituent states, enjoy greater powers and resources than the union government, and participate equally in the affairs of the union government. The proposed confederal structure would presumably be instituted at a sovereign national conference, which would comprise representatives of all Nigerian nationalities and special interest groups. The MNR's agenda is broadly supported by such groups as the Ijaw National Congress, the Itsekiri Leaders of Thought, the Movement for the Survival of the Ogoni People, and several prominent political and opinion leaders in all the geographic zones of southern Nigeria.

While it appears to be manifestly more profound than the clamor for power sharing, the campaign for territorial restructuring often suffers basically from the same moral, analytical, and practical limitations associated with Nigerian power-sharing proposals. Above all, it enjoys practically no support in the northern half of the country. Yet the proposal seeks to restructure not only the states of the South but also those of the North into some big geoethnic zones. Basically, the idea of restructuring not only excites northern fears about a southern campaign to weaken or sever access by the North to the resources of the South but also seems to be violently incongruous with the much more complex ethnic composition of the northern region. Surprisingly, proponents of restructuring inadequately address the reasons behind this northern opposition.[56]

Also, it is quite obvious that proponents of territorial restructuring are neither speaking with the same voice nor sufficiently individually clear-minded about the political specificities or administrative logistics of a restructured Nigerian state. Rather, the clamor for restructuring is characterized by confusion or disagreement over such basic issues as the proposed number of regions or units in a restructured Nigeria; the specific geopolitical or ethnic configuration of such units; the position that the current states and localities would occupy in a restructured Nigeria; and the appropriate distribution of functions, powers, and resources among the governmental tiers of the reformed Nigerian union.

The Patriots, a group of some seventeen eminent southern Nigerians led by Chief Rotimi Williams, published a memorandum in January 2000 that sought to address a number of these issues. Yet the limitations of the group's approach were underscored by the exclusion of northerners from the body, by the swift repudiation of the group's proposals on resource and power distribution by at least one of its leading members, and by the self-acknowledged inconclusiveness of some of the proposals contained in the memorandum.[57] It is not sufficient to assume

that all gray areas will be resolved or clarified in a constitutional conference. It is simply unlikely that the majority of the Nigerian citizenry
would voluntarily embark upon a grandiose but analytically superficial
and potentially contentious program of territorial restructuring.[58]

Moreover, it is by no means certain that the ethnic, political, and
bureaucratic interests that have developed around the current structure
of states would consent to the dissolution of such states into bigger
zones or regions. Indeed, as P. C. Asiodu has observed, given the intense
rancor and competition that have accompanied recent reorganizations
of states and local boundaries in Nigeria, it is difficult to imagine any
"state that is ready to be suppressed in a region."[59] To be sure, these
state-based ethnopolitical and bureaucratic interests may be largely
politically manipulative and economically exploitative. Because these
interests can hardly be wished away, their potential opposition to
regionalization ought to be acknowledged and realistically addressed by
the proponents of restructuring.

In addition, it is quite unlikely that a territorial reconfiguration of
the Nigerian state on the scale being proposed by most supporters of
restructuring would preserve the positive impact of the initial multistate federal system in weakening the ethnoregional identities that
assailed the First Republic; in generating a more fluid, decentralized,
shifting, and crosscutting pattern of ethnic political alignments; and in
providing a viable federal authority as a potential focus of attraction for
the development of a common Nigerian identity and citizenship. In
short, the structural pathologies of state-proliferation and balkanization
in Nigeria should neither obscure the initial advantages of the multistate framework in the country nor lead to a revisionist romanticization
of the First Republic's regionalized—yet flawed—federal model.

Further, although largely designed to incorporate more ethnically
compatible or homogeneous populations, many of the new constituent
units being proposed for a restructured Nigerian union are actually culturally artificial and potentially politically controversial, especially the six-
region structure. Only three of the six proposed regions are significantly
ethnically homogeneous: the Yoruba South-West, the Igbo South-East,
and the Hausa-Fulani North-West. Yet the six-region arrangement would
still leave substantial Yoruba, Igbo, and Hausa-Fulani populations literal-
ly politically stranded in the Middle Belt, South-South, and North-East

zones, respectively. The arbitrariness of the six-region structure is further underscored by the classification of such cultural borderline northern states like Kaduna, Taraba, and Kwara into zones with which significant sections of the populations in these states can hardly identify. In the South, groups like the Ijaws (who have consistently pushed for a separate, homogeneous Ijaw zone) and the Edos have explicitly opposed their inclusion in the South-South zone, calling instead for the fragmentation of the zone into two or more regions.[60] Virtually the same contradictions are inherent in the MNR's proposed eight-unit Nigerian union. Quite instructively the MNR itself has often vacillated between its original support for an eight-unit arrangement and intermittent endorsement of the six-region scheme.[61]

All of these objections would tend to underscore the limitations of constructing the constituent units of a multiethnic union on explicitly ethnic grounds. Rather, reality speaks to the wisdom of adopting more consciously and consistently ethnically flexible or mixed solutions. In other words, because it is largely impossible to erect ethnically discrete internal boundaries in a multiethnic union, it is unwise and dangerous to adopt formulas that make ethnicity the sole or primary basis for defining the internal configuration of the union.[62]

For the many who are committed to the vision of a strong and united Nigerian state-nation, a scheme for zonal or regional territorial restructuring would appear undesirable as it could reinforce or inflame the deep, centrifugal tensions inherent in Nigeria's ethnic fragmentation. The ultimate result, in their view, could be the violent dissolution of the Nigerian entity. Thus in 1996, the radical Northern Elements Progressive Union–PRP political group denounced proposals for "restructuring" as a formula for "balkanizing Nigeria into a confederation of ethnic republics, which will lead to national disintegration and protracted civil wars and all forms of chronic, violent and destructive ethnic, subethnic, communal, and religious conflicts."[63] Similarly, Alex Ekwueme has alluded to the manner in which the campaign to enshrine the six-region arrangement in the 1995 draft constitution was stymied by the "scare, alarm, panic, and unease" that was created at the 1994–95 NCC by those who believed that "this truly federal proposal amounted to confederation, and that confederation was the first stage to the dismemberment of Nigeria."[64]

Yet one more flaw in the argument for territorial restructuring as a blueprint for genuine self-governance in Nigeria is the proposition's complete neglect of what arguably should be the quintessential element in any effort to reform the country's structure of governance and self-rule: the empowerment of grassroots, self-help institutions at home-town, district, village, or local community levels. Known variously as community development associations, town unions, improvement leagues, progressive associations, or descendants' unions, these institu-tions constitute the primary organ of collective action in many of Nigeria's estimated 90,000 basic, primary, or autonomous communi-ties.[65] To varying degrees of success, these fundamental institutions have fulfilled several roles, including nurturing a structure of civil soci-ety at the grassroots, the planning and delivery of social welfare (espe-cially through the construction of schools, hospitals, markets, commu-nity halls, parking lots, and roads), the enforcement of public account-ability, the promotion of linkages between the local communities and governmental and international institutions, and the encouragement of a civic sense of community identity, solidarity, and pride.[66] Yet Jane Guyer has highlighted the limitations of these institutions in "collective endeavors beyond a certain scale, and the danger and futility of self-help for kinds of enterprises that cannot do without expertise and access to corporate financing."[67] What is more, these grassroots associ-ations have also been implicated in violent intercommunal boundary disputes and other forms of subethnic conflicts.[68]

Nevertheless, community-level institutions have one important advantage over the current states and local government units, both of which have been created and sustained largely by the central state appa-ratus. These institutions have remained self-defining, self-regulating, and substantially self-financing in the best tradition of self-rule. Several studies attest to the ubiquity, flexibility, and vitality of these institutions as "a potent force for mobilizing local resources to meet specific needs."[69] Clearly, these basic communities (and not the more recently "imagined" and often structurally weak local government, state, ethnic, or regional units) constitute the foundational constituents of the Nigerian state.

If such entities can be explicitly empowered and recognized con-stitutionally as an informal, nonpartisan tier of the federal system and financially strengthened with guaranteed matching grants from the federal revenue-sharing system, community-level institutions can help to enhance the authenticity (or "rootedness"), viability, and vitality of the Nigerian system of federalism. Along with the local, state, regional (zonal), and central tiers of the Nigerian federation, the community-level units can serve to nurture and sustain the institutional flexibility, diversity, and creativity necessary to sustain a dynamic federal system.

In sum, the only real value in the proposals for regional restructuring in Nigeria appears to lie in (1) the opportunities that broad regional groupings of states can provide as an additional (and distinctively horizontal) axis of intergovernmental collaboration or interactions; (2) the specific possibility that such intergovernmental relations could lead to the establishment of joint interstate services or ventures, especially where individual state initiatives may be impossible, unviable, or unprofitable; and (3) the flexibility that bigger regions or zones, especially the relatively popular six-region format, can offer as the basis for reflecting the federal character "when it is unreasonable or impossible to mandate the representation of every state."[70]

RECONSTRUCTING THE DEMOCRATIC BASIS OF NIGERIAN FEDERALISM

The excesses of the military rulers who governed Nigeria from 1984 to 1999 effectively shattered the intellectually fashionable illusions regarding the ability of the Nigerian military to sustain a functioning federal system. The repressive hypercentralization of that era not only put federalism virtually in abeyance until the military's departure in May 1999 but also bequeathed a problematic institutional legacy for the succeeding federal democratic dispensation. Nigeria thus entered its Fourth Republic with some profound institutional dilemmas that were either created, exacerbated, or left unresolved by the preceding military regime. The military's perverse political legacy for the Fourth Republic included such institutional pathologies as a zero-sum presidential system, a vulnerable electoral process, a tainted judiciary, and, most important, an imposed and potentially contentious constitution.

The rise of significant pressures in Nigeria for the abandonment or modification of the country's American-style presidential system has been noted. While retaining the presidential system, for instance, the 1995 draft constitution contained such significant departures from the American model as the provisions for the regional rotation of the presidency, for a system of multiple vice presidents, for nonsuccessive presidential terms, and for a federal executive (ministerial) cabinet that should be selected predominantly from, and that would continue to sit in, the National Assembly.[71] Yet, despite its own occasional flirtations with the idea of a mixed presidential-parliamentary system, the Nigerian military establishment has generally resisted civilian pressures and proposals for the discontinuation of the pure presidential system. Instead, it has promoted a strong executive presidency as an antidote to Nigeria's ethnic fragmentation. Arguably, the basic problem here is not with presidentialism per se, but with the military's authoritarian prevention of all opportunity for the open democratic contestation, revalidation, modification, or adaptation of this basic institutional choice.

A similar authoritarian imposition in the name of national integration involves the requirements for the registration and operation of political parties in Nigeria. Beginning with those of the Second Republic, Nigerian political associations have been required to fulfill certain constitutional conditions before they can function as political parties. The most important of these conditions include registration by the national electoral agency; a membership that is open to every Nigerian citizen, irrespective of religion or ethnic grouping; a governing body or executive committee that includes members from at least two-thirds of the states in the federation and the Federal Capital Territory; the absence of any sectional (religious, ethnic, geographical) connotation in the name, emblem, or motto of the association; and the location of the headquarters of the association in the capital of the federation.[72] However, as if these general constitutional provisions are not restrictive enough, successive "democratizing" military administrations imposed additional conditions on party formation.

The most bizarre regulation was imposed by the Babangida government, which constitutionally restricted electoral competition to only two government-designated and state-funded political parties.[73] While avoiding the democratic aberration of a mandatory two-party system, both the Abacha and Abubakar administrations imposed novel conditions of their own. The Abacha government required each prospective political party to establish offices in two-thirds of the local councils in each state of the federation, to enlist at least 40,000 members in each state, and to recruit not fewer than 10,000 members in the Federal Capital Territory.[74] Under the Abubakar regime, political associations were required to win at least 10 (later reduced to 5) percent of the votes in national local government polls in each of at least two-thirds of the states in the federation, and in the FCT, to qualify for permanent registration.[75]

For critics, the tight regulation of party formation in Nigeria is both antidemocratic and antifederalist: It negates the freedom of individuals to associate freely and effectively in partisan associations and denies autonomous political expression to legitimate ethnoterritorial or local interests.[76] Yet the more fundamental problem with the regulation of party formation in Nigeria lies not so much in the restriction of democratic choice or interest articulation, but in the evident structural artificiality and fragility of the parties so regulated, as well as the opportunity the regulatory process has often offered for the arbitrary control and undemocratic manipulation of party registration procedures by the party licensing authority—namely, the national electoral agency.

In a fundamental sense, the official promotion of both presidentialism and a regulated party system as integrative devices in Nigeria evokes a broader intellectual discourse over the appropriateness of integrative, as distinct from accommodative, institutions in divided societies.[77] In essence, while integrative institutions seek to transcend or overcome the fault lines of a divided society, accommodative institutions seek to recognize and conciliate such divisions explicitly. Comparative experience suggests that to avoid destructive sectional conflicts, divided societies must maintain a delicate and endogenously apt balance between integrative and accommodative institutions or processes. Consequently, the path to a viable party system in Nigeria probably lies in both the retention of the initial general constitutional provisions for the formation of nonsectarian national political parties and the abandonment of the democratically abusive accretions to these provisions from the Babangida, Abacha, and Abubakar political transition programs.

One of the more compelling reasons for a relatively regulated party system in Nigeria concerns the need to maintain a manageable and stable electoral process. The capacity to conduct free and fair elections may seem to be the most mundane or elementary of democratic tasks, but in Nigeria the endemic failure of the electoral process is perhaps the most urgent threat to the country's federal democratic political development. This is how historian J. F. Ade-Ajayi describes the dilemma:

> The clearest evidence of our failure to nurture the Nigerian nation . . . [and] the essence of the national question . . . is that we cannot conduct a free and fair election. . . . Unless we have enough feeling of community to be able to choose lawmakers and rulers who represent our wishes, and therefore command our loyalty and voluntary consent, and to be able to change rulers who no longer enjoy that loyalty, we will not be able to achieve stability or legitimacy, and development will remain elusive.[78]

Essentially, Nigerian elections have been corrupt, violent, and chaotic. These "elections," as former governor Chukwuemeka Ezeife put it, "test the differential availability of resources to the competitors and not, at all, the preferences of the electorate."[79] Thus, far from serving to renew the Nigerian federal democratic process, elections have often precipitated its collapse. Astute observers recognize this electoral incapacity to be a deep-rooted, structural—rather than primarily administrative—problem. It derives significantly from the enormous socioeconomic premium on political office in Nigeria, from a reactionary elite mentality that perceives and pursues elections as a competition for the control of the electoral machinery and not for popular support, and from the fragility of civil society and other independent institutions of political restraint.[80]

Nevertheless, Akin Mabogunje has outlined a number of basic institutional reforms for securing electoral rectitude in Nigeria: (1) making the delimitation of wards and polling districts a matter of easy and publicly accessible knowledge; (2) designating a permanent public site as the polling station in each polling district or neighborhood; (3) exhibiting on a permanent basis the names of eligible voters in each polling district; (4) massively involving residents of each polling district in certifying all legitimate (registered and resident) voters in the respective districts; (5) organizing voter registration as a scheme for updating the voters list and not as an excuse for the repeated compilation of entirely new, and invariably freshly inflated or manipulated, voters lists; (6) entrenching the tradition of announcing electoral results at local collation stations in order to prevent the "centralized rigging of (election) results"; (7) immediately implementing the long-planned national identity-card scheme to provide a basis for verifying the authenticity of voters lists; and (8) using more regularly the electoral process for decision making, especially at the local level, to entrench the notion of free and fair elections in the mass political culture.[81] These reforms could, of course, be greatly facilitated through continued international involvement in exercising independent external oversight of the electoral process, in improving or enhancing the logistics or techniques of the process, and in collaborating with domestic election monitors.

An important course of electoral reform could involve the appointment of the national electoral agency by a nonpartisan oversight agency, rather than by the incumbent executive president, who invariably has a personal political stake in the activities of the electoral commission.[82] Nigeria could also mediate the perverse, zero-sum outcomes associated with its simple-plurality electoral system through the residual application of some form of proportional representation. Such an electoral system could be designed to ensure complete proportionality in the partisan distribution of national and state legislative seats through the "topping off" of representation in the legislature by drawing "from each party's best losers within the various constituencies."[83] Ultimately, however, even when all other forces and factors falter, an independent and competent judiciary can play a crucial, final role in enforcing electoral rectitude. What is more, the judiciary is indispensable to the resolution of such other potentially intractable conflicts as the disputes, since May 1999, over the application of Shari'a law and the scope of the economic and political rights of the states.

Yet the Nigerian judiciary, although it includes a number of competent and independent judges, has been broadly victimized by both civilian chicanery and military misrule. Under the military, in particular, the Nigerian judiciary was tamed and tainted by executive decrees that precluded judicial review of military laws and actions, blunt authoritarian intimidation, corrupt inducement, ethnopolitical manipulations, and financial strangulation. Under both civilian and military regimes, the independence of the judiciary has also been gravely undermined by considerable executive control of the funding and appointment of the judicial branch. Thus, perhaps more than any other institution in Nigeria, the judiciary ought to be effectively shielded from partisan control. Only then can this branch undertake success-fully the indispensable "umpiring" and "enforcing" roles that the judi-ciary (especially the supreme or constitutional court) plays in all feder-ations. Significantly, this outcome may be greatly facilitated by the work of the National Judicial Council, which was established under the 1999 Constitution to recommend and supervise (admittedly in a rather centralizing manner) the appointment and funding of the judi-ciary at all levels in Nigeria.

An underlying source of the fragility of Nigeria's democratic insti-tutions is the country's flawed constitution-making procedure. Nigeria's constitutions generally, and the postindependence constitutional frameworks particularly, have hardly involved an active, extensive, effective, or decisive—in short, sovereign—role in constitution making for the whole of the Nigerian citizenry and for the constituent units of the federation. Instead, the Nigerian military authorities, in particular, effectively dictated or dominated the process of constitution making by unilaterally selecting members of constitutional review or drafting committees, by manipulating or diluting the composition of elected constituent assemblies, by excluding certain institutional questions ("no-go areas") from the purview of open constitutional debate, by sub-stituting institutional preferences of their own for more widely sup-ported options, and by exercising the right to edit, amend, ratify, and, ultimately, promulgate the Nigerian constitutions. In essence, Nigerians have hardly had an opportunity to debate and decide freely their country's constitutional future.[84]

Consequently, pressures have persisted in Nigeria for the introduc-tion of significant amendments to the constitutional framework inherit-ed from the military. Other Nigerians demand a fresh constitution-making process that would involve the widest and freest consultation, negotiations, and participation possible. The process would preferably culminate in the ratification of the final constitutional product in a pop-ular referendum. For other Nigerians, however, the solution to Nigeria's constitutional problems lies not in a renewed constitution-making proc-ess but in a full-fledged sovereign national conference that would con-sider and resolve the whole gamut of issues concerning Nigeria's political future, including the legitimacy of the Nigerian union and strategies for its possible reconstruction or dissolution.

CAN THE NIGERIAN FEDERATION SURVIVE?

In a 1991 speech, Anthony Enahoro posed some probing and sobering questions:

> Can Nigeria survive as one country? Should it survive as one country? If it does so survive, will federalism survive? If federalism does survive, will democracy . . . survive? Can the component groups of Nigeria secure for themselves an honourable and equitable share of power and of the nation's resources?[85]

To reiterate, the pathologies of the Nigerian federation have engendered not only a national preoccupation with the agenda of federal reform, but also significant doubts about the viability of the federation and periodic calls for its confederalization or amicable dissolution. In 1981, for example, Hezekiah Oluwasanmi, a Yoruba and former university professor and vice chancellor, queried: "Do the constitutional arrangements we have essayed to wear since Independence fit the Nigerian reality? Can we run an essentially confederal state as a unitary or federal entity without the turbulence and instability that have afflicted us for the past twenty years?"[86]

For Ola Oni, an erstwhile Marxist scholar and activist who subsequently became leader of the ethnic Yoruba movement Apapo Omo Oduduwa, confederation indeed represents the best option for Nigeria. In his words: "Given the population . . . [of] the various [Nigerian] nationalities, our analysis has convinced us that it is a confederal union that can best eliminate ethnic domination and ethnic conflicts in our politics . . . and not any form of federalism, whether it is a true federalism or not."[87]

In calling for the reconstitution of Nigeria into a six-unit confederation, Chike Obi, an Igbo and Nigeria's pioneering professor of mathematics, was blunt enough to admit that this option would effectively mean the dissolution of the Nigerian state. "Left to me," Obi declared, "I would say let the Yoruba be an independent country. I am sure they will succeed. If the Yoruba become independent, the others must follow."[88]

In 1994, prominent leaders of the minority South-South zone dismissed the Nigerian federation as unworkable and inequitable, and demanded "a federation of Akwa Ibom, Cross River, Delta, Edo, and

Rivers States, where we can control our resources and destiny, and enjoy a sense of belonging and brotherhood."[89] And even the Council of Ulama in northern Nigeria's Zaria has argued that "if a proper federal arrangement, with full recognition of Muslim rights to apply Shari'a law in Muslim states . . . is not implementable, then the only workable alternative in our circumstances is a confederation."[90] At least two noted external academic observers have also expressed skepticism about the viability of the Nigerian federation. While Max Frenkel surmises that "politically, Nigeria would be more stable if it were split into two or three federations," Jeffrey Herbst simply asks, "Is Nigeria a viable state?"[91]

All things considered, a federal solution seems to remain the most feasible, peaceable, and acceptable, although by no means inevitable, option for Nigeria. In the first place, despite significant and growing voices of dissent, a federal solution still appears to remain the choice of an overwhelming majority of Nigerians. This conclusion is supported by the findings of various panels and commissions that indicate a significant national consensus behind federalism in Nigeria. For these Nigerians, federalism seems to represent the pragmatic compromise, or the sensible middle-ground, between the contending pulls of diversity and unity in the country. Indeed, despite the intensity of Nigeria's ethnic fragmentation, the country is also profoundly united by age-old commercial and cultural links among the various ethnicities, by a shared colonial and postcolonial political history, by the poignant lessons of the "war of national unity," and by "an undeniable economic interdependence."[92] Consequently, federalism seems to respond best to the paradoxical reality of Nigeria as a "country that can seemingly never be united nor divided," in the words of Adekeye Adebajo.[93]

Second, because federalism has never really been truly practiced in Nigeria, the federal solution can hardly be said to have foundered in the country. Rather, the enormous opportunities and creative possibilities of federalism have been squandered by the country's succession of abusive or repressive civilian and military leaders. With a more imaginative political leadership that is willing to learn from the accumulated lessons of past political mistakes, the federal solution may yet thrive in Nigeria.

Third, proponents of confederation and other alternatives to federation have not demonstrated that these options in Nigeria are intrinsically superior to, or practically more viable than, the federal framework. Instead, they have often proffered fuzzy, contradictory, unrealistic, or deeply contentious strategies or "solutions" that would compound the country's political problems.

Fourth, given Nigeria's ethnic complexity—and, indeed, the tragic enormity of the Biafran adventure—it is unlikely that a peaceable formula can be crafted for the confederalization or dissolution of the Nigerian entity. Rather, a scheme to unscramble Nigeria would be riddled with intractable conflict over competing ethnoterritorial claims and would also invite stiff and violent resistance from pro-Nigerian forces.

Fifth, and finally, on purely moral and intellectual grounds, the challenges of nurturing a multiethnic Nigerian union via federalism are far more humanistic, edifying, or elevating than the parochial struggles for ethnic secessionism. Federalism, of course, does not repudiate the principle of ethnic self-determination; it simply seeks to accommodate, mediate, or moderate the principle within a broader, civic political framework that combines self-rule (self-determination) with shared rule and limited rule. For the federalist, the repudiation of ethnicity is as unwise and dangerous as its deliberate elevation above all other principles of social organization and interaction, including multiculturalism, liberalism, and constitutionalism. If the Nigerian federation survives and succeeds, it could provide for multiethnic countries in Africa and beyond a model of how a developing society can sustain some modicum of constitutional governance or "civicness" amidst the dilemmas of ethnic fragmentation and competition.

CONCLUSIONS

The multifaceted crisis of Nigerian federalism is reflected in the ongoing melee over the intergovernmental distribution of constitutional responsibilities and economic resources, the sharing of federal political power among ethnic blocs of the population, the internal territorial configuration of the federation, the democratic institutions of the federal system, and the very legitimacy or sustainability of the Nigerian federal union. Undoubtedly, these conflicts have been greatly exacerbated by the irregularities associated with the prolonged domination of the Nigerian political system by centralizing military juntas.

Yet underlying and complicating the contemporary crisis of the

Nigerian state is the institutionalization of a largely distributive, and invariably deeply conflictive, system of federalism. In other words, the federal institutional structure in Nigeria serves primarily to process the struggles among diverse governments and segments for access to centrally controlled resources and opportunities. The core chapters of this work (chapters 3 through 6) were devoted to the narration and explication of the processes associated with these distributive struggles in the four arenas of revenue allocation, territorial demarcations, application of the "federal character" principle, and population enumeration. To reiterate, the "boomerang effects" of this distributive federalism are largely reflected in the current angst in Nigeria over intergovernmental overcentralization, geoethnic marginalization, the structural deformation of the federation, and the presumed failure of federalism.[94]

If the primary logic of a federal system is simply to sustain a process of centralized cake sharing, then such a system is unlikely to develop the civility, flexibility, and creativity associated with a functioning, noncentralized political order. On the contrary, the system will be prone to coercion, corruption, and manipulation by the central authorities; to divisive and destructive sectional struggles to control the patronage-oriented central-state apparatus; to the imposition of authoritarian solutions as a means to regulate the turbulence of raw distributive politics; and to profound and palpable frustrations about the perceived iniquities or inequities of the overpoliticized and overcentralized distributive process.

Nigeria may never overcome the pathologies that vex its federal system until it begins to utilize federalism not as a mechanism for processing the allocative conflicts of a fundamentally overcentralized state but as an instrument for promoting genuine institutions and processes of self-rule, shared rule, and limited rule in both the polity and the economy.

Although there may be no better alternative to federalism in Nigeria, the challenges involved in overcoming the pathologies of the country's federal system are truly enormous. Beyond the ongoing debates about the operational failings and institutional deficiencies of their country's federal system, Nigerians must begin to redress the underlying structural pressures that have reduced Nigerian federalism into a source of perverse, distributive contention rather than a vehicle for regenerative, rule-based governance.

NOTES

CHAPTER 1: INTRODUCTION

1. Daniel Elazar, "Federalism and Consociational Regimes," *Publius: The Journal of Federalism* 15, no. 2 (1985): 33.

2. See, for instance, John P. Mackintosh, "Federalism in Nigeria," *Political Studies* 10, no. 3 (1962): 223–242; and Eghosa E. Osaghae, "The Status of State Governments in Nigeria's Federalism," *Publius: The Journal of Federalism* 22, no. 3 (1992): 181–200.

3. Ivo Duchacek, "State Constitutional Law in Comparative Perspective," *Annals* 496 (1988): 134.

4. Donald Horowitz, "Democracy in Divided Societies," *Journal of Democracy* 4, no. 4 (1993): 37.

5. Larry Diamond, "Nigeria: Pluralism, Statism, and the Struggle for Democracy," in *Democracy in Developing Countries: Africa,* ed. Larry Diamond, Juan Linz, and S. M. Lipset (Boulder, Colo.: Lynne Rienner, 1988), 65; and Daniel Elazar, *Exploring Federalism* (Tuscaloosa: University of Alabama Press, 1987), 241.

6. Lawrence Rupley, "Revenue Sharing in the Nigerian Federation," *The Journal of Modern African Studies* 19, no. 2 (1981): 275.

7. See Gavin Williams, *State and Society in Nigeria* (Idanre, Nigeria: Afrografika, 1980), 100.

8. Mackintosh, "Federalism in Nigeria," 223.

9. James Barber, "South Africa: The Search for Identity," *International Affairs* 70, no. 1 (1994): 73.

10. Crawford Young, "Patterns of Social Conflict: State, Class and Ethnicity," *Daedalus* 3, no. 2 (1982): 73; and Larry Diamond, "Issues in the Constitutional Design of a Third Nigerian Republic," *African Affairs* 86, no. 343 (1987): 212.

11. Arend Lijphart, *Democracy in Plural Societies: A Comparative Exploration* (New Haven, Conn.: Yale University Press, 1977), 164.

12. Donald Rothchild, "An Interactive Model for State-Ethnic Relations," in *Conflict Resolution in Africa,* ed. Francis M. Deng and I. William Zartman (Washington, D.C.: Brookings Institution, 1991), 39.

13. See John Paden, "National System Development and Conflict Resolution in Nigeria," in *Conflict and Peacemaking in Multiethnic Societies,* ed. Joseph V. Montville (Lexington, Mass.: Lexington Books, 1990), 421.

14. Daniel Elazar, "International and Comparative Federalism," *Political Science and Politics* 26, no. 2 (1993): 194.

15. Robert L. Hardgrave, "India: The Dilemmas of Diversity," *Journal of Democracy* 4, no. 4 (1993): 55.

16. See Ronald Watts, "West German Federalism: Comparative Perspectives," in *German Federalism Today*, ed. Charlie Jeffrey and Peter Javigear (New York: St. Martin's, 1991), 25.

17. Charles Tarlton, "Symmetry and Asymmetry as Elements of Federalism: A Theoretical Speculation," *The Journal of Politics* 27, no. 4 (1965): 861–74; Eric Nordlinger, *Conflict Resolution in Divided Societies* (Cambridge, Mass.: Harvard University, Center for International Affairs, 1972).

18. Elazar, *Exploring Federalism,* 253.

19. Ibid., 77–78.

20. Adele Jinadu, "The Constitutional Situation of the Nigerian States," *Publius: The Journal of Federalism* 12, no. 1 (1982): 159.

21. Henry Bienen, *Political Conflict and Economic Change in Nigeria* (London: Frank Cass, 1985), 2; Henry Bienen, "The Politics of Income Distribution: Institutions, Class and Ethnicity," in *The Political Economy of Income Distribution in Nigeria,* ed. Henry Bienen and V. P. Diejomaoh (New York: Holmes and Meier, 1981), 162.

22. Tom Forrest, *Politics and Economic Development in Nigeria* (Boulder, Colo.: Westview, 1993), 69.

23. Ibid., 2.

24. James R. Scarritt, "Communal Conflict and Contention for Power in Africa South of the Sahara," in Ted Robert Gurr, *Minorities at Risk: A Global View of Ethnopolitical Conflicts* (Washington D.C.: United States Institute of Peace Press, 1993), 286.

25. Goran Hyden, "Reciprocity and Governance in Africa," in *The Failure of* *the Centralized State: Institutions and Self-Governance in Africa,* ed. James S. Wunsch and Dele Olowu (Boulder, Colo.: Westview, 1990), 264–65.

26. Rothchild, "An Interactive Model," 193–97.

27. Ibid., 198.

28. Daniel Bach, "Managing a Plural Society: The Boomerang Effects of Nigerian Federalism," *Journal of Commonwealth and Comparative Politics* 27, no. 2 (1989): 218–45.

29. *Daily Times* (Lagos), January 22, 1993, 1, 12.

30. "Text of 1992 Budget Address by President Babangida," *National Concord* (Lagos), January 1, 1992, iii.

31. Claude Ake, "Points of Departure," *Nigerian Tribune* (Ibadan), December 17, 1992.

32. Kenneth D. McRae, "Canada: Reflections on Two Conflicts," in Montville, ed., *Conflict and Peacemaking in Multiethnic Societies,* 212.

33. Izoma P. C. Asiodu, "The Political Economy of Fiscal Federalism," *Daily Times* (Lagos), February 19, 1993, 19, 36.

34. See Richard Joseph, "Class, State, and Prebendal Politics in Nigeria," *Journal of Commonwealth and Comparative Politics* 21, no. 3 (1983): 32.

35. See, in particular, Diamond, "Issues in the Constitutional Design," 210.

36. Douglas Rimmer, "The Overvalued Currency and Overadministered Economy of Nigeria," *African Affairs* 84, no. 336 (1985): 444.

37. Ronald May, "Decision-Making and Stability in Federal Systems," *Canadian Journal of Political Science* 3, no. 1 (1970): 87.

38. Larry Diamond, "Ethnicity and Ethnic Conflict," *The Journal of Modern African Studies* 25, no. 1 (1987): 123.

39. Richard Joseph, *Democracy and Prebendal Politics in Nigeria: The Rise and Fall of the Second Republic* (New York: Cambridge University Press, 1987), 4.

40. Asiodu, "The Political Economy of Fiscal Federalism," 36.

41. T. M. Yesufu, "The Politics and Economics of Nigeria's Population Census," in *The Population of Tropical Africa,* ed. J. C. Caldwell and C. Okonjo (London: Longman, 1968), 106.

42. Martin Dent, "Federalism in Africa, with special reference to Nigeria," in *Federalism and Nationalism,* ed. Murray Forsyth (New York: St. Martin's, 1989), 197.

43. Elazar, "International and Comparative Federalism," 193.

44. Elazar, *Exploring Federalism,* 170–71; Dean E. McHenry, "Stability of the Federal System in Nigeria: Elite Attitudes at the Constituent Assembly toward the Creation of New States," *Publius: The Journal of Federalism* 16, no. 2 (1986): 91.

45. Diamond, "Issues in the Constitutional Design," 211.

46. Ibid., 212.

47. Ladipo Adamolekun and John Kincaid, "The Federal Solution: Assessment and Prognosis for Nigeria and Africa," *Publius: The Journal of Federalism* 21, no. 4 (1991): 178.

48. See Paul Beckett, "Elections and Democracy in Nigeria," in Fred M. Hayward, *Elections in Independent Africa* (Boulder, Colo.: Westview, 1987), 95; and Richard L. Sklar, "Democracy in Africa," in *African Politics and Problems in Development*, ed. Richard L. Sklar and C. S. Whitaker (Boulder, Colo.: Lynne Rienner, 1991), 251.

CHAPTER 2: THE EVOLUTION OF THE NIGERIAN FEDERATION

1. See William D. Graf, *The Nigerian State: Political Economy, State Class and Political System in the Post-Colonial Era* (London: James Currey, 1988), 17.

2. Elazar, *Exploring Federalism,* 77; and R. L. Watts, *New Federations: Experiments in the Commonwealth* (New York: Oxford University Press, 1966), 27.

3. See Graf, *The Nigerian State,* 5; and S. E. Oyovbaire, *Federalism in Nigeria: A Study in the Development of the Nigerian State* (London: Macmillan, 1985), 29.

4. See, in particular, Adiele E. Afigbo, "Background to Nigerian Federalism: Federal Features in the Colonial State," *Publius: The Journal of Federalism* 21, no. 4 (1991): 13–29; Uma O. Eleazu, *Federalism and Nation-Building: The Nigerian Experience 1945–1964* (Devon, UK: Arthur Stockwell, 1977); and S. E. Oyovbaire, "Structural Change and Political Processes in Nigeria," *African Affairs* 82, no. 326 (1983): 8.

5. See A. H. Birch, "Approaches to the Study of Federalism," *Political Studies* 14, no. 1 (1966): 23.

6. As cited in Jide Osuntokun, "The Historical Background of Nigerian Federalism," in *Readings on Federalism,* ed. A. B. Akinyemi, P. D. Cole, and Walter Ofonagoro (Lagos: Nigerian Institute of International Affairs, 1979), 99.

7. See R. E. Wraith, "Local Government," in J. P. Mackintosh, *Nigerian Government and Politics* (London: Allen and Unwin, 1966), 202; and J. A. Ballard, "Administrative Origins of Nigerian Federalism," *African Affairs* 70, no. 281 (1971): 335.

8. Graf, *The Nigerian State,* 7.

9. Frederick A. O. Schwarz, *Nigeria: The Tribes, The Nation or The Race: The Politics of Independence* (Cambridge, Mass.: MIT Press, 1965), 34.

10. See *Nigeria: Report of the Commission Appointed to Enquire into the Fears of Minorities and the Means of Allaying Them* (London: HMSO, 1958), 1.

11. See Watts, *New Federations,* 85.

12. See Afigbo, "Background To Nigerian Federalism," 15; and Oyovbaire, "Structural Change and Political Processes in Nigeria," 9.

13. Ladipo Adamolekun and Bamidele Ayo, "The Evolution of the Nigerian Federal Administration System," *Publius: The Journal of Federalism* 19, no. 1 (1989): 157.

14. Eme Awa, *Federal Government in Nigeria* (Berkeley: University of California Press, 1964), 48.

15. Billy Dudley, "Federalism and the Balance of Political Power in Nigeria," *Journal of Commonwealth Political Studies* 4, no. 1 (1966): 16–17. The "Wheare model" of federalism refers to the ideal system of federation, in which central and regional governments would be "coordinate and independent" in both constitutional design and political practice. The formulation is that of Kenneth C. Wheare in his classic treatise *Federal Government* (New York: Oxford University Press, 1964). This "dualistic" model of federalism is often contrasted with the more centripetal, or center-dominated, systems that have been instituted in most colonially created or developing federations. However, many Third World scholars consider the Wheare model not only politically impossible or undesirable in the developing world but also an inaccurate depiction of the evolution and operation of the American, Swiss, or any other classical federation; see Akinyemi, Cole, and Ofonagoro, eds., *Readings on Federalism.*

16. Mackintosh, "Federalism In Nigeria," 226–27; Kalu Ezera, *Constitutional Developments in Nigeria* (New York: Cambridge University Press, 1964), 266–69.

17. Dudley, "Federalism and the Balance of Political Power," 19.

18. Mackintosh, "Federalism in Nigeria," 240.

19. Mackintosh, *Nigerian Government and Politics,* 68.

20. Mackintosh, "Federalism in Nigeria," 238.

21. C. S. Whitaker, "Second Beginnings: The New Political Framework," *Issue* 2, no. 1/2 (1981): 4.

22. Dudley, "Federalism and the Balance of Political Power," 21.

23. Larry Diamond, "Class, Ethnicity, and the Democratic State: Nigeria, 1950–1966," *Comparative Studies in Society and History* 25, no. 3 (1983): 474.

24. Dudley, "Federalism and the Balance of Political Power," 21–22.

25. Kenneth Post and Michael Vickers, *Structure and Conflict in Nigeria, 1960–1966* (London: Heinemann, 1973), 200.

26. Richard Sklar, "Nigerian Politics: The Ordeal of Chief Awolowo," in Sklar and Whitaker, eds., *African Politics and Problems in Development,* 146.

27. Larry Diamond, "Nigeria: Pluralism, Statism, and the Struggle for Democracy," in Diamond, Linz, and Lipset, eds., *Democracy in Developing Countries: Africa,* 40.

28. See, for instance, Adewale Ademoyega, *Why We Struck: The Story of the First Nigerian Coup* (Ibadan, Nigeria: Evans Brothers, 1981), 67–68; compare with Ben Gbulie, *Nigeria's Five Majors* (Onitsha, Nigeria: Africana, 1981), 38–41.

29. See J. Isawa Elaigwu, "The Military and State Building: Federal-State Relations in Nigeria's Military Federalism 1966–1976," in Akinyemi, Cole, and Ofonagoro,, eds., *Readings on Federalism*, 161; and Oyovbaire, *Federalism in Nigeria*, 110–111.

30. J. Isawa Elaigwu, "Nigerian Federalism Under Civilian and Military Regimes," *Publius: The Journal of Federalism* 18, no. 1 (1988): 183.

31. See, for instance, Richard Joseph, "Principles and Practices of Nigerian Military Government," in *The Military in African Politics*, ed. John W. Harbeson (New York: Praeger, 1987), 71.

32. Rupley, "Revenue Sharing," 257.

33. Ibid., 257–77.

34. See Alex Gboyega, *Political Values and Local Government in Nigeria* (Lagos: Malthouse Press, 1987).

35. See Keith Panter-Brick, "Nigeria and the Uncertainties of Pluralism," in *Three Faces of Pluralism*, ed. Stanislaw Ehrlich and Graham Wootton (Westmead, UK: Gower Publishing Company, 1980), 273; see also Whitaker, "Second Beginnings," 6.

36. Whitaker, "Second Beginnings," 10.

37. Michael Joye and Kingsley Igweike, *Introduction to the 1979 Nigerian Constitution* (London: Macmillan, 1982), 94.

38. See Federal Republic of Nigeria, *Proceedings of the Constituent Assembly* (Lagos: Federal Ministry of Information, 1978), 49, 509; see also Lijphart, *Democracy in Plural Societies*, 33.

39. See "Address by the Head of State at the Inaugural Session of the Constitution Drafting Committee on October 18, 1975" in *The Constitution of the Federal Republic of Nigeria, 1979* (Kaduna, Nigeria: New Nigerian Publishers, 1981 [reprint]).

40. See *Constitution of the Federal Republic of Nigeria, 1979*, especially sections 135, 173, 188, and 202–203.

41. Diamond, "Nigeria: Pluralism, Statism, and the Struggle for Democracy," 65.

42. See Forrest, *Politics and Economic Development in Nigeria*, 73–92.

43. See Rotimi T. Suberu, "Political Opposition and Intergovernmental Relations in the Second Nigerian Republic," *Journal of Commonwealth and Comparative Politics* 28, no. 3 (1990): 269–87.

44. Otwin Marenin, "The Nigerian State as Process and Manager: A Conceptualization," *Comparative Politics* 20, no. 2 (1988): 226.

45. See Sam Oyovbaire, "New Guidelines for Local Government," *The Guardian* (Lagos), November 28, 1991, 17.

46. See Larry Diamond, *Class, Ethnicity, and Democracy in Nigeria: The Failure of the First Republic* (London: Macmillan, 1988), 155; and Lijphart, *Democracy in Plural Societies*, 163.

CHAPTER 3: THE POLITICS OF REVENUE SHARING

1. See Adebayo Adedeji, *Nigerian Federal Finance: Its Development, Problems, and Prospects* (London: Hutchinson, 1969), 260.

2. Rupley, "Revenue Sharing," 257–58.

3. Gini F. Mbanefoh, "Unsettled Issues in Nigerian Fiscal Federalism and The National Question," in *The National Question and Economic Development in Nigeria*, ed. F. E. Onah (Ibadan, Nigeria: Nigerian Economic Society, 1993), 68.

4. Pauline H. Baker, *The Economics of Nigerian Federalism* (Washington, D.C.: Battelle Memorial Institute, 1984), 10.

5. Ibid., v.

6. See Adedeji, *Nigerian Federal Finance*, 49.

7. Ibid., 53.

8. Baker, *The Economics of Nigerian Federalism*, 11.

9. Adedeji, *Nigerian Federal Finance*, 86–87.

10. Ibid., 113.

11. Ibid., 112–113.

12. Ibid., 134.

13. Ibid., 236–238.

14. Ibid., 243.

15. Baker, *The Economics of Nigerian Federalism*, 15–16.

16. Ibid., 16.

17. See, for instance, Rupley, "Revenue Sharing," 258, 266.

18. Federal Republic of Nigeria, *Report of the Presidential Commission on Revenue Allocation*, vol. 1 (Apapa, Lagos: Federal Government Press, 1980).

19. See Federal Republic of Nigeria, "Allocation of Revenue Act, 1981 (No. 1 of 1982)," supplement to *Official Gazette Extraordinary* 69, no. 8 (February 18, 1982), A1–5.

20. See press statement by Vice President Augustus Aikhomu on new revenue allocation formulas in *The Guardian on Sunday* (Lagos), June 7, 1992, A10.

21. Anthony Ani, "Press Briefing of the Minister of Finance on the 1998 Budget of Transition," *The Guardian* (Lagos), January 7 and 8.

22. Adedotun Phillips, *Nigeria's Fiscal Policy, 1998–2010*. Monograph Series, no. 17 (Ibadan, Nigeria: Nigerian Institute of Social and Economic Research, 1997), 18.

23. Ibid., 33.

24. Federal Republic of Nigeria, *Report of the Political Bureau* (Lagos: Federal Government Printer, 1987), 166–67.

25. Ifedayo Sayo, "Senate Panel Wants Revenue Formula to Favor States, Councils," *The Guardian* (Lagos), December 23, 1999.

26. *The Guardian* (Lagos), June 23, 2000.

27. Adedotun Phillips, "Managing Fiscal Federalism: Revenue Allocation Issues," *Publius: The Journal of Federalism* 21, no. 4 (1991): 104.

28. Federal Republic of Nigeria, *Report of the Presidential Commission,* vol. 1, 90.

29. See, for instance, ibid., 28.

30. Federal Republic of Nigeria, *Report of the Presidential Commission on Revenue Allocation,* vol. 4: *Minority Views* (Lagos: Federal Government Press, 1980), 35.

31. See Federal Republic of Nigeria, *Report of the Presidential Commission on Revenue Allocation,* vol. 3 (Lagos: Federal Government Press, 1980), 112.

32. Chiichii Ashwe, *Fiscal Federalism in Nigeria.* Research Monograph, no. 46 (Canberra: Australian National University, Centre for Research on Federal Financial Relations, 1986), 88.

33. See Lt. General T. Y. Danjuma, "Revenue Sharing and the Political Economy of Federalism" (paper prepared for the National Conference on Federalism and Nation-Building in Nigeria, Abuja, December 14–18, 1992), 32.

34. See A. G. Adebayo, *Embattled Federalism: History of Revenue Allocation in Nigeria, 1946–1990* (New York: Peter Lang, 1993), 142.

35. See Adedeji, *Nigerian Federal Finance.*

36. Ibid., 254.

37. Melford Okilo, "Derivation: A Criterion of Revenue Allocation" (paper presented at the postgraduate seminar, Command Staff College, Jaji, July 1980), 13–14.

38. A. G. Adebayo, "The 'Ibadan School' and the Handling of Federal Finance in Nigeria," *The Journal of Modern African Studies* 28, no. 2 (1990): 255.

39. Mbanefoh, "Unsettled Issues," 75.

40. See *The Guardian on Sunday* (Lagos), June 7, 1992, 37.

41. See Ken Saro-Wiwa, "Federalism and the Minority," *The Guardian* (Lagos), November 30, 1992, 37.

42. See Federal Republic of Nigeria, *Report of the Constitutional Conference,* vol. 2 (Abuja: National Assembly Press, 1995), 142.

43. Mbanefoh, "Unsettled Issues," 76.

44. Danjuma, "Revenue Sharing," 34–36.

45. Ibid., 35.

46. Federal Republic of Nigeria, *Government's Views on the Report on the Presidential Commission on Revenue Allocation* (Lagos: Federal Government Press, 1980), 16–17.

47. Danjuma, "Revenue Sharing," 36.

48. Ibid., 35.

49. Federal Republic of Nigeria, *Report of the Presidential Commission on Revenue Allocation,* vol. 1, 117.

50. See Federal Republic of Nigeria, *Government's Views,* 19.

51. See Suberu, "Political Opposition," 275–77.

52. See *The Guardian on Sunday* (Lagos), June 7, 1992, A10.

53. Federal Republic of Nigeria, *Report of the Presidential Commission on Revenue Allocation,* vol. 1, 117.

54. Danjuma, "Revenue Sharing," 17.

55. David Edevbie, "The Politics of the 13 Percent Derivation Principle" (text of a statement by the Commissioner for Finance and Economic Planning, Asaba, Delta State, May 15, 2000), 6.

56. *The News* (Lagos), May 17, 1993, 25.

57. See J. Isawa Elaigwu, "Federalism and National Leadership in Nigeria," *Publius: The Journal of Federalism* 21, no. 4 (1991): 141.

CHAPTER 4: THE STRUGGLE FOR NEW STATES AND LOCALITIES

1. See Bach, "Managing a Plural Society," 221.

2. McHenry, "Stability of the Federal System in Nigeria," 94.

3. Bach, "Managing a Plural Society," 226.

4. Diamond, "Class, Ethnicity, and the Democratic State," 424, 475.

5 Ibid., 474.

6. See Mackintosh, "Federalism in Nigeria," 229. Because the southern Cameroons constituted the fourth region of Nigeria in 1958, a majority of regions was assumed to mean three out of four, rather than two out of three.

7. See, for instance, Eghosa Osaghae, "Ethnic Minorities and Federalism in Nigeria," *African Affairs* 90, no. 359 (1991): 243.

8. Mackintosh, "Federalism in Nigeria," 230.

9. See Donald Rothchild, "Safeguarding Nigeria's Minorities," *Duquesne Review* (1963): 42.

10. For details, see Post and Vickers, *Structure and Conflict in Nigeria,* 92, 96.

11. Ibid., 117.

12. See E. Alex Gboyega, "The Making of the Nigerian Constitution," in *Nigerian Government and Politics Under Military Rule, 1966–79,* ed. Oyeleye Oyediran (New York: St. Martin's, 1979), 236–37.

13. A. H. M. Kirk-Greene, *Crisis and Conflict in Nigeria: A Documentary Sourcebook 1966–1969,* vol. 1 (London: Oxford University Press, 1971), 309.

14. Ibid., 309.

15. Ibid., 309.

16. Ibid., 401.

17. Ibid., 414.

18. Ibid., 447.

19. Ibid., 447.

20. Ibid., 447.

21. See Federal Republic of Nigeria, *Federal Military Government Views on the Report of the Panel on Creation of States* (Lagos: Federal Ministry of Information, 1976), 9.

22. Brian Smith, "Federal-State Relations in Nigeria," *African Affairs* 80, no. 320 (1981), 359.

23. Federal Republic of Nigeria, *Federal Military Government Views,* 8.

24. Ibid., 9.

25. Ibid., 11.

26. Ibid., 13.

27. Ibid., 10.

28. Ibid., 10.

29. Ibid., 10.

30. Ibid., 15.

31. Ibid., 30.

32. Ibid., 22.

33. Ibid., 18.

34. Ibid., 26.

35. Ibid., 28.

36. See A. D. Yahaya, "The Creation of States," in *Soldiers and Oil: The Political Transformation of Nigeria,* ed. Keith Panter-Brick (London: Frank Cass, 1978), 219.

37. See *A Time For Action: Collected Speeches of Murtala Mohammed* (Lagos: Federal Ministry of Information, 1976), 55.

38. See *West Africa,* August 1, 1977, 1605 and August 15, 1977, 1702.

39. See Rotimi T. Suberu, "The Struggle for New States in Nigeria, 1976–1990," *African Affairs* 90, no. 361 (1991): 506.

40. Graf, *The Nigerian State,* 141.

41. See *Nigerian Herald* (Ilorin), January 29, 1983; and Dean E. McHenry, Jr., "Political Struggle in Nigeria's Second Republic: The State Creation Issue in the Politics of Cross River State," *Journal of Commonwealth and Comparative Politics* 24, no. 2 (1986): 131.

42. See "Address by the Head of State," 123–25.

43. James Reed, "The New Constitution of Nigeria, 1979: The Washington Model," *Journal of African Law* 23 (1979): 164.

44. See Federal Republic of Nigeria, *Political Party Leaders' Recommended Guidelines on the Creation of States in the Federal Republic of Nigeria* (Lagos: Executive Office of the President, 1982), appendix 2.

45. Federal Republic of Nigeria, *Supplement to Official Gazette,* 69, 58 (November 18, 1982), A115–A121.

46. See the statement by Professor Ayodele Awojobi in *New Nigerian* (Kaduna), June 3, 1983.

47. See Federal Republic of Nigeria, *National Assembly Debates (Senate),* June 14, 1982, col. 9485.

48. *Daily Sketch* (Ibadan), September 2, 1980, 2.

49. See Aaron T. Gana, "The Politics and Economics of State Creation in Nigeria," *Nigerian Journal of Policy and Strategy* 2, no. 1 (June 1987): 14.

50. Federal Republic of Nigeria, *Political Party Leaders' Recommended Guidelines,* 7.

51. Federal Republic of Nigeria, *Report of the Political Bureau,* 168–81.

52. Ibid., 170.

53. Ibid., 170–72.

54. Ibid., 171.

55. Ibid., 176–80.

56. Federal Republic of Nigeria, *Government Views and Comments on the Findings and Recommendations of the Political Bureau* (Lagos: Federal Government Printer, 1987), 61.

57. Federal Republic of Nigeria, *Report of the Political Bureau,* 176.

58. See *The Guardian* (Lagos), September 24, 1987, 14.

59. Ibid., and *The Guardian* (Lagos), May 12, 1988, 17.

60. See, for instance, Rotimi T. Suberu, "The 1991 State and Local Government Reorganizations in Nigeria," *Travaux et Documents,* no. 41 (1994).

61. See *For Their Tomorrow We Gave Our Today: Selected Speeches of IBB,* vol. 1 (Ibadan, Nigeria: Safari Books Limited, 1991), 53.

62. See *Daily Times* (Lagos), April 17, 1991.

63. *National Concord* (Lagos), December 6, 1991.

64. See *Daily Times* (Lagos), October 2, 1996, 21.

65. Ibid., 21.

66. Ibid., 21.

67. Federal Republic of Nigeria, "States Creation and Transitional Provisions, Decree No. 41," *Official Gazette Extraordinary* 54, no. 78 (October 2, 1991), A287–A303.

68. Suberu, "The 1991 State and Local Government Reorganizations," 22–29.

69. *Daily Times* (Lagos), October 2, 1996, 21.

70. See also Rotimi T. Suberu, "The Travails of Federalism in Nigeria," *Journal of Democracy* 4, no. 4 (October 1993): 45–46.

71. Saro-Wiwa, "Federalism and the Minority," 37.

72. Bach, "Managing a Plural Society," 234.

73. Olusegun Obasanjo, "The Nigerian Society and the Third Republic," *The Guardian* (Lagos), March 14, 1992, 9.

CHAPTER 5: THE "FEDERAL CHARACTER" PRINCIPLE

1. Diamond, "Issues in the Constitution Design," 212; Forrest, *Politics and Economic Development in Nigeria*, 59; and "Federal Character is Federal Discrimination," *Daily Sketch* (Ibadan), August 15, 1981, 2

2. See "Address by the Head of State," 124.

3. *The Constitution of the Federal Republic of Nigeria, 1979*, section 272 (1).

4. See J. A. Ayoade and R. T. Suberu, "Federalism," *The Quarterly Journal of Administration* (special issue on "The New Nigerian Constitution") 24, no. 3 (1990): 157.

5. Ibid., 157.

6. See "Seventy Key Decisions of Confab '94," *Sunday Champion* (Lagos), December 11, 1994, 4.

7. See Federal Republic of Nigeria, *Guiding Principles and Formulae for the Distribution of Posts in the Public Service* (Abuja: Federal Character Commission, 1996).

8. See Alex Gboyega, "The 'Federal Character' or the Attempt to Create Representative Bureaucracies in Nigeria," *International Review of Administrative Sciences* 51, no. 1 (1984): 17–24; Anthony H. M. Kirk-Greene, "Ethnic Engineering and the 'Federal Character' of Nigeria: Boon of Contentment or Bone of Contention?" *Ethnic and Racial Studies* 6 (1983): 457–76; and J. A. Ayoade "Ethnic Management in the 1979 Nigerian Constitution," *Publius: The Journal of Federalism* 16 (1986): 73–90.

9. See *Report of the Constitution Drafting Committee Containing the Draft Constitution,* vol. 1 (Lagos: Federal Ministry of Information, 1976), ix.

10. See Billy J. Dudley, *An Introduction to Nigerian Government and Politics* (London: Macmillan, 1982), 169–78.

11. See, for instance, "Party Registration," *The Guardian* (Lagos), June 25, 1996, 16.

12. Forrest, *Politics and Economic Development in Nigeria,* 76; Alex Gboyega, "Choosing a New Cabinet," in *The Nigerian 1979 Elections,* ed. Oyeleye Oyediran (Lagos: Macmillan 1981), 153–65.

13. Despite the rhetoric of economic rationalization and adjustment, for instance, the Babangida administration created several new agencies or ministries as part of its extensive political patronage system.

14. T. Y. Danjuma, "Revenue Sharing and the Political Economy of Nigerian Federalism," *The Nigerian Journal of Federalism* 1, no. 1 (1994): 52.

15. See Alex Ekwueme, "More Than a Government of National Consensus," *The Guardian* (Lagos), March 21, 1992, 9. Regarding the NEC, it should be noted here that FEDECO, NEC, and now, the Independent National Electoral Commission (INEC) are different constitutional designations for the same institution— namely, the national electoral agency. The agency was referred to as FEDECO in the 1979 Constitution, as NEC in the 1989 Constitution and 1995 draft constitution, and as INEC in the 1999 Constitution.

Geographic zones—or, as some Nigerian politicians call them, "geopolitical" zones—and the associated concept of zoning reflect an increasingly fashionable principle of federal distribution and reorganization in Nigeria. The principle maintains that, in order to promote the equitable and stable distribution of powers and resources in the country, Nigeria's many constituent governments and segments may be profitably aggregated into a smaller number of more or less equivalent zones, reflecting broad regional, cultural, or ethnopolitical divisions in the federation. See, for example, Diamond, "Issues in the Constitutional Design," 213–14; and John N. Paden, "Nigerian Unity and the Tensions of Democracy: Geocultural Zones and North-South Legacies," in *Dilemmas of Democracy in Nigeria,* ed. Paul A. Beckett and Crawford Young (Rochester, N.Y.: University of Rochester Press, 1997), 243–64.

16. Ayoade, "Ethnic Management," 86; Ben Nwabueze, *Nigeria's Presidential Constitution, 1979–83* (London: Longman, 1985), 306.

17. The exception was Yoruba Chief Ernest Shonekan, who headed a military-backed interim national government for eighty-two days, from August 26, 1993, to November 17, 1993.

18. See also Rotimi T. Suberu, "Federalism, Ethnicity, and Regionalism in Nigeria," in Beckett and Young, eds., *Dilemmas of Democracy in Nigeria,* 343–46.

19. Dudley, *An Introduction to Nigerian Government and Politics,* 162.

20. See "Manifesto of the NPN" in Chuba Okadigbo, *Mission of the NPN* (Enugu, Nigeria: Nwankwo Associates, 1980).

21. See Suberu, "The Travails of Federalism in Nigeria," 48.

22. *Sunday Champion,* "Seventy Key Decisions," 4.

23. See *Daily Times* (Lagos), October 2, 1995, 27.

24. Bola Dauda, "Fallacies and Dilemmas: The Theory of Representative Bureaucracy with Particular Reference to the Nigerian Public Service, 1950–1986," *International Review of Administrative Sciences* 56 (1990): 467–95.

25. See "For a Balanced Public Service," *The Guardian* (Lagos), July 15, 1985, 8.

26. Gray Longe, "Federal Perceptions," in *Federal Character and National Integration in Nigeria,* ed. Ukwu I. Ukwu (Kuru, Nigeria: National Institute for Policy and Strategic Studies, 1987), 46.

27. S. A. Musa, "Developments at the Federal Level," in *Nigerian Public Administration 1960–1980,* ed. Ladipo Adamolekun (Ibadan, Nigeria: Heinemann, 1985), 117.

28. Federal Republic of Nigeria, *Implementation Guidelines on the Civil Service Reforms* (Lagos: Federal Government Printer, 1988), 7–9.

29. Ibid., 9.

30. Ibid., 9.

31. Ibid., 9.

32. "Two Rights Can't Make a Wrong," *The Guardian* (Lagos), July 22, 1986, 12.

33. "Federal Character," *This Day* (Lagos), October 11, 1996.

34. *New Nigerian* (Kaduna), December 17, 1984, 1.

35. See J. Bayo Adekanye, "The Quota Recruitment Policy: Its Sources and Impact on the Nigerian Military," in *Federal Character and Federalism in Nigeria,* ed. P. Ekeh and E. Osaghae (Ibadan, Nigeria: Heinemann, 1989), 230–55; also Robin Luckham, *The Nigerian Military: A Sociological Analysis of Authority and Revolt* (New York: Cambridge University Press, 1971).

36. Adekanye, "The Quota Recruitment Policy," 242.

37. See Luckham, *The Nigerian Military,* 231; Ademoyega, *Why We Struck,* 23–24; and Gbulie, *Nigeria's Five Majors,* 10.

38. J. Bayo Adekanye, "Federal Character Provisions of the 1979 Constitution and Composition of the Nigerian Armed Forces: The Old Quota Idea by New Name," *Plural Societies* 14, nos. 1–2 (1983): 66–78.

39. David Akpode Ejoor, *Reminiscences* (Lagos: Malthouse Press, 1989), 169, 170.

40. J. S. Attah, "National Education Policy," in Ukwu, ed., *Federal Character and National Integration,* 134–35.

41. Ibid., 136; Longe, "Federal Perceptions," 46.

42. Attah, "National Education Policy," 137; Longe, "Federal Perceptions," 46.

43. E. A. Yoloye, "Federal Character and Institutions of Higher Learning," in Ekeh and Osaghae, eds., *Federal Character and Federalism*, 68.

44. Ibid., 67.

45. Ibid., 66.

46. *The Guardian* (Lagos), October 6, 1988, 1–2.

47. See *West Africa,* February 4, 1980, 223.

48. *Daily Times* (Lagos), August 5, 1980; *New Nigerian* (Kaduna), August 10, 1992, 15, 19.

49. *New Nigerian* (Kaduna), August 24, 1992, 14.

50. *Daily Times* (Lagos), September 18, 1992, 14.

51. See Monday Idiong, "Resolving the Language Question in Akwa Ibom," *The Guardian* (Lagos), April 18, 1991, 12.

52. *Vanguard* (Lagos), June 15, 1992, 3.

53. *The Guardian* (Lagos), August 20, 1996, 34.

54. Robert Gulkani, "An Alternative to State Creation," *This Day* (Lagos), August 20, 1996.

55. *The Guardian* (Lagos), April 19, 1988, 10.

56. *Nigerian Tribune* (Ibadan), January 12, 1990, 1.

57. *African Concord* (Lagos), February 5, 1990, 36–37.

58. *Africa Confidential* (London), March 4, 1987, 1. The military administration of President Babangida launched the Mass Mobilization for Self-Reliance, Social Justice, and Economic Recovery (MAMSER) in 1987 as a national program of political socialization, education, and mobilization.

59. *The Comet* (Lagos), April 24, 2000.

60. *The News* (Lagos), May 9, 2000.

61. *The Guardian* (Lagos), April 29, 2000; see also *Vanguard* (Lagos), April 29, 2000.

62. *The News* (Lagos), April 25, 1994, 12; *Sunday Tribune* (Ibadan), December 15, 1991, 7.

63. *Vanguard* (Lagos), March 3, 2000.

64. *The Guardian* (Lagos), December 24, 2000.

65. See *Vanguard* (Lagos), March 3 and May 29, 2000.

66. *The Guardian* (Lagos), January 30, 2000.

67. Nath Maitakama, "Recipe for Kaduna Crisis," *The Comet* (Lagos), April 27, 2000.

68. *The Guardian* (Lagos), March 25, 2000.

69. See David Laitin, *Hegemony and Culture: The Politics of Religious Change among the Yoruba* (Chicago: University of Chicago Press, 1986).

70. *National Concord* (Lagos), February 4, 1986, 20.

71. See *Vanguard* (Lagos), September 13, 1990, 16.

72. *Nigerian Tribune* (Ibadan), January 17, 1989, 1; *Daily Sketch* (Ibadan), June 6, 1990, 11.

73. *Daily Sketch* (Ibadan), November 6, 1991, 3.

74. See *The Herald* (Ilorin), November 5, 1988, 1; also *Nigerian Tribune* (Ibadan), November 5, 1988, 1.

75. Kirk-Greene, "Ethnic Engineering," 457.

76. Peter Ekeh, "The Structure and Meaning of Federal Character in the Nigerian Political System," in Ekeh and Osaghae, eds., *Federal Character and Federalism,* 32, 36.

77. See *West Africa,* September 18–24, 1995, 1483–84.

78. *Daily Champion* (Lagos), November 22, 1994, 3.

CHAPTER 6: THE POLITICS OF POPULATION COUNTS

1. See Danjuma, "Revenue Sharing and the Political Economy of Nigerian Federalism," 61–62.

2. Federal Republic of Nigeria, *Federal Military Government Views,* 15.

3. Sam Oyovbaire and Tunji Olagunju, eds., *Crisis of Democratization: Selected Speeches of IBB* (Lagos: Malthouse Press, 1996), 30.

4. See *Daily Times* (Lagos), October 2, 1996, 21.

5. Cited in Douglas Rimmer, "Development in Nigeria: An Overview," in Bienen and Diejomaoh, eds., *The Political Economy of Income Distribution in Nigeria,* 58.

6. Rimmer, "Development in Nigeria," 46.

7. National Population Commission, *Questions and Answers on the 1991 Population Census* (Lagos: Public Affairs Department, National Population Commission, 1994), 22–23.

8. The phrase "population manipulation" is from Alex Ekwueme, "The Bones Shall Rise Again," *This Day* (Lagos), October 26, 1998, 34. Ekwueme contends that such "manipulation" has been a major source of "Igbo political emasculation" in Nigeria.

9. Isiaka A. Yahaya and Mannir Dan-Ali, *Breaking the Myth: Shehu Musa and the 1991 Census* (Ibadan, Nigeria: Spectrum Books, 1997), 7.

10. See S. A. Aluko, "How Many Nigerians? An Analysis of Nigeria's Census Problems, 1901–63," *The Journal of Modern African Studies* 3, no. 3 (1965): 372.

11. Ibid., 375.

12. Ibid., 376.

13. See, among many other sources, ibid., 371–92; Mackintosh, *Nigerian Government and Politics;* I. I. Ekanem, *The 1963 Nigerian Census: A Critical Appraisal* (Benin City, Nigeria: Ethiope Publishing Corporation, 1972); and Diamond, *Class, Ethnicity, and Democracy in Nigeria.*

14. Ekanem, *The 1963 Nigerian Census,* 19, 194–95.

15. Ibid., 101, 202.

16. Aluko, "How Many Nigerians?" 385.

17. Diamond, *Class, Ethnicity, and Democracy in Nigeria,* 149.

18. See, among other sources, Aluko, "How Many Nigerians?"; and Reuben K. Udo, "Geography and Population Censuses in Nigeria," in *Fifty Years of Geography in Nigeria: The Ibadan Story,* ed. Olusegun Areola and Stanley I. Okafor (Ibadan, Nigeria: Ibadan University Press, 1998), 348–72.

19. See Anthony Kirk-Greene and Douglas Rimmer, *Nigeria since 1970: A Political and Economic Outline* (London: Hodder and Stoughton, 1981), 5.

20. Ibid., 5.

21. See his "Introduction to the Census Report," as reproduced in Olusegun Obasanjo, *Not My Will* (Ibadan, Nigeria: University Press Limited, 1990), 242.

22. See Olukunle Adegbola, "The Philosophy of Census: Theory and Practice in Nigeria," in *Philosophy of Population Census in Nigeria,* ed. O. O. Arowolo and O. Daramola (n.p. National Population Commission, n.d.), 130.

23. Ibid., 130.

24. Obasanjo, *Not My Will,* 243.

25. S. O. Adekanye, "Acceptability of an Accurate Headcount: The Need for a Public Enlightenment Programme," in Arowolo and Daramola, eds., *Philosophy of Population Census in Nigeria,* 112.

26. See *The Guardian on Sunday* (Lagos), April 12, 1992, A1–A2.

27. See Obafemi Awolowo, *Voice of Courage* (Akure, Nigeria: Fagbamigbe Publishers, 1981), 77–78.

28. Cited in ibid., 80.

29. See Udo, "Geography and Population Censuses in Nigeria," 360.

30. Awolowo, *Voice of Courage,* 81.

31. Obasanjo, *Not My Will,* 16.

32. Ibid., 15; and Aderanti Adepoju, "Military Rule and Population Issues in Nigeria," *African Affairs* 80, no. 318, (January 1981): 35.

33. See Ian Campbell, "The Nigerian Census: An Essay in Civil-Military Relations," *Journal of Commonwealth and Comparative Politics* 14, no. 3 (November 1976): 242–54.

34. Ibid., 249.

35. For a general review of the design and execution of the 1991 census, see National Population Commission, *1991 Population Census of the Federal Republic of Nigeria: Analytical Report at the National Level* (Abuja: National Population Commission, 1998).

36. See Chris Ugokwe, *The Path to a Successful Census* (Lagos: National Population Commission, 1993), 9.

37. See ibid., 15; and Yahaya and Dan-Ali, *Breaking the Myth*, 125.

38. Ugokwe, *The Path to a Successful Census*, 14–15.

39. See *New Nigerian* (Kaduna), April 25, 1990, 16.

40. Yahaya and Dan-Ali, *Breaking the Myth*, 36–53.

41. See "Constitution of the Federal Republic of Nigeria Decree No. 12 of 1989," section 211; "National Population Commission Decree No. 23 of 1989," section 26; and Federal Republic of Nigeria, *Constitution of the Federal Republic of Nigeria 1999* (Lagos: Federal Government Press, 1999), section 213.

42. See *Newswatch* (Lagos), November 16, 1998, 9.

43. See Yahaya and Dan-Ali, *Breaking the Myth*, 121.

44. Ibid., 131–32.

45. See ibid., 97–99.

46. See Frank Hobbs, "Where Have All Nigeria's People Gone?" *The Guardian on Sunday* (Lagos), October 18, 1992, B2.

47. See, in particular, *Sunday Tribune* (Ibadan) April 19, 1992, 5; and *The Guardian* (Lagos), April 28, 1992, 12.

48. National Population Commission, "Brief on 1991 Census to State Governors," *Census News* (Lagos) 3, no. 1 (September 1992), 39.

49. Samuel Adamu, "Census '91: A 'Hidden' Agenda," *The Guardian* (Lagos), June 15, 1998, 49.

50. Andrew Obeya, "The 1963 Census Was Credible," *Nigerian Tribune* (Ibadan), June 18, 1992, 15.

51. See M. N. Ekwerekwu, H. S. Usman, and Ray Okafor, "The Second Census Tribunal: Suit No. CT/ BO/7/LG 9" (Abuja: April 28, 1993), 240–41.

52. M. N. Ekwerekwu, H. S. Usman, and Ray Okafor, "The Second Census Tribunal: Suit No CT/BN/6/LG 6" (Abuja: May 13, 1993), 105.

53. M. N. Ekwerekwu, H. S. Usman, and Ray Okafor, "The Second Census Tribunal: Suit No CT/KG/18/LG1A" (Abuja: May 28, 1993), 131.

54. M. N. Ekwerekwu, H. S. Usman, and Ray Okafor, "The Second Census Tribunal: Suit No. CT/OY/25/LG13" (Abuja: May 28, 1993), 169.

55. Titilola Mabogunje, I. M. Inuwa, and V. I. Isibor, "The First Census Tribunal: Suit No CT/KN/I5/LG 19" (Abuja: June 22, 1993), 2.

56. See Titilola Mabogunje, I. M. Inuwa, and V. I. Isibor, "The First Census Tribunal: Suit No. CT/KW/19" (Abuja: June 24, 1993), 2, 4; M. N. Ekwerekwu, H. S. Usman, and Ray Okafor, "The Second Census Tribunal: Suit No. CT/OG/22/INDV/2" (Abuja: May 24, 1993), 127; and Titilola Mabogunje, I. M. Inuwa, and V. I. Isibor, "The First Census Tribunal: Suit No. CT/OD/23/LG 13" (Abuja: June 23, 1993), 10.

57. National Population Commission, "Brief on 1991 Census to State Governors," 40.

58. M. N. Ekwerekwu, H. S. Usman, and Ray Okafor, "The Second Census Tribunal: Suit No. CT/RV/27/INDV/3/1" (Abuja: April 26, 1993), 316.

59. Titilola Mabogunje, I. M. Inuwa, and V. I. Isibor, "The First Census Tribunal: Suit No. CT/AK/3/LG24" (Abuja: June 23, 1993), 2.

60. Titilola Mabogunje, I. M. Inuwa, and V. I. Isibor, "The First Census Tribunal: Suit No. CT/DT/9/LG 13" (Abuja: June 22, 1993), 2.

61. Titilola Mabogunje, I. M. Inuwa, and V. I. Isibor, "The First Census Tribunal: Suit No. CT/TR/29/LG7" (Abuja: June 23, 1993), 3.

62. Titilola Mabogunje, I. M. Inuwa, and V. I. Isibor, "The First Census Tribunal: Suit No CT/OY/25" (Abuja: June 25, 1993), 14.

63. Ibid., 13.

64. Ibid., 14.

65. *Vanguard* (Lagos), May 18, 2000.

66. See Yahaya and Dan-Ali, *Breaking the Myth,* 110.

67. Ibid., 115.

68. See *Daily Sketch* (Ibadan), May 8, 1992, 6

69. See, among other sources, the proceedings of the two census tribunals; Olatunde Oloko, "Resolving Nigeria's 1991 Census Controversy," *Daily Times* (Lagos), December 8, 1994, 7; and Adamu, "Census '91," 49.

70. Chris Ugokwe, "Text of a World Press Conference on 13 May 1997 on the Final Tabulations of the 1991 National Population Census," 12.

71. See P. O. Olusanya, *Nigeria's Demographic Delusion: A Critical Examination of the Census Controversy* (Lagos: Lagos University Press, 1983); and Babatunde A. Ahonsi, "Deliberate Falsification and Census Data in Nigeria," *African Affairs* 87, no. 349 (October 1988): 553–62.

72. See Abdurrahman Okene, "Keynote Address," in Arowolo and Daramola, eds., *Philosophy of Population Census in Nigeria,* 7.

73. Sam Aluko, "Reflections on the 1991 Census," *The Guardian on Sunday* (Lagos), April 5, 1992, A7.

74. See Obasanjo, *Not My Will,* 243.

CHAPTER 7: ISSUES IN THE REFORM OF THE NIGERIAN FEDERAL SYSTEM

1. See *AM News* (Lagos), January 7, 1996, 14.

2. Wole Soyinka, "The Federal Quest," *Daily Champion* (Lagos), March 22, 1999, 27.

3. Dele Olowu, "Centralization, Self-Governance, and Development in Nigeria," in *The Failure of the Centralized State: Institutions and Self-Governance in Africa,* ed. James Wunsch and Dele Olowu (San Francisco: Institute for Contemporary Studies Press, 1995), 207.

4. See Federal Republic of Nigeria, *Constitution of the Federal Republic of Nigeria, 1979,* sections 13–22 and second schedule, part 1, item 59; idem, *Constitution of the Federal Republic of Nigeria, Decree No. 12 of 1989,* sections 14–24 and second schedule, part 1, item 58; idem, *Report of the Constitutional Conference Containing the Draft (1995) Constitution,* vol. 1, sections 14–25 and second schedule, part 1, item 58; idem, *Constitution of the Federal Republic of Nigeria,* 1999, sections 13–34 and second schedule, part 1, item 60.

5. See Joye and Igweike, *Introduction to the 1979 Nigerian Constitution,* 94.

6. Ibid., 40.

7. See Federal Republic of Nigeria, *Report of the Constitutional Conference Containing the Draft (1995) Constitution,* vol. 1, second schedule, pp. 157–67; and Human Rights Watch/Africa, *Nigeria: Transition or Travesty?* (New York: Human Rights Watch, 1997), 11–12.

8. See Sam Oyovbaire and Tunji Olagunju, eds., *Crisis of Democratization in Nigeria: Selected Speeches of IBB,* vol. 11 (Lagos: Malthouse Press Ltd., 1996), 26.

9. See Peter P. Ekeh, ed., *Wilberforce Conference on Nigerian Federalism* (Buffalo, N.Y.: Association of Nigerian Scholars for Dialogue, 1997), 11.

10. Ibid., 12.

11. See Abraham Adesanya, "What Yorubas Expect of Their Elected Leaders," *This Day* (Lagos), March 22, 1999, 28.

12. See *The Guardian* (Lagos), March 27, 1992, 2.

13. See *West Africa,* November 3, 1986, 2312.

14. See Phillips, *Nigeria's Fiscal Policy,* 18; "How FG Cheats States on Revenue," *This Day* (Lagos), October 19, 1998, 1; and Ayo Arowolo, "Sharing the National Cake Equitably," *This Day* (Lagos), November 1, 1998, 40.

15. The Aboyade Technical Committee recommended that the state should administer companies' income taxes; the Okigbo Commission argued that mining rents should be assigned to the mineral-producing states "as of right"; and Dotun

Phillips opined that "each state should administer the (value added) tax and retain the revenue collected within the state." See, respectively, Oladunjoye Fajana, "Intergovernmental Fiscal Relations in the Report of the Technical Committee on Revenue Allocation," *The Quarterly Journal of Administration* 14, no. 2 (1980), 184; Federal Republic of Nigeria, *Report of the Presidential Commission on Revenue Allocation*, vol. 1, 93; and Phillips, *Nigeria's Fiscal Policy*, 22.

16. See Fajana, "Intergovernmental Fiscal Relations," 179–96. See also Oyeleye Oyediran and Olatunji Olagunju, "The Military and the Politics of Revenue Allocation," in Oyediran, ed., *Nigerian Government and Politics under Military Rule*, 192–211.

17. Federal Republic of Nigeria, *Report of the Presidential Commission on Revenue Allocation*, vol. 4, 12–39.

18. Federal Republic of Nigeria, *Report of the Constitutional Conference*, vol. 2, 141.

19. See Danjuma, "Revenue Sharing and the Political Economy of Nigerian Federalism," 61.

20. Federal Republic of Nigeria, *Constitution of the Federal Republic of Nigeria, 1999*, section 162 (2); also Federal Republic of Nigeria, *Report of the Constitutional Conference Containing the Draft (1995) Constitution*, section 163 (2).

21. Tam David-West, "Thoughts on the Constitution," *Vanguard* (Lagos), October 10, 1995, 5.

22. Ken Saro-Wiwa, *A Month and a Day: A Detention Diary* (Harmondsworth, U.K.: Penguin Books, 1995), 91.

23. Edet Akpan, "Why They Cry," *Newswatch* (Lagos), November 9, 1998, 10–11.

24. See C. O. Ikporukpo, "Federalism, Political Power, and the Economic Power Game: Conflict over Access to Petroleum Resources in Nigeria," *Environment and Planning* 14 (1996): 159–77.

25. Federal Republic of Nigeria, *Report of the Presidential Commission on Revenue Allocation*, vol. 1, 93.

26. See, for instance, G. B. Leton, "Minority Recommendations," in Federal Republic of Nigeria, *Report of the Presidential Commission on Revenue Allocation*, vol. 4, 5–11.

27. See Human Rights Watch, *The Price of Oil: Corporate Responsibility and Human Rights Violations in Nigeria's Oil-Producing Communities* (New York: Human Rights Watch, 1999), 53–90.

28. See Rotimi T. Suberu, "Revenue Allocation and Intergovernmental Relations: Old Practices and New Perspectives," in *Perspectives on Nigerian Federalism*, ed. Peter P. Ekeh (Buffalo, N.Y.: Association of Nigerian Scholars for Dialogue, forthcoming).

29. The ensuing discussion of Nigerian power-sharing proposals draws largely from Suberu, "Federalism, Ethnicity, and Regionalism in Nigeria," 343–46.

30. See Alex Ekwueme, "The Question of Rotation," *AM News* (Lagos), August 7–10, 1995.

31. Ekwueme, "More Than a Government of National Consensus," 9.

32. See *Sunday Concord* (Lagos), March 14, 1993, 6.

33. Federal Republic of Nigeria, *Report of the Political Bureau,* 74.

34. See Julius Ihonvbere, "Rotational Presidency is Plain Nonsense," *This Day* (Lagos), October 11, 1998, 4.

35. Eskor Toyo, "Cake-Sharers' Presidency," *The Guardian* (Lagos), January 11, 1999, 33.

36. *The Guardian* (Lagos), November 24, 1995, 28.

37. See, for instance, Federal Office of Statistics, *Socio-Economic Profile of Nigeria, 1996* (Lagos: Federal Office of Statistics, n.d.), 142.

38. Toyo, "Cake-Sharers' Presidency," 33.

39. Richard Sklar, "African Polities: The Next Generation," in *State, Conflict, and Democracy in Africa,* ed. Richard Joseph (Boulder, Colo.: Lynne Rienner, 1999), 171.

40. *This Day* (Lagos), November 18, 1998, 34.

41. See, for instance, Ekwueme, "The Question of Rotation."

42. See, for instance, Federal Republic of Nigeria, *Report of the Constitutional Conference Containing the Draft (1995) Constitution,* sections 142–143, 229; and *Daily Times* (Lagos), October 2, 1995, 27.

43. Bola Ige, "Share Powers, Not Positions," *Sunday Tribune* (Ibadan), September 3, 1995, 2.

44. Wole Soyinka, "A Year of Rapid Reverses," *The News* (Lagos), January 18, 1999, 44.

45. *This Day* (Lagos), January 28, 1999.

46. Soyinka, "A Year of Rapid Reverses," 44.

47. See, "Report of the Constitutional Debate," *This Day* (Lagos), January 3, 1999, 23.

48. *See Nigerian Tribune* (Ibadan), August 31, 1991, 5; *Nigerian Tribune* (Ibadan), October 4, 1994, 13; Ahmed Joda and Ukpabi Asika, "On the Question of Creation of New States," *Sunday Times* (Lagos), June 2, 1991, 15; and Tekena Tamuno, "A New Model Nigeria," *Nigerian Tribune* (Ibadan), November 4, 1991, 13.

49. Olusegun Obasanjo, "Keynote Address," in *Nigeria: The State of the Nation and the Way Forward,* ed. A. Mahadi, G. A. Kwanashie, and A. M. Yakubu (Kaduna, Nigeria: Arewa House, 1994), 27.

50. Ekwueme, "More Than a Government of National Consensus," 9.

51. Alex Ekwueme, "Nigerian Federation: Which Way Forward?" *Nigerian Tribune* (Ibadan), May 16, 1997, 18.

52. See *West Africa,* August 3–16, 1998, 602.

53. Abraham Adesanya, "Towards Restructuring the Nigerian Federation," *Nigerian Tribune* (Ibadan), August 4, 1998, 21.

54. Patrick Ani, "That Oil Communities May Survive," *This Day* (Lagos), November 15, 1998, 3.

55. Movement for National Reformation, "Position Paper," *The Guardian* (Lagos), January 29, 1993, 18.

56. In March 1993, the Kaduna-based *New Nigerian* reported a meeting between the MNR and some members of the northern intelligentsia, including Mahmud Tukur and Suleiman Kumo. The northern elements reportedly endorsed the MNR's proposal for a "union government with viable federations and a return to parliamentary democracy as a way out of the country's malaise." However, this attempt to involve the North in the MNR was not sustained, and the movement and its campaign remained purely southern-led. See *New Nigerian on Sunday* (Kaduna), March 28, 1993, 1.

57. See *The Guardian* (Lagos), January 26 and 27, 2000.

58. See Chuba Okadigbo, "The People Know Best," *African Concord* (Lagos), August 7, 1986, 11–12.

59. P. C. Asiodu, "Realizing the Dream of a Renascent Nigeria," *The Guardian* (Lagos), November 11, 1998, 8; and *Vanguard* (Lagos), October 12, 1998, 1.

60. See, for instance, Ijaw National Congress, "Communiqué," *This Day* (Lagos), December 27, 1998, 3.

61. See, for instance, Edet Uno, "MNR Advocates Derivation as New Revenue Allocation Formula," *The Guardian* (Lagos), July 30, 1998, 7.

62. Compare Timothy Sisk, *Power Sharing and International Mediation in Ethnic Conflicts* (Washington, D.C.: United States Institute of Peace Press, 1996), 47–75; and Elazar, "International and Comparative Federalism," 194.

63. *Nigerian Tribune* (Ibadan), May 1, 1996, 2.

64. Ekwueme, "Nigerian Federation," 18.

65. See J. D. Barkan, M. L. McNulty, and M. A. O. Ayeni, "Hometown Voluntary Associations, Local Development, and the Emergence of Civil Society in Western Nigeria," *The Journal of Modern African Studies* 29, no. 3 (1991): 462, note 18.

66. Ibid., 457–80.

67. Jane Guyer, "Local Government, Chiefs, and Office-Holders in a Rural Area: An Interpretation Based on Ibarapa, Oyo State," in *Transition without End: Nigerian Politics and Civil Society under Babangida,* ed. L. Diamond, A. Kirk-Greene, and O. Oyediran (Ibadan, Nigeria: Vantage Publishers, 1997), 428.

68. See, for instance, Pita O. Agbese, "Ethnic Conflicts and Hometown Associations: An Analysis of the Experience of the Agila Development Association," *Africa Today* 43, no. 2 (1996), 139–56.

69. Barkan, McNulty, and Ayeni, "Hometown Voluntary Associations," 479.

70. Diamond, "Issues in the Constitutional Design," 213.

71. Federal Republic of Nigeria, *Report of the Constitutional Conference Containing the Draft (1995) Constitution,* vol. 1, sections 229, 138, 140, 142–143, and 148.

72. See Federal Republic of Nigeria, *The Constitution of the Federal Republic of Nigeria, 1979,* sections 210–209; idem, "The Constitution of the Federal Republic of Nigeria (promulgation), Decree No. 12 of 1989," sections 219–227; idem, *Report of the Constitutional Conference Containing the Draft (1995) Constitution,* sections 220–228; idem, *Constitution of the Federal Republic of Nigeria, 1999,* sections 221–229.

73. Federal Republic of Nigeria, "The Constitution of the Federal Republic of Nigeria (promulgation), Decree No. 12 of 1989," section 220 (1).

74. Human Rights Watch/Africa, *Nigeria: Transition or Travesty,* 12–15.

75. See Peter M. Lewis, "Nigeria: An End to the Permanent Transition," *Journal of Democracy* 10, no. 1 (1999): 154.

76. See, in particular, "Party Registration," *The Guardian* (Lagos), June 25, 1996, 16.

77. Compare with Sisk, *Power Sharing and International Mediation,* 34–45.

78. J. F. Ade-Ajayi, "The National Question in Historical Perspective," *The Guardian* (Lagos), November 5, 1992, 17.

79. *The Punch* (Lagos), March 4, 1999, 17.

80. See, in particular, Diamond, "Issues in the Constitutional Design," 209–10; and Joseph, *Democracy and Prebendal Politics in Nigeria,* 155.

81. See Akin Mabogunje, "On a Platter of Gold? Reflections on Four Decades of Governance in Nigeria" (text of the Obafemi Awolowo Lecture, Nigerian Institute of International Affairs, Lagos, May 2, 1997, mimeo.), 8–10.

82. Diamond, "Issues in the Constitutional Design," 216–17.

83. Larry Diamond, *Prospects for Democratic Development in Africa.* Hoover Essays in Public Policy, no. 74 (Stanford, Calif.: Hoover Institution Press, 1997), 30.

84. Peter P. Ekeh, *Comments and Viewpoints on the Nigerian Constitution* (Buffalo, N.Y.: Association of Nigerian Scholars for Dialogue, 1998).

85. Anthony Enahoro, "Nigeria in Ferment," *Daily Times* (Lagos), December 9, 1991, 48.

86. See *Daily Sketch* (Ibadan), March 7, 1981, 9.

87. *Nigerian Tribune* (Ibadan), November 25, 1998, 2.

88. *The Guardian* (Lagos), September 21, 1998, 8.

89. *The Guardian* (Lagos), February 28, 1994, 40.

90. Council of Ulama of Nigeria, Zaria, "A Time to Speak," *New Nigerian* (Kaduna), November 4, 1988, 14.

91. Max Frenkel, *Federal Theory* (Canberra: Australian National University, Center for Research on Federal Financial Relations, 1986), 180; and Jeffrey Herbst, "Is Nigeria a Viable State?" *Washington Quarterly* 19, no. 2 (1996): 151–72.

92. See Tekena Tamuno, "Separatist Agitations in Nigeria since 1914," *The Journal of Modern African Studies* 8, no. 4 (1970): 583.

93. Adekeye Adebajo, "Remembering Biafra," *Newswatch* (Lagos), January 29, 1996, 8.

94. Bach, "Managing a Plural Society," 281–45.

INDEX

Land mass and terrain entitlement
    principle, 59, 68–69
Lijphart, Arend, 46
Local governments
    census tribunal and, 163–65
    devolution of powers to, xvii, 175,
        176
    direct federal funding, 34–35
    distributive contention, 2
    federal character principle and,
        115, 131–33
    Federation Account and, 52–56
    marginalization of subnational
        authorities, 176–77
    operational revenues, 48
    reforms and reorganizations under
        second phase of military rule,
        39–41, 46
    reforms of 1976, 34–35, 173–74
    reorganizations, 106–8, 143
    responsibility for social services, 48
    revenue sharing and, 49, 75–76
    statutory grants, 48

Mabogunje, Akin, 200
Macdonald, Alfonso, 160–61, 161
Macpherson Constitution of 1951, 19
Majority vote, federal character and,
    113
Marginalization, 43, 45
May, Ronald, 12
Mbakwe, Samuel, 140
Mbanefoh, Chief Arthur, 102
Mbanefoh, Gini, 69
Mexico, xi
Mid-West Region, 15, 28, 29, 82–85,
    109
Mid-West State Movement, 83
Militant ethnic youth organizations,
    43–44
Military
    federal character principle and, 16,
        113, 126–28

military coups, xiii, 1, 128
"military federalism," 32, 46
military governors, 32–33
national integration under, 35
Military rule, first phase
    (1966–1979), xxiv, 30–35, 46
    revenue allocation in, 13–14,
        51–53
Military rule, second phase
    (1984–1999), xiv, xxv–xxvi,
        39–42, 46
    pathologies of federalism and,
        171–72, 197
    revenue sharing, 53, 55–56
Mineral-producing areas. See also Oil
        operations; Oil revenues
    derivation principle and, xvii,
        63–68, 179–82
    and mineral revenues, 54n, 65–68
    NDDC and, 75
    OMPADEC, 72–75
    special grants to, 66–68, 74
Ministries and branches of govern-
        ment
    ministerial positions and appoint-
        ments, 117
    sectional domination, 118
Ministry of State and Local
        Government Affairs, 174
Ministry of the Federal Capital
        Territory, 76
MNR. See Movement for National
        Reformation
Modernization, 22–23
Mohammed, Brigadier Murtala, xxiv,
    30, 37, 90, 112
Mohammed-Obasanjo administration
    nineteen-state structure and, 93
    seven additional states, 33
    state governors and, 32
Motor fuel import duties, 51, 64
Movement for National Reformation
    (MNR), 192

Rotimi T. Suberu is a senior lecturer in the Department of Political Science, University of Ibadan, Nigeria, where he obtained his Ph.D. in 1990. During 1993–94, Suberu was a fellow in the Jennings Randolph fellowship program at the United States Institute of Peace, during which he conducted further research for this book. Most recently, Suberu was a fellow at the Woodrow Wilson International Center for Scholars' International Studies Division during 1999–2000. Suberu's research has focused on the problems of ethnic conflict, democracy, and federalism in Nigeria. He is a contributing coeditor of *Federalism and Political Restructuring in Nigeria* (1998) and the author of *Ethnic Minority Conflicts and Governance in Nigeria* (1996, reprinted in 1999), and *Public Policies and National Unity in Nigeria* (1999).

Jennings Randolph Program for International Peace

This book is a fine example of the work produced by senior fellows in the Jennings Randolph fellowship program of the United States Institute of Peace. As part of the statute establishing the Institute, Congress envisioned a program that would appoint "scholars and leaders of peace from the United States and abroad to pursue scholarly inquiry and other appropriate forms of communication on international peace and conflict resolution." The program was named after Senator Jennings Randolph of West Virginia, whose efforts over four decades helped to establish the Institute.

Since 1987, the Jennings Randolph Program has played a key role in the Institute's effort to build a national center of research, dialogue, and education on critical problems of conflict and peace. Nearly two hundred senior fellows from some thirty nations have carried out projects on the sources and nature of violent international conflict and the ways such conflict can be peacefully managed or resolved. Fellows come from a wide variety of academic and other professional backgrounds. They conduct research at the Institute and participate in the Institute's outreach activities to policymakers, the academic community, and the American public.

Each year approximately fifteen senior fellows are in residence at the Institute. Fellowship recipients are selected by the Institute's board of directors in a competitive process. For further information on the program, or to receive an application form, please contact the program staff at (202) 457-1700, or visit our web site at www.usip.org.

JOSEPH KLAITS
DIRECTOR

FEDERALISM AND ETHNIC CONFLICT IN NIGERIA

This book was set in the typeface American Garamond; the display type is American Garamond Bold. Cover design by the Creative Shop in Rockville, Md. Interior design and page makeup by Mike Chase. Map adaptation and design by Michael Sonesen. Copyediting and proofreading by EEI Communications in Alexandria, Va. Production supervised by Marie Marr. Peter Pavilionis was the book's editor.